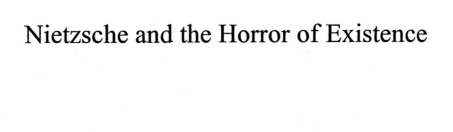

Nietzsche and the Horror of Existence

Nietzsche and the Horror of Existence

PHILIP J. KAIN

LEXINGTON BOOKS

A division of
ROWMAN & LITTLEFIELD PUBLISHERS, INC.
Lanham • Boulder • New York • Toronto • Plymouth, UK

LEXINGTON BOOKS

A division of Rowman & Littlefield Publishers, Inc.
A wholly owned subsidiary of The Rowman & Littlefield Publishing Group, Inc.
4501 Forbes Boulevard, Suite 200
Lanham, MD 20706

Estover Road
Plymouth PL6 7PY
United Kingdom

British Library Cataloguing in Publication Information Available

Library of Congress Cataloging-in-Publication Data

Kain, Philip J., 1943–
  Nietzsche and the horror of existence / Philip J. Kain.
    p. cm.
  Includes bibliographical references and index.
  ISBN 978-0-7391-2694-3 (cloth : alk. paper)
  ISBN 978-0-7391-3517-4 (electronic)
  1. Nietzsche, Friedrich Wilhelm, 1844–1900. I. Title.
  B3317.K24 2009
  193—dc22   2008050903

Printed in the United States of America

♾™ The paper used in this publication meets the minimum requirements of American
National Standard for Information Sciences—Permanence of Paper for Printed Library
Materials, ANSI/NISO Z39.48–1992.

Contents

Abbreviations

AC	Nietzsche, *The Anti-Christ*
BGE	Nietzsche, *Beyond Good and Evil* (Kaufmann translation)
BGE (Cowan)	Nietzsche, *Beyond Good and Evil* (Cowan translation)
BT	Nietzsche, *The Birth of Tragedy* (Kaufmann translation)
BT (Golffing)	Nietzsche, *The Birth of Tragedy* (Golffing translation)
CPR	Kant, *Critique of Pure Reason*
CWFN	Nietzsche, *The Complete Works of Friedrich Nietzsche* (Magnus edition)
CWFN (Levy)	Nietzsche, *The Complete Works of Friedrich Nietzsche* (Levy edition)
D	Nietzsche, *Daybreak*
EH	Nietzsche, *Ecce Homo*
GM	Nietzsche, *On the Genealogy of Morals* (Kaufmann translation)
GM (Smith)	Nietzsche, *On the Genealogy of Morals* (Smith translation)
GS	Nietzsche, *The Gay Science*
HAH, I	Nietzsche, *Human, All Too Human, I*
HAH, II	Nietzsche, *Human, All Too Human*
KGS	Kant, *Kant's gesammelte Schriften*
NE	Aristotle, *Nicomachean Ethics*
NW	Nietzsche, *Nietzsche's Werke*
NWKG	Nietzsche, *Nietzsche Werke: Kritische Gesamtausgabe*
T&L	Nietzsche, "On Truth and Lies in a Nonmoral Sense"
TI	Nietzsche, *Twilight of the Idols*
U&DHL	Nietzsche, *On the Uses and Disadvantages of History for Life*
UM	Nietzsche, *Untimely Meditations*
WP	Nietzsche, *The Will to Power*
WW&R	Schopenhauer, *The World as Will and Representation*
Z	Nietzsche, *Thus Spoke Zarathustra*

Acknowledgments

I would like to thank Robert Audi, William Parent, Calvin Stewart, and Christopher Kulp for offering me advice on earlier portions of this book. I would also like to acknowledge my debt to the late Stanley Moore, in whose seminars during the 1970s I learned a lot of Nietzsche, and also to the late S. Robert Smith, who gave me helpful comments on this book and in whose seminars I learned a great deal during the 1960s.

Parts of Chapter 4 first appeared as "Nietzsche, Skepticism, and Eternal Recurrence," *Canadian Journal of Philosophy* 13 (1983): 365-87. Parts of Chapter 6 first appeared as "Nietzschean Genealogy and Hegelian History in the *Genealogy of Morals,"* *Canadian Journal of Philosophy* 26 (1996): 123-48. Parts of Chapter 3 and 4 first appeared as "Nietzsche, the Kantian Self, and Eternal Recurrence," *Idealistic Studies* 34 (2004): 225-37. Parts of Chapter 1 and 2 first appeared as "Nietzsche, Truth, and the Horror of Existence," *History of Philosophy Quarterly* 23 (2006): 41-58. Parts of Chapter 4 and 5 first appeared as "Eternal Recurrence and the Categorical Imperative," *The Southern Journal of Philosophy* 45 (2007): 105-116. Parts of Chapter 1, 4, and 5 first appeared as "Nietzsche, Eternal Recurrence, and the Horror of Existence," *The Journal of Nietzsche Studies* 33 (2007): 49-63. Parts of Chapters 1, 2, 4, 5, and 6 first appeared as "Nietzsche, Virtue, and the Horror of Existence," *British Journal for the History of Philosophy* 17 (2009): 153-67.

Chapter One

Horror

Nietzsche's stature as a philosopher has risen dramatically since his death. His writings increasingly captivate philosophical readers. There are many reasons for this. One reason is the depth of his thought. Philosophers like Aristotle, Kant, or Hegel impress us with the scope and breadth of their thinking. Philosophers like Plato, Descartes, or Berkeley impress us with an original insight that they unfold and elaborate. Nietzsche is different. He thinks deeply. He digs beneath other philosophies. He forces us to look at traditional philosophical assumptions from a different angle. He undermines and subverts them. He opens up the possibility of thinking in radically new ways.

This fascinates us even if we worry about the consequences. We may have believed in those traditional philosophical perspectives. We may regret their collapse. We may wish they could have been defended. But Nietzsche forces us to see them from a new perspective such that it becomes very difficult to return to our old way of understanding things. Nietzsche's depth, his ability to subvert, enchants us even if we rue the consequences.

The first seven chapters of this book attempt to illuminate the depth of Nietzsche's thinking—indeed, to show that it is even more subversive than has been recognized. The eighth chapter asks whether, finally, we must accept Nietzsche's views.

I. The Horror of Existence

This book will argue that at the center of Nietzsche's vision lies his concept of the "terror and horror of existence."[1] As he puts it in his first book, *The Birth of Tragedy:*

"There is an ancient story that King Midas hunted in the forest a long time for the wise Silenus, the companion of Dionysus. . . . When Silenus at last fell into his hands, the king asked what was the best and most desirable of all things for man. Fixed and immovable, the demigod said not a word, till at last, urged by the king, he gave a shrill laugh and broke out into these words: 'Oh, wretched ephemeral race, children of chance and misery, why do you compel me to tell you what it would be most expedient for you not to hear? What is best of all is utterly beyond your reach: not to be born, not to *be*, to be *nothing*. But the second best for you is—to die soon.'"[2]

Why is it best never to have been born? Because all we can expect as human beings is to suffer.[3] Yet, still, this is not precisely the problem. In a passage most central to my interpretation of the horror of existence, a passage to which I will return again and again, and a passage found not in Nietzsche's early but in one of his very late writings (at *Genealogy of Morals,* III, §28), Nietzsche tells us that human beings can live with suffering, what they *cannot* live with is *meaningless* suffering—suffering for no reason at all.[4] In Nietzsche's view, we are "surrounded by a fearful *void*. . . ."[5] We live in an empty, meaningless cosmos. We cannot look into reality without being overcome. In *Beyond Good and Evil,* Nietzsche even says that "it might be a basic characteristic of existence that those who would know it completely would perish. . . ."[6]

Moreover, it was not just intellectual reflection that led Nietzsche to a belief in the horror of existence. He lived it himself.[7] In a letter of 10 April 1888, he writes: "Around 1876 my health grew worse. . . . There were extremely painful and obstinate headaches which exhausted all my strength. They increased over long years, to reach a climax at which pain was habitual, so that any given year contained for me two hundred days of pain. . . . My specialty was to endure the extremity of pain . . . with complete lucidity for two or three days in succession, with continuous vomiting of mucus."[8] In 1889, in *Nietzsche Contra Wagner,* he tells us how significant this suffering was for him:

> I have often asked myself whether I am not much more deeply indebted to the hardest years of my life than to any others. . . . And as to my prolonged illness, do I not owe much more to it than I owe to my health? To it I owe a *higher* kind of health, a sort of health which grows stronger under everything that does not actually kill it!—*To it, I owe even my philosophy.* . . . Only great suffering is the ultimate emancipator of the spirit. . . . Only great suffering; that great suffering, under which we seem to be over a fire of greenwood, the suffering that takes its time—forces us philosophers to descend into our nethermost depths.[9]

In general, Nietzsche thinks that "every great philosophy . . . has been . . . the personal confession of its author and a kind of involuntary and unconscious memoir. . . ."[10] I think Nietzsche's suffering allowed him an insight into the horror of existence and I hope to show that this allowed him to develop a serious and radically different philosophical vision.

II. Dionysian Terror

There was another source of Nietzsche's belief in the horror of existence. He was trained as a philologist and his study of classical antiquity convinced him that the Greeks had a special insight into this horror. To get at this insight, however, Nietzsche had to overthrow the reigning paradigm that had been established by Winckelmann and Schiller.[11]

Schiller characterized the ancient Greek world as an age of beauty, naturalness, and unity.[12] The Greeks experienced a harmony and oneness with nature that Schiller called naive. Homer was the naive poet *par excellance.* Schiller contrasts this to the modern world which lacks such unity with nature and sentimentally strives for it as a lost ideal. Schiller says of the Greeks:

> They *are* what we *were;* they are what we *should become* once more. We were nature like them, and our culture should lead us along the path of reason and freedom back to nature. Thus they depict at once our lost childhood, something that remains ever dearest to us, and for this reason they fill us with a certain melancholy.[13]

> Recall the beauty of nature surrounding the ancient *Greeks.* . . . consider how very much nearer to the simplicity of nature lay its manner of thinking, its way of feeling, its mores. . . . For them the culture had not degenerated to such a degree that nature was left behind in the process. . . . One with himself and content in the feeling of his humanity, the Greek had to stand quietly by this humanity as his ultimate and to concern himself with bringing everything else closer to it.[14]

Schiller looks back to ancient Greece as a unified culture in harmony with itself and with nature, which then collapsed and gave rise to a sentimental striving after such unity as a lost ideal. The aspiration here is to set the Greek against the modern and to hope for a revival of Greek unity. Schiller wants to remake the modern world on Greek lines.

For Nietzsche, this vision of the ancient world sees only surface appearance. It completely misses the deeper reality. *There was no unity.* Greece was split, in violent opposition,[15] in contradiction, *from the start:*

> this harmony which is contemplated with such longing by modern man, in fact, this oneness of man with nature (for which Schiller introduced the technical term "naïve"), is by no means a simple condition that comes into being naturally and as if inevitably. It is not a condition that, like a terrestrial paradise, *must* necessarily be found at the gate of every culture. Only a romantic age could believe this, an age which conceived of the artist in terms of Rousseau's *Emile* and imagined that in Homer it had found such an artist Emile, reared at the bosom of nature. Where we encounter the "naïve" in art, we should recognize the highest effect of Apollinian culture—which always must first overthrow an empire of Titans and slay monsters, and which must have triumphed over an abysmal and terrifying view of the world and the keenest susceptibility to suffering through recourse to the most forceful and pleasurable illusions.[16]

The Apollonian, for Nietzsche, derives from the Olympian gods of Homer. It refers to a realm of clear, beautiful, plastic images. The Apollonian heals us with its beauty. It allows us to escape from pain. It makes life possible and brings calm. It is beautiful illusion. It captures Schiller's concept of the naive.[17] The Apollonian, however, is mere surface appearance. The Dionysian, on the other hand, derives from the older Orphic tradition of the Orient—from the pre-Olympian Titans. Dionysian ritual brings the collapse of appearance. It destroys one's sense of being a coherent individual. We are absorbed into a cosmic oneness. This involves a mixture of blissful ecstasy as well as pure blind terror—terror at the loss of self and blissful ecstasy over an intoxicating unity with nature, earth, the animal, the cosmos. The Dionysian is the reality behind surface appearance.[18]

Nietzsche describes the Dionysian experience as ceasing to be an artist and becoming the work of art.[19] The individual is no longer an observer, contemplator, or creator. The individual is overwhelmed, absorbed into a primordial unity in which all individuality and separateness are annihilated. There is no longer a difference between subject and object: "nature which has become alienated, hostile, or subjugated, celebrates once more her reconciliation with her lost son, man."[20] The Dionysian, Nietzsche tells us, reveals in nature "a sentimental trait; it is as if she were heaving a sigh at her dismemberment into individuals."[21] Nietzsche himself suggests that the Dionysian is like Schiller's sentimental. It seeks a lost unity with nature. But the Dionysian is not modern. It already existed way back in ancient Greece, even before the Apollonian.

The Apollonian, then, is a veil that hides the terrifying Dionysian world from consciousness. This is the horrible need that forced the creation of the Olympian gods. They are an ideal version of ourselves which hide the terror of the cosmos that the Dionysian is aware of:

> The Greek knew and felt the terror and horror of existence. That he might endure this terror at all, he had to interpose between himself and life the radiant dream-birth of the Olympians. That overwhelming dismay in the face of the titanic powers of nature, the Moira enthroned inexorably over all knowledge, the vulture of the great lover of mankind, Prometheus, the terrible fate of the wise Oedipus, the family curse of the Atridae. . . . All this was again and again overcome by the Greeks with the aid of the Olympian *middle world* of art; or at any rate it was veiled and withdrawn from sight. It was in order to be able to live that the Greeks had to create these gods. . . . So that now, reversing the wisdom of Silenus, we might say of the Greeks that "to die soon is worst of all for them, the next worst—to die at all."[22]

Dionysian terror was original and the Homeric Apollonian was a necessary response to veil it. Nietzsche links the Apollonian to Schiller's naive, but rejects the view that the naive-Apollonian was original and natural.[23] For Schiller, the sentimental only arises after the collapse of the naive and as a longing for the lost unity of the naive. For Nietzsche, it is precisely the reverse. The Dionysian-sentimental is original and fundamental, and the naive-Apollonian arises to hide the terrifying reality of the Dionysian. Homeric naiveté was the victory of Apollonian illusion. Only moderns can look back to Homer and see an undisturbed unity. They miss the terrible battle that had to be fought against the Dionysian.

What makes the Dionysian so terrible is not just the horror that it threatens but the fact that it can also evoke the prospect of a blissful ecstasy—an intoxicating unity with nature. This must be further explained.

At the biological-organic-natural level, human beings are one with nature. We are a part of nature and nature is the source of all life, activity, and creativity. At the biological level we are dependent upon nature and can be in harmony with it, but only as part of a primordial unity. To approach this unity can be intoxicating, an ecstasy, and we can have a sentimental longing for it—but it involves the total loss of human consciousness and individuality. We are just an element of nature, one with it, without consciousness, without any conscious distinction from it.[24]

Besides being biological-organic-natural beings, however, we are also individual-conscious-human beings. Our unity with nature at the unconscious biological level is paralleled by a terrible alienation from nature at the level of consciousness. As conscious beings we find nature threatening and terrifying. It inevitably produces pain, suffering, and death. It cares nothing for consciousness and gets along quite well without it. Conscious individuals are terrified by nature's lack of concern for their needs—needs for meaning, purpose, and value.[25] For consciousness, nature is meaningless and valueless.

Individuation, Nietzsche tells us, is the source of all our suffering.[26] If we were not individuals, if we were simply one with primordial nature, we would not suffer. It is our separation from nature, our alienation from it, our individual consciousness, that brings suffering. Individuation, separation, dismemberment, Nietzsche suggests, are "the properly Dionysian *suffering*. . . ."[27] As a young boy, Dionysus was dismembered, torn into pieces, by the Titans. He was then restored and brought back to life by Zeus.

Aristotle, in identifying the human essence, set aside the life of nutrition and growth common to the rest of nature, as well as the life of perception common to all animals, and argued that rational activity is the proper and unique function of humans.[28] It is *precisely* the latter, for Nietzsche, that makes for the horror of existence. Lacking rational consciousness, we could be one with existence like the rest of nature. Instead, we find that nature does not care about our need for meaning. Consciousness cannot bear this emptiness, this threat to its existence, this terrifying void. If we come to see that existence really is meaningless, that we suffer for no reason at all, that existence simply cannot provide what is required by the sort of consciousness we possess, and if this realization sinks in, if it gains possession of us, it will paralyze us and may even actually kill us.

Nietzsche is not out to dismiss individual conscious life and just embrace an ecstatic Dionysian affirmation of the organic. Nor is he out to do just the opposite: we cannot eliminate, close out, totally suppress, the Dionysian—that would be to cut ourselves off from life, creativity, nature. Nietzsche thinks that the Apollonian did tend to close out the Dionysian more than was desirable—and he certainly thinks that since then philosophy, science, and Christianity have done so even more. Nietzsche rejects both the pure Dionysian and the pure Apollonian.

III. Tragedy

Nietzsche wants a balance between the Apollonian and the Dionysian, and he finds that balance in Greek tragedy.[29] It gives us the proper blend of reality and illusion, the Dionysian and the Apollonian. The Dionysian chorus discharges itself in the Apollonian world of images, dialogue, and dramatic action that is epic in nature—but which is only a veneer.[30] The outcome of tragedy is never redemption at the Apollonian level, Nietzsche thinks, but always the destruction, the crushing, by a cruel and uncaring cosmos, of the conscious individual—the dramatic, active, heroic, Homeric individual.

Tragic drama and music allow us to understand the delight felt at this crushing of the individual. They reveal eternal life continuing beyond all phenomena and in spite of destruction. They allow us to take a metaphysical joy in the negation of the tragic hero—the negation of all phenomena and the affirmation of eternal life unaffected by annihilation. We take deep joy in this reality behind appearance.[31]

The tragic hero, Nietzsche thinks, is simply Dionysus—and all other characters too are mere masks for that original hero. The hero is the Dionysus who experiences the suffering of individuation in being dismembered by the Titans. And tragic art is the joyful hope that the spell of individuation can be broken and oneness restored.[32] In tragedy:

> we are forced to look into the terrors of the individual existence—yet we are not to become rigid with fear. . . . We are really for a brief moment primordial being itself, feeling its raging desire for existence and joy in existence; the struggle, the pain, the destruction of phenomena, now appear necessary to us, in view of the excess of countless forms of existence which force and push one another into life, in view of the exuberant fertility of the universal will. . . . In spite of fear and pity, we are the happy living beings, not as individuals, but as the *one* living being, with whose creative joy we are united.[33]

The tragic hero, "like a powerful Titan, takes the whole Dionysian world upon his back and thus relieves us of this burden."[34] The individual is crushed, not in the Hegelian sense in which the individual is sacrificed so that ethical principles can evolve at the Apollonian level. Rather the individual is crushed and fused with primal being—with Dionysian reality. The Apollonian gives us enough distance, provides enough of a veil, so that we can feel this collapse and fusion with primal Dionysian being as powerful and creative—without being annihilated by it.[35]

Tragedy gives us an explanation of suffering, as well as of the dignity of the human condition. There is a metaphysical contradiction at the heart of reality that is revealed in tragedy as a clash of the divine and the human,[36] the Olympians and the Titans, and the suffering that results for humans. It is Dionysian wisdom that recognizes this very un-Apollonian reality.

Nietzsche profoundly disagrees with Aristotle's conception of tragedy.[37] Aristotle often considers the views of other thinkers and tries to give them a place in his own thought, but not the tragedians, not the wisdom that there is a metaphysical contradiction at the heart of existence, not the view that it is best never to have been born. Aristotle cannot and will not accept the horror of existence. And thus tragedy cannot express the essence of the human condition for him. Instead, tragedy must occur due to the fault of the tragic hero. The whole idea of a tragic flaw, Nietzsche might have said, was a ruse designed to make the tragic hero responsible for what the tragedians, certainly Sophocles, correctly understood as the horror of existence. And the tragic hero's suffering arouses pity in us because, for Aristotle, such suffering is not the human condition generally, after all, but merely something that happened to this poor fellow. It also arouses fear because it could happen even to us, but, Aristotle hastens to add, tragic drama is designed to *purge* this pity and fear and bring about catharsis.[38] Among the sorts of plots to be avoided by proper tragedy are those in which a good man passes to bad fortune.[39] For Nietzsche, on the other hand, that is *exactly and precisely* what tragedy is about.[40] Suffering *is* the human condition. The tragic hero is all of us.

IV. Rebirth of the Greek Ideal

As we begin to read the *Birth of Tragedy*, it seems that Nietzsche completely rejects Schiller's ideal of ancient Greece and the hope for its rebirth in the modern world. But it becomes clearer and clearer as we proceed, first, that Nietzsche *does* see Greek culture as an ideal. Every age and culture, he says, has tried to free itself from the Greeks because their own achievement seemed to lose life and become shriveled in comparison.[41] It is negatively put, but the Greeks are clearly taken as an ideal. In another passage, Nietzsche puts it as follows:

> One feels ashamed and afraid in the presence of the Greeks . . . the Greeks, as charioteers, hold in their hands the reins of our own and every other culture, but . . . almost always chariot and horses are of inferior quality and not up to the glory of their leaders, who consider it sport to run such a team into an abyss which they themselves clear with the leap of Achilles.[42]

But, second, more than this, it eventually becomes clear that Nietzsche even thinks that there *can* be a rebirth of the Greek ideal. "Let no one," he says, "try to blight our faith in a yet-impending rebirth of Hellenic antiquity; for this alone gives us hope for a renovation and purification of the German spirit through the fire magic of music."[43] Nietzsche clearly wants a return of the Greek ideal, but not Schiller's Homeric-Apollonian-naive ideal. He wants the Dionysian-tragic ideal of music. And he sees the gradual awakening of this Dionysian spirit in

Bach, Beethoven, and especially Wagner.[44] One day the Dionysian spirit will awaken in Germany with "all the morning freshness following a tremendous sleep: then it will slay dragons, destroy vicious dwarfs, wake Brünnhilde—and even Wotan's spear will not be able to stop its course!"[45]

It is true that Nietzsche's discussion of the rebirth of the Greek ideal through German music occurs in sections 16 to 25 of the *Birth of Tragedy,* which were only added to the second edition of the text. Kaufmann thinks these sections on the rebirth of tragedy should not have been added, that they weaken the book, and that they were soon regretted by Nietzsche.[46]

It is quite true that Nietzsche soon regretted his views on Wagner,[47] but it is not at all clear that Nietzsche regretted his belief in the rebirth of the Greek ideal. Even in *Ecce Homo,* one of Nietzsche's last books, he says:

> In the end I lack all reason to renounce the hope for a Dionysian future of music. Let us look ahead a century; let us suppose that my attempt to assassinate two millennia of antinature and desecration of man were to succeed. That new party of life . . . would again make possible that excess of life on earth from which the Dionysian state, too, would have to awaken again. I promise a tragic age: the highest art in saying Yes to life, tragedy, will be reborn.[48]

Moreover, I think we will see as we proceed that Nietzsche's ultimate solution to the horror of existence, that is, eternal recurrence, can itself be seen as reviving the tragic ideal.

V. Dionysian Life

We must also notice, as the passage just quoted at the end of the previous section implies, that tragedy is important and valuable because it sees deeply into the horror of existence and yet, nevertheless, it is able to *affirm life.* Silenus told us that it is best never to have been born, second best to die as soon as possible. That, I think we must conclude, is the perspective of an immortal for whom the suffering of us mortals is pitiful. Mortals at times will be tempted to agree with his advice, but they also are capable of mustering the strength to reject it. The reason Nietzsche is so attracted to the Greeks is not simply because they recognized the horror of existence, but because they overcame it. For Nietzsche, while existence is horrible, nevertheless, *life* is of the highest value.

For Nietzsche, the concept of life, we must be careful to notice, includes both the life of the individual and the life of the whole—the vast, teeming, indestructible, overwhelming flow of the totality of life. The latter involves the death of individuals, even individual species. *Individual* life must perish for the life of the *whole* to proceed. *Life,* we must remember, is a concept that includes *both* of these sides.[49]

Life is a "dark, driving power that insatiably thirsts for itself."[50] Life, we will come to see, is will to power. It will assert itself whatever happens. Life is larger than the individual. The individual may perish, indeed, *must* perish, but life continues. Insofar as the individual identifies only with itself, it sees that life does not need it or care about it. It will suffer and die while life as a whole continues to flourish—and *that* is the horror of existence. Insofar as the individual identifies with the primordial life of the whole, however, the individual can experience an intoxicating, blissful unity and has no difficulty in affirming life.

Dionysus is the god of life—life in *both* its senses. Dionysus affirms life. Despite death and destruction, despite the loss of individual life, despite painful and cruel dismemberment, despite the horror of existence, overpowering life always returns and continues. Life "is counted as *holy enough* to justify even a monstrous amount of suffering. The tragic man affirms even the harshest suffering: he is sufficiently strong, rich, and capable of deifying to do so. . . . Dionysus cut to pieces is a *promise* of life: it will be eternally reborn and return again from destruction."[51] The Dionysian, Nietzsche tells us, means:

> an ecstatic affirmation of the total character of life as that which remains the same, just as powerful, just as blissful, through all change; the great pantheistic sharing of joy and sorrow that sanctifies and calls good even the most terrible and questionable qualities of life; the eternal will to procreation, to fruitfulness, to recurrence; the feeling of the necessary unity of creation and destruction.[52]

Nietzsche uses the term 'Dionysian' ambiguously. Sometimes it refers to that pure raging torrent of life which includes death for the individual. To enter the Dionysian in this sense involves ecstasy, but it means that we do not return, we perish—or at least we are likely to perish. At other times, the term 'Dionysian' is used to refer to that situation where we have enough of a veil so that we can experience this raging torrent of life without succumbing to it, without perishing, indeed, while being invigorated by it.

The issue, then, is to embrace life, to be invigorated by it, without succumbing to the horror of existence, without perishing. What is required, we have seen, is illusion, lies, or to put it more congenially—*art*. We need enough of a veil so that we can be invigorated by the life of the whole without being destroyed by the horror of existence.

This raises a serious tangle that we will have to face. Clark writes: "Nietzsche seems to take as his measure of value what is 'life-promoting. . . .' If his commitment to truth came into conflict with the affirmation of life or the promotion of its interests, Nietzsche would have to consider life the higher value." I think this is correct and I fully agree with this interpretation. However, Clark continues: "But it is difficult to see how his commitment to truth could conflict with his affirmation of life."[53] It is not at all difficult to see this, unless one has failed to appreciate the centrality for Nietzsche of the horror of existence. Truth and life are opposed. To have one is to lose the other. Get too close to truth and you lose your life. To remain alive requires that we keep a distance from the truth. This will have to be explored at length in the next chapter.

VI. Three Visions

Nietzsche's belief in the horror of existence is largely, if not completely, over-looked by most scholars.[54] I hope to show that it had a profound effect on his thought. I do not want to *reduce* Nietzsche's thought to the horror of existence. I do not want to claim that it is the *essence* of his thought—a magic key to it. I do not want to oversimplify the thought of a very complex thinker. My claim is more modest and limited. It is simply that Nietzsche cannot be adequately understood without seeing the significance the horror of existence had for him. To begin to understand its importance, let us consider three different visions of the human condition.

The first holds that we live in a benign cosmos. It is as if it were purposively planned for us and we for it. We fit, we belong, we are at home in this cosmos. We are confirmed and reinforced by it. Our natural response is a desire to know it, and thus to appreciate our fit into it. Let us call this the *designed cosmos*. Roughly speaking, it is the traditional view held by most philosophers from Plato and Aristotle through the medievals. And it has largely disappeared in the modern world—few really believe in it any more.

The second vision backs off from the metaphysical assumptions required by the first. This view starts with Francis Bacon, if not before, and is the view of most moderns. Here the cosmos is neither alien nor is it designed for us. It is neither terrifying nor benign. The cosmos is neutral and, most importantly, it is malleable. Human beings must come to understand the cosmos through science and control it through technology. We must *make* it fit us. It does not fit us by design. We must work on it, transform it, and mold it into a place where we can be at home. We must create our own place. For such modern thinkers, we actually end up with more than the ancients and medievals had. We end up with a fit like they had, but we have the added satisfaction of bringing it about *ourselves,* accomplishing it through our own endeavor, individuality, and freedom. Let us call this the *perfectible cosmos.*

The third vision takes the cosmos to be alien. It was not designed for human beings at all, nor they for it. We do not fit. We do not belong. *And we never will.* The cosmos is horrible, terrifying, and we will never surmount this fact. It is a place where human beings suffer for no reason at all. Let us call this the *horrific cosmos.* This is Nietzsche's view.

Nietzsche simply dismisses the first view, the designed cosmos, which few believe in anymore anyway.[55] On the other hand, Nietzsche takes the second view, that of a perfectible cosmos, very seriously. He resists it with every fiber of his being.[56] For Nietzsche, we must stop wasting time and energy hoping to change things, improve them, make progress[57]—the outlook of liberals, socialists, feminists, even Christians, all of whom Nietzsche tends to lump together and excoriate. For Nietzsche, we cannot eliminate suffering and to keep hoping we can will only weaken us. Instead, we must conceal an alien and terrifying cosmos if we hope to live in it. And we must develop the strength to do so. We must toughen ourselves. We need more suffering, not less. It has "created all enhancements of man so far. . . ."[58]

Danto thinks that Nietzsche has a "blind spot with regard to social reform." And Danto thinks it "misleading and absurd to counter programs for the elimination of pain with the broad statement that *life* is pain and struggle. . . ."[59] After all, we might imagine a philosophy of medicine whose view of suffering was that it cannot be reduced and perhaps should even be increased? Such a position would not be a popular one. Nevertheless, it is a serious mistake to think that what we have on Nietzsche's part is a "blind spot"—some sort of *hang-up.* Nietzsche has thought through the horror of existence thoroughly and deeply. The fact that most people we know do not feel that existence is horrible does not make Nietzsche's position absurd. After all, most people in the world, even today, *do* in fact lead a pretty miserable existence, one that at the very least involves some serious suffering of one sort or another.

If we look deeply into the essence of things, into the horror of existence, Nietzsche thinks we will be overwhelmed—paralyzed. Like Hamlet we will not be able to act, because we see that action can "not change anything in the eternal nature of things."[60] We must see, Nietzsche says, that "a profound *illusion* . . . first saw the light of the world in the person of Socrates: the unshakeable faith that thought . . . can penetrate the deepest abysses of being, and that thought is capable not only of knowing being but even of *correcting* it. This sublime metaphysical illusion accompanies science as an instinct. . . ."[61] In Nietzsche's view, we cannot change things. Instead, with Hamlet we should "feel it to be ridiculous or humiliating that [we] should be asked to set right a world that is out of joint."[62]

One might think this silly. After all, isn't it just obvious that we can change things, reduce suffering, improve existence, make progress? Isn't it just obvious that modern science and technology have done so? Isn't it just absurd for Nietzsche to reject the possibility of significant change? Hasn't such change already occurred?

Well, perhaps not. Even modern environmentalists might resist all this *obviousness.* They might respond in a rather Nietzschean vein that technology may have caused as many problems as it has solved. The advocate of the perfectible cosmos, on the other hand, would no doubt counter such Nietzschean pessimism by arguing that even if technology does cause some problems, the solution to those problems can only come from better technology. Honesty requires us to admit, however, that this is merely a *hope,* not something for which we already have evidence, not something which it is absurd to doubt—not at all something *obvious.* Further technology may or may not improve things. The widespread use of antibiotics seems to have done a miraculous job of improving our health and reducing suffering, but we are also discovering that such antibiotics give rise to even more powerful bacteria that are immune to those antibiotics. We have largely eliminated diseases like cholera, smallpox, and tuberculosis, but we have produced cancer and heart disease. We can cure syphilis and gonorrhea, but we now have AIDS.

Even if we could show that it will be possible to continuously reduce suffering, still we must admit that it is very unlikely that we will ever eliminate it. If that is so, if there will always be some suffering, then it remains a real question whether it is not better to face suffering, use it as a discipline, perhaps even increase it, so as to toughen ourselves, rather than let it weaken us, allow it to dominate us, by our continually hoping to overcome it. We will have to address this issue at length as we proceed.

But whatever we think about the possibility of reducing suffering, the question may well become moot. Nietzsche tells a story:

> Once upon a time, in some out of the way corner of that universe which is dispersed into numberless twinkling solar systems, there was a star upon which clever beasts invented knowing. That was the most arrogant and mendacious minute of "world history," but nevertheless, it was only a minute. After nature had drawn a few breaths, the star cooled and congealed, and the clever beasts had to die.[63]

Whatever progress we might think we are making in reducing suffering, whatever change we think we are bringing about, it may all amount to nothing more than a short and accidental moment in biological time, whose imminent disappearance will finally confirm the horror and meaninglessness of existence.

The disagreement here is not so much about the quantity of suffering that we can expect to find in the world, but its *nature.* For proponents of the designed cosmos, suffering is basically accidental. It is not fundamental or central to life. It is not a necessary part of the nature of things. It does not make up the essence of existence. We must develop virtue, and then we can basically expect to fit and be at home in the cosmos. For the proponents of a perfectible cosmos, suffering is neither essential nor unessential. The cosmos is neutral. We must work on it to reduce suffering. We must bring about our own fit. For Nietzsche, even if we can change this or that, even if we can reduce suffering here and there, what cannot be changed for human beings is that suffering is fundamental and central to life. The very *nature* of things, the very *essence* of existence, means suffering.[64] Moreover, it means *meaningless* suffering—suffering for no reason at all. That cannot be changed—it can only be concealed.

Nietzsche does not reject *all* forms of change—after all, as we will see, he has a theory of will to power and of the *Übermensch.* What he rejects is the sort of change necessary for a perfectible cosmos. He rejects the notion that science and technology can transform the eternal nature of things—he rejects the notion that human effort can end or significantly reduce physical suffering. Instead, he only thinks it possible to build up the power necessary to construct meaning in a meaningless world and thus to hide the horror of existence. The horror of existence cannot be eliminated. It can only be concealed.

We cannot prove the opposite and I do not think we can dismiss Nietzsche's view simply because it goes counter to the assumptions of Christianity, science, liberalism, socialism, feminism, and so forth. And we certainly cannot dismiss this view if we hope to understand Nietzsche. At any rate, for Nietzsche, we cannot eliminate suffering, we can only seek to mask it.

Still, one might want to insist that Nietzsche cannot be committed to a horrific cosmos because he very obviously believes in joy. While it is quite true that Nietzsche does believe in joy, it does not follow from this that he cannot also believe in a horrific cosmos. If Nietzsche held that the horror of existence could simply be eliminated or significantly reduced and a certain amount of joy produced, then he *would* be rejecting a horrific cosmos (and endorsing a perfectible one). I do not think evidence can be found to show that Nietzsche believes that this sort of transformation of the world is possible. On the other hand, one might concede that Nietzsche does not think we can change the world to significantly reduce horror and produce joy, but that the world *itself* is just mixed—some aspects of it produce horror and other aspects joy. In other words, here we would need a fourth model—that of a *mixed cosmos*. There is, however, another possibility. It is that Nietzsche does not believe in a mixed cosmos at all, he believes in a horrific one, not in the sense that every last detail must be horrific, but in the sense that the world is *essentially* horrific. Joy can arise in this world, but it arises *despite* the horror of existence, *along* with it, *without* removing the horror or significantly reducing it. I will argue that this is Nietzsche's view.[65] At any rate, if Nietzsche's belief in the horror of existence has somehow not yet been sufficiently demonstrated, support for this belief will be reinforced again and again by text after text as we proceed.

Chapter Two

Truth

I. The True and the Good

Let us try to draw out the philosophical implications that follow from the horror of existence. If existence really is horrible, if to know it completely, as Nietzsche suggests in *Beyond Good and Evil,* means we are likely to perish,[1] then knowledge of the truth cannot be good for us. The horror of existence, if we think through its consequences, will put us radically at odds with perhaps the most fundamental assumption of philosophy since Plato and Aristotle, namely, that the true and the good coincide. Philosophers assume that the truth—far from being harmful—will be good for us. And what is really good for us will necessarily be something that is not an illusion or a lie but the truth. As Nietzsche puts it, they hold that: "All supreme values are of the first rank, all the supreme concepts . . . the good, the true . . . neither can these supreme concepts be incommensurate with one another, be incompatible with one another. . . ."[2] Nietzsche also says, "I seek to understand out of what idiosyncrasy that Socratic equation reason = virtue = happiness derives: that bizarrest of equations and one which has in particular all the instincts of the older Hellenes against it."[3] For Socrates, the true, the good, and happiness coincide.

So also, in Book X of the *Nicomachean Ethics,* Aristotle tells us that the highest happiness is activity in accord with the highest excellence, that is, the contemplative activity of the intellect.[4] Let us grant Aristotle, for the sake of argument, that the life of the intellect is the highest life. Still, we would have to ask why such a life would necessarily make us happy? There is a hidden assumption buried in Aristotle's argument.

If we were to look back to Sophocles, for example, it would not at all be the case for him that the life of the intellect—theoretical wisdom—could be expected to make us happy. Such wisdom would allow us to see more deeply into the truth of things and thus to see what a miserable, terrible, and alien cosmos we live in. We would see into the horror of existence. Both Sophocles and Nietzsche quote the wisdom of Silenus. Best never to have been born; second best, die as soon as possible. All we can expect in this world is to suffer.[5]

This, obviously, is not Aristotle's view. In the *Eudemian Ethics,* Aristotle tells us, approvingly, "that Anaxagoras answered a man who was raising problems . . . and asking why one should choose rather to be born than not by saying 'for the sake of viewing the heavens and the whole order of the universe.'"[6] For Aristotle, "existence is to all men a thing to be chosen and loved. . . ."[7] For Aristotle, human beings fit the cosmos, they belong, they are at home. It is as if the cosmos and human beings were designed for each other. And so at least a part of pursuing the contemplative life would mean contemplating one's fit into the cosmos—and this quite plausibly could make one happy.

For virtue to be compatible with happiness it is necessary that the individual acting virtuously fit the world. We cannot be happy if we continually grate against existence. So also, if knowing the truth about existence is to be compatible with happiness, the truth cannot be that existence is horrible and terrifying. If to be happy, we must avoid knowing the truth, if we must conceal it, if we must lie about it, then the true and the good are not compatible. If the truth is that existence is horrible and terrifying, then the life of the intellect cannot produce happiness, and the good for human beings cannot be the contemplative life of the intellect. Truth, goodness, and happiness would not accord.

But Plato and Aristotle insist they do accord. If we could just free ourselves from our chains, for Plato, if we could climb up out of the cave, if we could get used to looking at the sun, we would see that the idea of the good is not only compatible with, but is the very source of, the true as well as the beautiful.[8] The last thing we would want would be to return to the bottom of the cave. Contemplating the true and the good, for Plato, would be the highest happiness.[9] Here, the truth is not horror and terror. Though, it must be admitted that this is not the perspective of those still at the bottom of the cave. Like Jocasta, they seem to think it best not to know.[10]

But the view of most, and certainly the view of modern science, is that human rationality can discover the truth, that this is good for human beings, and that it will lead to overall progress for humanity, that is, to increasing happiness. As Lange argues in his *History of Materialism,* which Nietzsche carefully read,[11] "Holbach starts from the principle that the truth can never be injurious. He derives this from the wider proposition that theoretical principles . . . can never be dangerous."[12] Lange goes on to say that science needs to build up:

> a kingdom of the true, the good, and the beautiful. . . . With the attainment of truth, it results from this principle that a fuller and higher humanity is also attained. . . . Here, then, we have, in the full sense of the word, a *dogma* which not only is not proved, but which, in fact, when logically tested, is *not true,* but which, if held as an *idea,* may, indeed, like any other religious idea, edify mankind and raise him above the limits of sense.[13]

While Lange does not consider the agreement of the true and the good to be a truth, he nevertheless considers it to be an edifying idea which will benefit humankind. Nietzsche flatly rejects all of this: "For a philosopher to say, 'the good and the beautiful are one,' is infamy; if he goes on to add, 'also the true,' one ought to thrash him. Truth is ugly. . . . We possess *art* lest we *perish of the truth.*"[14] He also says, "There is no preestablished harmony between the further-ing of truth and the well-being," that is, the good, "of humanity."[15]

There is nothing Nietzsche would reject more, I think we can say, than Plato's allegory of the cave.[16] We cannot climb up out of the cave and look di-rectly at the truth. It would likely kill us. We are lucky to be down in the cave with our backs to the truth. All that advice that circulates at the bottom of the cave, that we should stay there, that it is lunacy to try to get out, is *damned* good advice. It is true that the shadows at the bottom of the cave are illusions, distor-tions, lies. But it is not true that the shadows lock us into a prison. They keep out the horror. They preserve life. Life exists, *only exists,* at the bottom of the cave.

The truth is not good for human beings—the truth is horror. Reality as it truly is, is not beautiful—it is terrifying. To pursue the truth, far from pursuing the good and achieving happiness, as most all philosophers have assumed, would have the consequence of plunging humankind into the abyss, of rubbing their noses in the horror of existence. Life requires lies, illusion, art, veiling. Life must shun the truth. Life is not possible with the truth. To pursue the good, what is best for human beings, requires rejection of the true. This is the radical and subversive position that real insight into the horror of existence drives one to hold.

One might try to respond that while it is obviously the case that some things are not good for us, nevertheless, *knowing the truth* is always good for us. It is certainly best for us to know what is bad, dangerous, threatening, and so forth. It might help us to avoid such things. But if existence is truly alien, if to come to know the truth means we are likely to perish, if it would put an end to human life, if existence is *ontologically* horrible (not just occasionally irritating), then Jocasta is right, knowing the truth is not good for us. Another way to put this is to say that Nietzsche raises the question: what is the *value* of truth?[17] As for Plato, this is to put the good above the true, but for Nietzsche it is not at all to value the truth positively. Nietzsche's answer is that from the perspective of life the true may well lack value. That is the subversive proposition Nietzsche wants to force us to think about.

Nietzsche's position is a difficult one. What is good for us, *really* good for us, is not the true. The good requires lies. But this means that what is usually taken to be good for us, what is traditionally called morality, to the extent that it really is good for us, to the extent that it masks the horror of existence, to the extent that it preserves life, to that extent it must deceive, to that extent, then, we must say it is immoral, that is, *not* good. The true and the good have been so welded together over the millennia that it is very difficult to separate them.

Nietzsche's attempt to break them apart leads us to see that most any phi-losophy (or science, or religion) wants to do two different things. It wants in a very straightforward way simply to get at the truth. It has a commitment to, even a deep passion for, the truth—Nietzsche calls this *will to truth.* It has a drive to weed out the false and discover the true. At the same time, and (it thinks) as a consequence of this commitment to the truth, it seeks meaning and purpose, it wants to achieve the good for human beings. What could be more obvious—

even trivial? So, on the one hand, we have a desire to get to the real truth—good old honest correspondence with reality. Secondly, we expect this also to give us meaning, purpose, the good.

Except that all of this is predicated upon a gross error, namely, that the true and the good coincide. If the truth is that existence is horrible, if the true is the furthest thing from the good, then at least since Socrates we have been involved in serious contradiction. In so far as we pursue the real truth, insofar as we approach the horror and meaninglessness of existence, we are not headed toward meaning, purpose, or the good at all. We progress toward meaninglessness. On the other hand, in so far as we seek meaning, purpose, and the good, we must mask the true, conceal it, create illusion. What emerges from this are two different conceptions of truth, the truth as correspondence to reality and a truth which requires illusion, that is, merely, what *we take to be* true. We must see that Nietzsche has and needs both of these conceptions and that to understand him we must explore both. Let us begin to do that.

II. Avoiding the Truth

Some scholars, like Kaufmann, Wilcox, and Clark, think that for Nietzsche there are truths and that knowledge of them is both possible and desirable.[18] Other scholars like Danto and Green think that Nietzsche rejects the possibility of truth, but they and others also think that this gives rise to problems of self-contradiction.[19] Nehamas asks whether we are to understand Nietzsche as holding his positions to be true: "If he does, how can this possibly be consistent with his view that all views are only interpretations? If he does not—that is, if he does not think that his views are true—why does he make the effort to present them in the first place?"[20] Others, like Schutte, simply think that Nietzsche is inconsistent. He "does not have a systematic theory of truth; if he did, he would be violating some of his major insights on the subject."[21]

If one thinks that Nietzsche believes in truth, one will naturally gravitate toward those passages in Nietzsche's texts that endorse such a view, and there are plenty of such passages to be found. There will also be a natural tendency to want to downplay, subordinate, or interpret away those passages where Nietzsche rejects the possibility of truth, and there are plenty of these sorts of passages also. On the other hand, if one does not think that Nietzsche believes that truth is possible, one will tend to favor those texts where Nietzsche rejects truth, endorses perspectivism, and claims that all is interpretation. And one will tend to ignore or de-emphasize passages where Nietzsche makes truth claims.

In short, in my opinion, textual support can be found for two different positions here, but each is based on half the texts and does not really do justice to the other half.[22] My position will try to do justice to both sets of texts, and do so without holding that Nietzsche is simply unsystematic and contradicts himself.

I will argue that there *is* truth for Nietzsche. The truth is that existence is horrible and terrifying. Truth exists. But truth *must be avoided*—which is different from, though it will often look the same as, claiming that truth simply does not exist. Truth not only *must* be avoided, but we have through long evolution actually learned to avoid it. We have interpreted, simplified, and falsified our world so as to make life possible. We have buried the truth under the sediment of millennia. Truth is possible—at least conceptually possible. We do not have to worry about self-contradiction. But truth is most difficult to get at and thus, *fortunately*, is unavailable to us. That, I shall argue, is Nietzsche's position.

In *The Birth of Tragedy,* Nietzsche makes it quite clear that he believes in truth: "The truth once seen, man is aware everywhere of the ghastly absurdity of existence, comprehends the symbolism of Ophelia's fate and the wisdom of the wood sprite Silenus: nausea invades him."[23] In the *Genealogy of Morals,* he speaks of a will to truth, "the awe-inspiring *catastrophe* of two thousand years of training in truthfulness that finally forbids itself the *lie involved in belief in God.* . . . After Christian truthfulness has drawn one inference after another, it must end by drawing its *most striking inference*, its inference *against* itself. . . ."[24] In the same text, he also speaks of "plain, harsh, ugly, repellant, unchristian, immoral truth.—For such truths do exist.—"[25]

Quite clearly, for Nietzsche, truth exists. What, then, is his response to this horrible truth? If we read carefully, we see that his response, time and again, is that we *must avoid* this truth. In *The Birth of Tragedy,* he says: "The Greek knew and felt the terror and horror of existence. That he might endure this terror at all, he *had to* interpose between himself and life the radiant dream-birth of the Olympians. . . . It was in order to be able to live that the Greeks *had to* create these gods. . . ."[26] In the same text he also says that "Apollonian masks—are the *necessary* productions of a deep look into the horror of nature. . . ."[27] In *Will to Power,* he says, "there is only *one* world, and this is false, cruel, contradictory, seductive, without meaning. . . . *We have need of lies* in order to conquer this reality, this 'truth,' that is, in order to *live*— That lies are necessary in order to live is itself part of the terrifying and questionable character of existence."[28]

Thus, truth exists, but we *must*, we *had* to, it was *necessary* to, avoid it. This 'must,' we should notice, is a very deep sort of 'must,' an evolutionary 'must.' We have learned over millennia and in myriad ways to hide the truth. Most people normally assume that biological as well as cultural evolution would tend to improve our ability to get at the truth, that is, that survival would depend on, and thus select for, an ability to know the truth. That, however, makes sense only in a world that fits us—where the true and the good coincide. The evolution of a species for whom existence is horrible would be quite different. Its evolution and development would depend upon an ability to conceal the truth. Truth is not necessary for our preservation, rather:

> In order for a particular species to maintain itself and increase its power, its conception of reality must comprehend enough of the calculable and constant for it to base a scheme of behavior on it. The utility of preservation—not some abstract-theoretical need not to be deceived—stands as the motive behind the

development of the organs of knowledge—they develop in such a way that their observations suffice for our preservation.[29]

As Nietzsche puts it in *The Gay Science:*

"Innumerable beings who made inferences in a way different from ours perished; for all that, their ways might have been truer."[30]

Over immense periods of time the intellect produced nothing but errors. A few of these proved to be useful and helped to preserve the species: those who hit upon or inherited these had better luck in their struggle for themselves and their progeny. . . . It was only very late that truth emerged—as the weakest form of knowledge. It seemed that one was unable to live with it: our organism was prepared for the opposite; all its higher functions . . . worked with those basic errors which had been incorporated since time immemorial.[31]

In Nietzsche's view, knowing reduces, simplifies, and falsifies the world. In *Will to Power,* he says: "The entire apparatus of knowledge is an apparatus for abstraction and simplification—directed not at knowledge but at taking possession of things. . . ."[32] In *Beyond Good and Evil,* he says that we live in "simplification and falsification,"[33] and also:

Our eye finds it more comfortable to respond to a given stimulus by reproducing once more an image that it has produced many times before, instead of registering what is different and new in an impression. . . . We make up the major part of the experience and can scarcely be forced *not* to contemplate some event as its "inventors." All this means: basically and from time immemorial we are—*accustomed to lying.* Or to put it more virtuously and hypocritically, in short, more pleasantly: one is much more of an artist than one knows.[34]

III. Taking to be True

What clearly begins to emerge here is the second sense in which Nietzsche uses the term 'truth.' Besides *real truth,* the horror of existence, Nietzsche regularly talks about what we *take to be true,* truths we have *constructed,* truths whose function it is to mask the real truth—that is, illusions. For example, in *Will to Power,* he says, "Truth is the kind of error without which a certain species of life could not live."[35] In "On Truth and Lies," he says: "What then is truth? . . . Truths are illusions which we have forgotten are illusions; they are metaphors that have become worn out and have been drained of sensuous force, coins which have lost their embossing and are now considered as metal and no longer as coins."[36] He also says, "life requires illusions, i.e. untruths which are taken to be truths."[37] Thus, Nietzsche will frequently speak of 'my truths,' as when he indicates a desire "to state a few truths about 'woman as such'—assuming that it is now known from the outset how very much these are after all only—*my* truths."[38]

Nietzsche's views on the relation of women and truth, while ugly and objectionable concerning women, are very informative concerning this second kind of truth.[39] Nietzsche says: "Supposing truth is a woman—what then? Are there not grounds for the suspicion that all philosophers, insofar as they were dogmatic, have been very inexpert about women. . . . What is certain is that she has not allowed herself to be won."[40]

Nietzsche also says:

> Woman wants to become self-reliant—and for that reason she is beginning to enlighten men about "woman as such." . . . We may in the end reserve a healthy suspicion whether woman really *wants* enlightenment about herself. . . . Unless a woman seeks a new adornment for herself that way. . . . But she does not *want* truth: what is truth to a woman? From the beginning, nothing has been more alien, repugnant, and hostile to woman than truth—her great art is the lie, her highest concern is mere appearance and beauty.[41]

> No, we are disgusted with this bad taste, this will to truth, this search after truth "at all costs." . . . We no longer believe that truth remains truth when it is unveiled. . . . Perhaps truth is a woman who has reasons for *not revealing her reasons?* . . . Perhaps her name, to use a Greek word is *Baubo?* . . . [I]t is needful to halt bravely at the surface . . . to worship appearance. . . . These Greeks were superficial—from *profundity.*[42]

This is the same point that we have been making all along. It is not that we cannot get to the naked truth. Truth exists, it is theoretically possible to get to it, but we *should not,* and we should not *want* to, get to it.[43] Instead, woman constructs a second kind of truth, that is, beauty, surface appearance, illusion, lie.[44]

There is one other matter that we should notice here. Lukács claims that Nietzsche has no criterion of truth other than usefulness and that he was an important precursor of pragmatism.[45] Pragmatic considerations may be at work in determining (and Nietzsche may even have a pragmatic theory of) what we *take to be* true, that is, illusions necessary to promote life. But that does not make what we take to be true *actually* true and Nietzsche certainly does not have a pragmatic theory of what makes something actually true. In *Will to Power,* he writes:

> The most strongly believed a priori "truths" are for me—*provisional assumptions;* e.g., the law of causality, a very well acquired habit of belief, so much a part of us that not to believe in it would destroy the race. But are they for that reason truths? What a conclusion! As if the preservation of man were a proof of truth![46]

IV. A Consistent Account of Truth

As I have already said, scholars who think that for Nietzsche truth is both possible and desirable tend to downplay those passages where Nietzsche rejects the possibility of truth, and scholars who think that Nietzsche rejects the possibility of truth tend to downplay those passages where Nietzsche clearly holds that there is knowledge of the truth. No commentator that I am aware of makes consistent sense out of both sets of passages. I suggest that the interpretation I have given does so. Nietzsche makes statements that clearly claim that there is truth and he makes statements that clearly claim that there is no truth. How do we reconcile these seemingly contradictory claims? Truth exists. The truth is that existence is horrible. We can know this truth, but it would likely mean our annihilation. Thus we must avoid it. Moreover, through millennia of evolution we have actually learned to avoid it. We have buried it and replaced it with what we *take to be* true, with *our* truths, that is, with illusions. And thus all those texts which suggest that there is no truth make perfect sense. There is, in fact, no truth—it has been buried. The claim that there is no truth, here, is not an ontological claim. It is a social, cultural, or historical claim. We have buried the truth. We could with great effort dig back through millennia of sediment to find it. Ontologically truth is possible, but socially, culturally, and historically it no longer exists.

Nor does Nietzsche have any problem with self-contradiction. As long as he admits that truth is possible, there is no contradiction at all in holding that we have buried it and live in illusion. There is no self-refutation here as there is supposed to be when one says, 'nothing is true'—it is usually held that if that statement were true, then it would be false. It is not the case that Nietzsche rejects the concept of truth, and thus cannot legitimately employ the concept, such that one can embarrass him by asking whether his rejection of truth is to be taken as true. He accepts the possibility of truth and thus can with full legitimacy employ the concept. The concept is not lost to him. He just thinks we must and have avoided truth, buried it, and created illusions that make life possible.

Still, a very common objection to Nietzsche runs as follows. Nietzsche claims that all is perspective, interpretation, or illusion. What then of Nietzsche's own view that all is perspective, interpretation, or illusion? Is it itself also merely a perspective, interpretation, or illusion? If we answer yes, as Nietzsche seems to do at *Beyond Good and Evil* §22,[47] then, as Smith puts it, doesn't this leave Nietzsche's view "open to dismissal as merely another groundless perspective?"[48]

But how did we all of a sudden arrive at the conclusion that perspectives, interpretations, or illusions are to be *dismissed as groundless?* Nietzsche would not agree. Some perspectives are far more valuable than the truth. If the truth is horror, if we might perish from the truth, then we dismiss perspective, interpretation, or illusion at our own risk. If perspectives are more valuable than the truth, if they promote life, if they save us from the truth, they are certainly not to be dismissed.[49] What must be dismissed is the notion that just because something is a perspective, interpretation, or illusion it is not to be taken seriously. It must be admitted, certainly, that such illusions are not true, but, then, their very function is to protect us from the truth. Thus, as far as I can see, Nietzsche has no problem in admitting that his views are perspectives, interpretations, or illusions. Smith also claims that "to assert that objective truth is a fiction is to make a statement of objective truth, which thereby denounces itself as a fiction."[50] But again this is only so if to call truth a fiction is to *denounce* it as a fiction. What if fiction has a greater value than truth? What if fiction preserves us from a horrible truth? Then to call it a fiction is certainly not to denounce it.

What about when Nietzsche makes such extreme claims as: "Nothing is true . . . ,"[51] "there is no truth . . . ," or "Everything is false!"[52] Are not such claims self-refuting? Maybe not. In the first place, we have seen that for Nietzsche truth is theoretically possible. That means there can be some truths. Could these statements be among them? That depends on what these statements are taken to mean. They could mean that given millennia of evolution, given the need to avoid the horror of existence, the need to create illusions that make life possible, there is in fact no truth left to be found. Thus, all is false, nothing is true. These claims need not mean that it would be impossible to dig back to the truth. They need not mean that it is absolutely impossible to get at the truth. And thus they need not rule out our use of the concept. They can very well mean merely that truth has systematically been buried. And then perhaps we must just admit that these claims are rhetorically overstated a bit for dramatic effect. At any rate, it would seem that this is the way such statements must be read if we are also to take seriously other passages where Nietzsche clearly claims that truth is possible.

But still we have not yet fully come to terms with the issue here. How much truth can there be in the world—can there be *any* at all—if we are to meaningfully claim that *everything* is false? Indeed, Nietzsche speaks of a will to truth, which is something we find especially in modern science, and he thinks that science can get us all the way to the ultimate truth. It can eventually bring us face to face with the horror of existence and plunge us into nihilism. Moreover, before we reach that catastrophe, Nietzsche's view seems to be, science can also get us a good deal of ordinary truth.[53] How much truth can it give us? And how is such truth compatible with Nietzsche's claim that there is no truth?

Science can ultimately get us to real truth. It can get us to the horror of existence and plunge us into the void. But short of this horror, short of ultimate truth, what does science get us? Does it, for example, continuously accumulate bits of *real* truth or merely what we *take to be* truth? If it only gets us the latter, what we *take to be* truth, that is, illusion, how could it ever through the accumulation of such illusions get us to the ultimate truth, the *real* truth—the horror of existence? On the other hand, if we admit that science does regularly accumulate *real* truth, then there would seem to be a *lot* of real truth sitting around. If science has been accumulating a lot of real truth, this would seem to call in question statements like: "Nothing is true . . . ," "there is no truth . . . ," "Everything is false!" Must we then just accuse Nietzsche of using language too loosely in such passages and thus of contradicting his concept of science as a will to truth? Well, Nietzsche at least would not seem to think so. In *Beyond Good and Evil,* he says that the will to ignorance is not the opposite of the will to knowledge, *but its refinement.*[54] We must see, I think, that the sorts of truths generated by will to knowledge, will to truth, or science, while they may in one sense be *real* truths, are yet in another sense also deceptions, thus merely what we *take to be* truths, that is, illusions. Let me try to explain.

We seek the truth, we seek knowledge, we gather up as much scientific understanding as we can, we make continuous progress at this, and doing so will for us mask the ultimate horror and meaninglessness of the cosmos. This is to say that the accumulation of scientific truth, which may be real truth, will deflect us from, prevent us from seeing, the horror, emptiness, and meaninglessness of existence—the ultimate truth. The scientific amassing of truth thus hides the truth. Truth conceals the truth—*truth,* don't we have to say it, *can lie.* There is a great deal of falsehood—simple and ordinary falsehood—that derives from the millennia of our avoiding the horror of existence. But there is even more falsehood in that truths—simple and ordinary truths, even *real* truths—can also serve to mask the horror of existence, that is, mask the truth. Our *search* for truth is really a deep and complex way of *hiding* the truth. I think we could even say that rigorous, syllogistic, logical truth, insofar as it absorbs us, insofar as we find it impossible to doubt, insofar as we find it meaningful and significant, deflects us from the ultimate truth, the horror, emptiness, and meaninglessness of existence—it *deceives.* Thus, while we can say that, for Nietzsche, a great deal of truth may exist, nevertheless, there is also a falseness about it. It functions to mask the ultimate truth. And so Nietzsche has not really contradicted his claims that "Nothing is true . . . ," "there is no truth . . . ," "Everything is false!"[55] It is much like what Nietzsche says of Sterne, the author of *Tristram Shandy.* The reader who demands to know exactly what Sterne "really thinks of a thing, whether he is making a serious or a laughing face, must be given up for lost; for [Sterne] knows how to encompass both in a *single* facial expression; he likewise knows how, and even wants to be in the right and in the wrong at the same time. . . ."[56]

Still, one might want to object to this, one might want to ask scholars like myself whether we take our own explanations of Nietzsche's views on truth to be accurate, correct—that is, true? And we would have to admit that we do. One might then think that this would contradict the Nietzschean dictum that 'nothing is true.' That, however, would be a mistake. An accurate explanation of Nietzsche's views, as much as any other truth, is capable of deflecting us from the ultimate truth, the horror of existence, and thus of being a deception.

Philosophy, science, religion, all of them, demand the truth, yet at the same time they all serve to mask the horror of existence—they falsify. They thus move in two opposed directions. When they are caught in this contradiction, or when they catch themselves, they are in a real fix. They cannot accept deception, lies, contradiction. They demand the truth. Art, on the other hand, does not have these problems. Art masks reality, constructs fictions, creates beautiful illusions, all with a perfectly good conscience.[57] Indeed, art can fully achieve its aims, even its own greatness, in doing so.

In philosophy, if one states the proposition, 'there is no truth,' it is usually taken to be self-refuting. It dismisses itself. If philosophy makes such a claim, it is usually taken to be bad philosophy, and we tend to think that it communicates nothing, or nothing of value. Art, however, can communicate such notions and may even impart a good deal of wisdom in doing so. Kurosawa's *Rashomon* is a good example. *Rashomon* is a film in which four participants in the same event each recount that event. Each tells the story of what happened, but each story is different. In fact, each story profoundly contradicts the other stories. We come away with the sense that no story could capture the truth of the event. Another story would just be another story. We are left with a bit of wisdom concerning the nature of the reality we live in, that it is unlikely we will ever know the truth about it. We are left with a powerful artistic experience and a bit of wisdom, not a self-refuting proposition.

Rather than it being the case that claims like 'there is no truth' are self-refuting, Nietzsche seems to think, instead, that any system that holds truth to be the highest value will be self-refuting. Any system that pursues truth rigorously and thoroughly will ultimately demonstrate its own falsehood—it will ultimately come to see that its pursuit of truth has in fact worked to hide the horror of existence, hide the ultimate truth, and thus that its pursuit of truth has contradicted itself. As Nietzsche says: "All great things bring about their own destruction. . . . In this way Christianity . . . was destroyed. . . . After Christian truthfulness has drawn one inference after another, it must end by drawing its *most striking inference,* its inference *against* itself. . . ."[58]

We must still say a bit more about truth. If we could actually know the truth, for Nietzsche, what exactly would that mean? We can approach truth, he thinks, but as we do we risk paralysis, the dissolution of our individuality, and even death. Any truth claim never quite makes it all the way to the truth. Truth and life are opposed. To get too close to truth can lose you your life. To remain alive you had better not get too close to the truth. Nevertheless, for Nietzsche, we can legitimately have a *concept* of truth—truth as a regulative idea. We are not condemned to self-refutation. Moreover, all of this is compatible with a correspondence theory of truth. We can *know that* existence is horrible. The general claim that 'existence is horrible' corresponds to, accurately describes, reality.

Nevertheless, we must see that such abstract knowing, for Nietzsche, already involves a distance from the truth,[59] a deflection of it, a making it less horrible, a preventing it from *truly* being horrible, from overwhelming us and causing us to perish. Such knowing, then, *distorts* the truth. That is, real truth, truth which really corresponds to reality, in so far as it interests us and absorbs us, serves to veil the horror of existence, distract us from it, hide the truth. Truth itself masks the truth.

In Nietzsche's view, we can get *closer* to truth than the correspondence theory allows, closer than the abstraction of a statement accurately describing reality. Tragic drama, in Nietzsche's opinion, can get us closer to the horror of existence, "it depicts reality more truthfully and more completely. . . ."[60] Tragedy allows us not merely to *know that* existence is horrible, but to *know of* this horror, to actually *know the horror,* that is, to experience it. But still there is an aesthetic veiling going on even in tragic drama. We still have a distance from the truth. We are not paralyzed, our individuality is not dissolved, and we do not perish.

We can get even closer to the truth than is possible in the tragic experience. We can do so in a pure Dionysian experience, an experience unmixed with an Apollonian (or any other sort of) veil. However, we might not return from such an experience. We might perish. And at any rate, we would not be conscious as individuals during such an experience. Nevertheless, this is to get as close to the truth as we can get.

What does it mean to hold that we can perish from the truth? Obviously writing or reading the proposition, 'existence is horrible,' will not kill anyone. We have millennia of evolutionary sediment protecting us. We would have to experience this horror, dwell in it, it would have to gain possession of us, it would have to overcome us.

Thus, generally speaking, truth must be avoided and has been avoided. Nevertheless, as we have seen, it would be possible with great effort to move back toward it. Indeed, Nietzsche even sees this as a test of our strength:

> Something might be true while being harmful and dangerous in the highest degree. Indeed, it might be a basic characteristic of existence that those who would know it completely would perish, in which case the strength of a spirit should be measured according to how much of the "truth" one could still barely endure—or to put it more clearly, to what degree one would *require* it to be thinned down, shrouded, sweetened, blunted, falsified.[61]

Nietzsche also says, "Truth has had to be fought for every step of the way, almost everything else dear to our hearts, on which our love and our trust in life depend, has had to be sacrificed to it. Greatness of soul is needed for it. . . ."[62] Thus, truth exists, but it is horrible and must be avoided. Indeed, for millennia we have been burying it. It would take great effort to get to it, and the test of our strength is how much of the truth we can bear. It would be heroic to gain as much truth as we are able.[63]

Sophocles, too, thought the truth was horrible. For Jocasta it was something to be shunned. But Oedipus plows ahead and demands the truth. Truth is terrible, but nevertheless we want it, need it, demand it. To suffer under illusion is demeaning. To stand in the light of truth is a deep spiritual need. We cannot get all the way there, up outside the cave, but we want as much as we can bear. What then is the value of truth? It is horrible and terrible. It must be avoided. Yet it is a test of our strength—our greatness.

Chapter Three

Chaos, the Self, and Will to Power

I. Meaningless Suffering

We have started to see what follows from the realization that existence is horrible, but before proceeding further, we must back up a bit and try to understand at a deeper level exactly why it is that existence is so terrible. In the process, we should again take care to notice that the horror of existence is not a concept found only or mainly in early texts like the *Birth of Tragedy*. It is absolutely central in very late texts like the *Genealogy of Morals*. At any rate, the horror of existence does not mean, we have seen, merely that existence involves suffering. Nietzsche explicitly rejects that explanation. At *Genealogy of Morals,* III, §28, he claims that man is:

> surrounded by a fearful *void*—he did not know how to justify, to account for, to affirm himself; he *suffered* from the problem of his meaning. He also suffered otherwise . . . but his problem was *not* suffering itself, but that there was no answer to the crying question, *"why* do I suffer?"
> Man . . . the one most accustomed to suffering, does *not* repudiate suffering as such; he *desires* it, he even seeks it out, provided he is shown a *meaning* for it, a *purpose* of suffering. The meaninglessness of suffering, *not* suffering itself, was the curse that lay over mankind.[1]

We live in an empty and meaningless cosmos, a cosmos that does not care about us, and we cannot face this. Suffering we can handle, but meaningless suffering, suffering for no reason at all, we cannot handle. So what do we do? We give suffering a meaning. We invent a meaning. We create an illusion. The Greeks constructed gods for whom wars and other forms of suffering were festival plays and thus occasions to be celebrated by the poets. Christians imagine a God for whom suffering is punishment for sin.[2]

Nietzsche even thinks we used to enjoy inflicting suffering on others:

> To see others suffer does one good, to make others suffer even more. . . . [I]n the days when mankind was not yet ashamed of its cruelty, life on earth was more cheerful than it is now. . . . Today, when suffering is always brought forward as the principal argument *against* existence, as the worst question mark,

one does well to recall the ages in which the opposite opinion prevailed because men were unwilling to refrain from *making* suffer and saw in it an enchantment of the first order, a genuine seduction *to* life.[3]

Why was the infliction of suffering so enjoyable? Why was it a seduction to life? The answer is not, I do not think, that people of past ages were just sadists, as Danto and others seem to think.[4] Rather, since meaningless suffering is unbearable, we give it a meaning. We make it a punishment and inflict it ourselves. In doing so, suffering is made to participate in the web of meaning we have created. That is why it is so enjoyable to inflict suffering. That is why it is a seduction to life. We engage in practices that invest suffering with the meaning it must have for us. We unconsciously participate in the imposition of meaning. We keep meaninglessness at bay. It is true that suffering in the world is thereby increased, but that, Nietzsche seems to be suggesting, is worth it as the price of removing *meaningless* suffering.

But we are not content, in Nietzsche's opinion, merely to inflict suffering on others. We go further. We inflict it upon *ourselves.* As society develops and we are unable to discharge our instincts outwardly, we direct them within. We create guilt.[5] And priests are quick to nurture this new development.[6] Just as we inflict suffering on others to keep meaningless suffering at bay, so we inflict it upon ourselves. We give *all* suffering a meaning. No meaningless suffering is allowed to remain—anywhere. "[W]here there was suffering, one always wanted punishment too."[7] We reinterpret "suffering as feelings of guilt, fear, and punishment; everywhere the scourge, the hair shirt, the starving body, contrition; everywhere the sinner breaking himself on the cruel wheel of a restless, morbidly lascivious conscience."[8] We make guilt "the *sole* cause of suffering."[9] And just as inflicting suffering on others was a seduction to life, so in inflicting it on ourselves, "life again became *very* interesting . . . one no longer protested *against* pain, one *thirsted* for pain; *'more* pain! *more* pain!'"[10]

To remove meaningless suffering, it is quite clear, we bring about *greater* suffering, "deeper, more inward, more poisonous, more life-destructive suffering. . . ."[11] Moreover, it is clear that in Nietzsche's view it is *desirable* to increase suffering: "You want, if possible—and there is no more insane 'if possible'—*to abolish suffering*. And we? It really seems that *we* would rather have it higher and worse than ever. . . . The discipline of suffering, of *great* suffering— do you not know that only *this* discipline has created all enhancements of man so far?"[12]

Nevertheless, Nietzsche wants to rid guilt and punishment so as to restore the innocence of existence:

> This instinct of revenge has so mastered mankind in the course of millennia that the whole of metaphysics, psychology, conception of history, but above all morality, is impregnated with it. . . . He has made even God ill with it, he has *deprived existence* in general *of its innocence;* namely, by tracing back every state of being thus and thus to a will, an intention, a responsible act. The entire doctrine of the will, this most fateful *falsification* in psychology hitherto, was

essentially invented for the sake of punishment. . . . [T]he priests at the head of the oldest communality: they wanted to create for themselves a right to take revenge—they wanted to create a right for *God* to take revenge. To this end, man was conceived of as "free"; to this end, every action had to be conceived of as willed. . . . [W]e halcyonians especially are trying with all our might to withdraw, banish, and extinguish the concepts of guilt and punishment from the world.[13]

There might seem to be a lack of clarity here as to whether Nietzsche wants to eliminate or intensify guilt, punishment, and suffering. To understand his position, we must be careful to distinguish between punishment and guilt, on the one hand, and suffering, on the other. Suffering is fine. In Nietzsche's view, we should even increase it. But suffering needs to be given a meaning. It has none of its own. We live in an empty, meaningless cosmos and we cannot stand meaningless suffering. One way that we have traditionally given suffering a meaning, we have just seen, has been by constructing a God who punishes us for what we take to be our sins. This does give suffering a meaning. It is better than meaningless suffering. But it produces guilt and eliminates the innocence of existence. It subordinates sufferers to their suffering. It produces a spirit of revenge. Nietzsche wants to rid punishment, guilt, and sin entirely. He wants to restore innocence. But he does not want to rid suffering—he does not think that is even possible. He wants to increase suffering. And he wants to give it a different meaning, one which, as we shall see, strengthens rather than weakens the sufferer.

Thus, Nietzsche's position here is that because we cannot accept meaningless suffering, we have given it a meaning—as punishment. We inflict punishment ourselves to invest it with a meaning. In fact, we go even further, we inflict suffering on ourselves internally—we invent guilt. We also invent a will and thus responsibility so that we can be held guilty and so that God can have a right to inflict punishment.[14] We create the spirit of revenge. Nietzsche wants to overthrow this whole set of meanings that have been given to suffering, return us to the innocence of existence, and construct a different meaning for suffering.

II. God Is Dead

Still, we must say more to explain why existence is horrible. We have said that it is so because it involves meaningless suffering. But why is it that existence is taken to be *meaningless?* For Nietzsche, there are two major reasons. The first is that God is dead. As he puts it in *The Gay Science:*

Have you not heard of that madman who lit a lantern in the bright morning hours, ran to the market place, and cried incessantly: "I seek God! I seek God!" . . . "Whither is God?" he cried; "I will tell you. *We have killed him*—you and I. All of us are his murderers. But how did we do this? How could we drink up the sea? Who gave us the sponge to wipe away the entire horizon? What were we doing when we unchained this earth from its sun? . . . God is dead. God remains dead. And we have killed him.[15]

Nietzsche does not believe in God, certainly not the Christian God. He thinks we have constructed God. His claim that God is dead means that we no longer believe in our construction.[16] Despite Nietzsche's atheism, however, there is still something peculiarly religious about his thought. He is anti-religious, but in such a way as to fall within the orbit of basic religious assumptions. Nietzsche seems to agree with traditional theology on a major point. Both hold that God is the center of all meaning and value—that without God we would be plunged into an empty and meaningless void.[17] The difference between traditional theology and Nietzsche is that for the former (fortunately, from its perspective) God does exist and we are saved from meaninglessness. For Nietzsche, on the other hand, God does not exist and we are thus condemned to a meaningless void.

We might contrast this to a very different sort of atheism, that of Feuerbach and Marx. They do not think that atheism eliminates all meaning and value. For them, God is our construction just as much as for Nietzsche, but we do not construct God to hide from ourselves an empty and meaningless void. Feuerbach and Marx do not believe in such nihilism. For them, meaning and value can be discovered—it is just that they have been impossible to realize in the human world. Existing conditions blocked their actualization and thus we projected them into a beyond. For Feuerbach and Marx, religion contains a great deal of real value and truth—it just misplaces it in an other world. For them, atheism means rejecting religion's beyond and realizing its values and truths in this world.[18] For Nietzsche, atheism plunges us into meaninglessness. Feuerbach and Marx believe in a perfectible cosmos, Nietzsche a horrific one.

III. Chaos

Even if we were to decide that Nietzsche's atheism is less acceptable than other forms of atheism, nevertheless, he has a second and independent reason why existence is meaningless. Reality just is not the sort of thing that *can* have any meaning. Reality is chaos. Nietzsche tells us that the world is chaos in that it lacks all order, arrangement, and form.[19] He speaks of a "formless unformulable world of the chaos of sensations. . . ."[20] He holds that reality is a "tremendous multiplicity." It is a ceaseless flux of coming to be and passing away.[21] Nothing remains the same, "what appears is always something new. . . ."[22] "Every moment devours the preceding one. . . ."[23] Reality is unfathomable. To look into reality is to see the emptiness, meaninglessness, and thus horror, of existence:

> The everlasting and exclusive coming-to-be, the impermanence of everything actual, which constantly acts and comes-to-be but never is, as Heraclitus teaches it, is a terrible, paralyzing thought. Its impact on men can most nearly

be likened to the sensation during an earthquake when one loses one's familiar confidence in a firmly grounded earth.[24]

Knowledge is impossible if all is sheer becoming. Thus most philosophers have rejected becoming and sought being.[25] But Nietzsche finds it impossible to accept the metaphysical notions these philosophers have traditionally used to fabricate being behind becoming. There is no substance or substratum, no unity, behind becoming. There is no thing-in-itself, no true world, distinct from appearance.[26] In Nietzsche's opinion, even the laws and categories of logic, the very principles of identity and non-contradiction, falsify the world.[27] The grammatical structure of language leads us into these errors.[28]

For Nietzsche, all knowing, perceiving, and sensing involve projection from a perspective. We simplify chaos, we impose familiar patterns, we establish sameness and identity, we exclude the new and different. These are necessary presuppositions for any knowledge or perception. But all are falsifications, distortions, lies, illusions. All are interpretations. There are no facts here, only interpretations.[29]

Thus, to say that reality is chaos is to say that it is so complex, so formless and disordered, so changing, that it cannot be grasped. Anything meaningful or significant about such reality, any knowledge or perception, requires simplification, fabrication, falsification.[30]

IV. The Kantian Self

It is not the case, however, that chaos is found merely in the world outside. If we turn within, we find chaos there too.[31] We might say we have a chaos facing a chaos, except that chaos is not the sort of thing that can be separated and individualized so neatly. For Nietzsche, neither the ego nor the will are simple entities. They are structures, nothing but complex multiplicities of sensations. And the simplest sensation is something infinitely composite. The notion of the ego as a simple unified entity is the result of interpretation—that is, simplification and falsification.[32] Furthermore, Nietzsche repeatedly says that if there is no unified subject, then there can be no unified object.[33] In this he is like Kant. Indeed, Nietzsche's entire epistemology, and especially his concept of the self, grow out of Kant's thought—and then attempt to subvert Kant's thought.

In the Transcendental Deduction of the first edition of the *Critique of Pure Reason*, Kant says: "If each representation were completely foreign to every other, standing apart in isolation, no such thing as knowledge would ever arise. For knowledge is [essentially] a whole in which representations stand compared and connected."[34] For knowledge to be possible, the manifold of sensation must be run through and held together. Coherent experience, Kant argues, requires a threefold synthesis: a synthesis of apprehension in intuition, a synthesis of reproduction in imagination, and a synthesis of recognition in a concept. These are not three separate steps; they are inseparable moments of one synthesis. In the synthesis of apprehension, for Kant, the imagination takes up impressions, apprehends them, forms them into an image, and makes them modifications of the mind belonging to inner sense and thus subject to time. Inner sense is thoroughgoingly temporal. Our representations appear to us successively in time. They are ordered, connected, and related in time.[35]

This synthesis of apprehension, however, cannot by itself give us ordered experience. A second synthesis is also necessary. The mind must be able to reinstate preceding perceptions alongside subsequent ones and hold them together in a temporal series. We need to retain, remember, and reproduce perceptions. We need a synthesis of reproduction in imagination.[36] If I try to "think of the time from one noon to another," Kant tells us, and "if I were always to drop out of thought the preceding representations . . . [if I] did not reproduce them while advancing to those that follow," then, he says, "not even the . . . most elementary representations . . . could arise."[37] We must be aware that what we think is the same as what we thought a moment before.[38] Otherwise we would have nothing but disjointed chaos. We would not be able to connect earlier with later perceptions of an event or object—they would not belong together for us. One sentence of a speech, even one word, since it would not be remembered, could not be connected with the next. We would have no experience that we would call experience.

Still, even this is not enough. Representations, if they are to give rise to knowledge, cannot be reproduced in any old order. The reproduction, Kant thinks, must conform to a rule according to which a perception is connected with some one representation rather than another.[39] The categories of the understanding provide these rules—rules for the necessary reproduction of the manifold.[40] A third synthesis, then, is also necessary. A synthesis of recognition in a concept is necessary to determine the specific order and relation of the reproduction of representations. The only way to grasp these successive and remembered moments in one cognition and the only way to unify these sensations into one object is through concepts that organize and unify them. Without these concepts we would not have an object, but merely a disjointed series of isolated, remembered sensations. Furthermore, this threefold synthesis requires a unity of consciousness—Kant calls it the transcendental unity of apperception.[41] For Hume, there was no fixed, stable, unified self that could be experienced. When we turn to inner sense, we experience nothing but a flux of shifting and changing ideas, images, impressions, feelings, and so forth.[42] Kant agrees with Hume that we never *experience* a unified self.[43] But for Kant there must be a unified self. If not, then the diverse multitude of sensations, the temporal flux that constitutes inner sense, would not belong to a single consciousness and thus could not belong to me. The flux must be unified within a single self for experience to be possible—or else this flux of images could not be *my* flux of images. It could not be *my* experience.[44] As Kant puts it in the second edition, it must be possible for an "I think" to accompany all my representations.[45] If not, I would have no experience—"merely a blind play of representations, less even than a dream."[46]

At the very same time, there is also a second unity involved here—that of the object. For the manifold of sensations to be unified as one object, it is also the case that this manifold must be contained in a unified self. If we cannot presuppose a transcendental unity of apperception, there is no way to understand the possibility of a unified object. The transcendental unity of apperception through the categories forms a unified object. Thus the transcendental unity of apperception is an *objective* condition of all experience. It is not merely a subjective condition that I require in order to have experience of an object. It is an objective condition under which representations must stand in order to become an object for me.[47] Representations for their part must be capable of association; they must have what Kant calls an affinity. They must be able to enter the mind, conform to the unity of apperception, and be subject to the rules of the categories.[48]

This might all seem to be just a bizarre problem that idealists are stuck with and that other philosophers can avoid. But that is not the case at all. Kant, it is true, suggests that our experience is constructed out of unconnected elements. This might strike some as an unacceptable view, but for it to be right, we must see, it need not at all be the case that things-in-themselves are unconnected. Let us assume, as a realist would, that things are fully organized and connected independently of our perception. Nevertheless, we must still *apprehend* these things, and in doing so we would have to organize and connect *our various representations*—whatever the character of the thing itself.

Suppose a house exists before us. We apprehend a foundation, walls, roof, chimney, windows, doors, and so forth. Even if they are organized and connected in themselves as for the best realist, we must still organize and connect them *in our apprehension,* or for us there would only be disconnected chaos. Each shingle on the roof, brick of the chimney, pane of the window, panel of the door—all the way down to the minutest aspects of the manifold of sensation— would have to be grasped in our apprehension, reproduced in memory, subsumed under concepts, and brought under the unity of apperception. If not, we would have unconnected chaos.[49] Our senses separate things. We apprehend the roof separately from the foundation; we can fail to remember one aspect of a perception as connected with preceding perceptions. We must organize each of these representations in our inner experience—whatever the world in itself might be like. A threefold synthesis and a transcendental unity of apperception are necessary presuppositions of any ordered experience—for any sort of theory of experience.

Postmodern theorists have attacked the notion of a unified subject. I do not think, however, that they can get away with simply rejecting Kant's notion of a unified self. It is true that selves may have more than one identity they are torn between or undecided about. They may also feel socially pressured toward a single identity as if it were supposed to be their essence and such that other parts of the self are denied, repressed, or marginalized. We may even admit that the self is undermined and subverted by an unconscious. Nevertheless, Kant convincingly shows us that there has to be enough unity in the first place for this self to have experience sufficiently organized to then go on to say that it wavers between multiple identities, feels pressured toward one and marginalizes others, or is undermined by an unconscious. We cannot dismiss Kant, though we can decide that things are more complicated than he thought they were.

What follows from the Kantian notion of a unified self, for Nietzsche, is that if all connection, unity, and organization are dependent upon and consti- tuted by a unified ego, then, if it turns out that the unity of this ego exists only as illusion, all organized objects too would only be illusions. Objects might appear unified, experience might appear organized, but really there would be total ab- sence of connection, unity, and organization in things—all would really be chaos. This is Nietzsche's view—and I want to work toward showing that it is. He says in *Will to Power:* "If we give up the effective subject, we also give up the object. . . ."[50] Nietzsche agrees, I think, that a unified subject and a threefold synthesis (or something very close to it) are necessary presuppositions for or- dered experience to be possible.[51] Nevertheless, he thinks that a unified subject is a fiction, that organized experience is mere appearance, and thus that the threefold synthesis falsifies reality. He says:

> If our "ego" is for us the sole being, after the model of which we fashion and understand all being: very well! Then there would be very much room to doubt whether what we have here is not a perspective illusion—an apparent unity that encloses everything like a horizon.[52]

> We need "unities" in order to be able to reckon: that does not mean we must suppose that such unities exist. We have borrowed the concept of unity from our "ego" concept—our oldest article of faith. If we did not hold ourselves to be unities, we would never have formed the concept "thing." Now, somewhat late, we are firmly convinced that our conception of the ego does not guarantee any actual unity.[53]

Nietzsche says in *Will to Power* that it is only on the model of the subject that we have invented the reality of things and projected them into our experi- ence. If we no longer believe in this subject, then belief will disappear in things.[54] It will also disappear in causes which produce things. In *Beyond Good and Evil,* Nietzsche tells us that while belief in the truth of causal judgments, or (to use Kant's language) synthetic a priori judgments, is necessary for the pres- ervation of creatures like ourselves, nevertheless such judgments are "nothing but false judgments."[55]

V. Forgetfulness

We must also notice that forgetfulness plays a central role in Nietzsche's epis- temology. In appropriating Kant's threefold synthesis, Nietzsche makes a very interesting addition. Kant, we have seen, made memory central to the constitu- tion of experience. The mind must be able to reinstate preceding perceptions alongside subsequent ones and hold them together through time. We must be aware that what we think is the same as what we thought a moment before. Otherwise experience would dissolve into disjointed chaos. Nietzsche too admits that such reproduction is necessary,[56] but he thinks that memory alone is only part of the story. We do not and cannot remember the myriad flux of sensations we are continually bombarded with. We would be overwhelmed. We must forget. We must reduce and simplify—or all we would have is chaos. As Nietzsche puts it:

> Imagine the extremest possible example of a man who did not possess the power of forgetting at all and who was thus condemned to see everywhere a state of becoming: such a man would no longer believe in his own being, would no longer believe in himself, would see everything flowing asunder in moving points and would lose himself in this stream of becoming . . . it is altogether impossible to *live* at all without forgetting.[57]

A unified self must be able to hold together all its experience. Experience must appear to me as *my* experience. If not, if things are too complex, if I am overwhelmed by a chaos of sensations, if I cannot unify the object, then I could not experience anything as *my* experience, and if I could not do that I would not be able to believe in myself. After all, as Hume showed, we have no *experience* of the self.[58] The most basic indication I can have of my self comes through the organization of experience as *my* experience. If I fail to do that, if things are too complex, what indication could there be that there is a self behind the chaotic flux of inner experience?[59] For the self to be sure of itself, it must reduce, simplify, forget enough so that it can construct the object as *its* experience.

In fact, in the *Genealogy of Morals,* Nietzsche even makes forgetfulness the more basic faculty. Memory, of course, is necessary for the moment to moment holding together and reproduction of perceptions, and longer term memory is also necessary for responsibility—the keeping of promises. For the latter sort of memory to develop it must overcome our basic tendency to forgetfulness. It is Nietzsche's view that overcoming forgetfulness is not easily accomplished. It requires some doing. A memory must actually be "burned" into human beings over a long period of time.[60] This suggests that forgetfulness is the more powerful faculty.

Moreover, Nietzsche thinks that forgetfulness is necessary even for memory itself to be possible: "memory is possible only with a continual emphasizing of what is already familiar, experienced.— Before judgment occurs, the process of assimilation must already have taken place."[61] We must forget the new and different, we must reduce the chaotic multiplicity of becoming, we must assimilate, we must establish the familiar. Until we do so, it is impossible to remember.

Nietzsche even thinks "there could be . . . no *present,* without forgetfulness."[62] If nothing remains the same, if "what appears is always something new," if every "moment devours the preceding one,"[63] if memory itself presupposes forgetfulness, then to hold a present out from the stream of becoming, to remember the present long enough for us to apprehend it, we must reduce and simplify, we must forget.

Forgetfulness is also necessary as a part of the third moment of the threefold synthesis. For Kant, the only way to grasp successive and remembered moments in one cognition and the only way to unify these sensations into one object is through concepts that organize and unify them. But for such categorization to occur, Nietzsche insists, there must be identical cases.[64] Since we are confronted with chaos, which hardly contains identical cases, we must again forget differences and exceptions. We must reduce and simplify. We must construct the identical.[65] Nietzsche tells us that "what appears is always something new," but we only include the new "to the extent that it is similar to the old."[66] We reproduce the image that we have produced many times before. We do not register what is new and different.[67]

Forgetfulness is also crucially important, for Nietzsche, because memory is very much connected to the horror of existence:

> A human being may well ask an animal: 'Why do you not speak to me of your happiness but only stand and gaze at me?' The animal would like to answer, and say: 'The reason is I always forget what I was going to say'—but then he forgot this answer too, and stayed silent: so that the human being was left wondering.
>
> But he also wonders at himself, that he cannot learn to forget but clings relentlessly to the past: however far and fast he may run, this chain runs with him. . . . It affects him like a vision of a lost paradise to see the herds grazing or, in closer proximity to him, a child which, having as yet nothing of the past to shake off, plays in blissful blindness between the hedges of past and future. Yet its play must be disturbed; all too soon it will be called out of its state of forgetfulness. Then it will learn to understand the phrase 'it was': that password which gives conflict, suffering, and satiety access to man so as to remind him what his existence fundamentally is. . . . If death at last brings the desired forgetting, by that act it at the same time extinguishes the present and all existence and therewith sets the seal on the knowledge that existence is only an uninterrupted has-been, a thing that lives by negating, consuming and contradicting itself.[68]

VI. The Composite Self

At any rate, to have ordered experience we must assume a unified self. If there is no unified self, there can be no unified object, no subsumption under categories, no judgment, no thinking.[69] How, then, do we know there is a unified self? We have no experiential evidence for it. For neither Hume nor Kant can it be experienced. There must be a unified self, Kant argues, because that is the *only* way to explain the possibility of organized experience.[70] But, then, what if we were able to offer an explanation of such experience without assuming a unified self? What if we were able to offer a different explanation? Then Kant's explanation would not be the *only* possible explanation—and his justification of a unified self would collapse.

And, indeed, Nietzsche *is* able to give us an alternative explanation. It is the case, for Nietzsche much as for Kant, that the manifold, the flux of experience, must be apprehended, reproduced, and categorized. It has to be held together as *my* experience for it to be experience. It must be possible for an "I think" to accompany all my representations. But it is not the case that this requires the sort of unified self that Kant thought it did.[71] Nietzsche writes:

> A thought comes when "it" wishes, and not when "I" wish, so that it is a falsification of the facts of the case to say that the subject "I" is the condition of the predicate "think." *It* thinks; but that this "it" is precisely the famous old "ego" is, to put it mildly, only a supposition, an assertion, and assuredly not an "immediate certainty."[72]

Nietzsche says, "The subject: this is the term for our belief in a unity underlying all the different impulses. . . . 'The subject' is the fiction that many similar states in us are the effect of one substratum."[73] For Nietzsche, this subject is a "fiction."[74] The ego is a "fable."[75] He suggests instead:

> The assumption of one single subject is perhaps unnecessary; perhaps it is just as permissible to assume a multiplicity of subjects, whose interaction and struggle is the basis of our thought and our consciousness in general? A kind of aristocracy of "cells" in which dominion resides. . . . *My hypothesis:* The subject as multiplicity.[76]

Instead of a unified self, Nietzsche wants to posit a composite bundle of drives that only become a self through organization. He says: "It is our needs that interpret the world; our drives and their For and Against. Every drive is a kind of lust to rule; each one has its perspective that it would like to compel all the other drives to accept as a norm."[77] We must envision the sphere of the subject as "constantly growing or decreasing, the center of the system constantly shifting; in cases where it cannot organize the appropriate mass, it breaks into two parts. On the other hand, it can transform a weaker subject into its functionary without destroying it, and to a certain degree form a new unity with it."[78] The best way to think of subjects, Nietzsche tells us, is "as regents at the head of a communality."[79]

Postmodern thinkers who reject the notion of a unified subject are correct in pointing out that individuals have many identities or personas. Nevertheless, Kant has done a persuasive job of showing us that we cannot have the ordinary experience we do have without a unified self. I must hold experience together from moment to moment or the chair I am about to sit on will not appear as the same chair. I must retain and reproduce it. And that means that I must remain unchanged. I can have different identities, adopt different personas, play different roles, develop a different personality, but I must remain myself. I cannot change into something else or some other self, or the chair would not be retained, reproduced, and remembered by *me,* thus would not by *my* experience, thus would not be *experience,* thus would not appear as a *chair.*

Nevertheless, for Nietzsche as for Hume, we have no experience of a fixed self, certainly not of a transcendental self. Kant merely insists that it is an assumption necessary to explain the possibility of organized experience. But is it? The self, I think we have to admit, must have a *certain* amount of unity for experience to hold together from moment to moment, but does the self need to be *really* unified? It certainly need not be a transcendental or noumenal self. Wouldn't a powerful drive dominating and organizing other drives, a regent at the head of a communality, give us plenty of unity, enough so that the chair I am about to sit on is retained and reproduced as the same chair? Wouldn't such a dominant drive give us a subject with sufficient unity, as Nietzsche puts it, to "comprehend enough of the calculable and constant for [us] to base a scheme of behavior on it?"[80] Such a unified subject, for Nietzsche, would thus be much like the unified object, a multiplicity held together, organized, and dominated. This subject *is* unified, it is just that its unity is forged, constructed, organized, brought about by domination.

But is there enough unity here to satisfy Kant? All we have, for Nietzsche, is a bundle of drives that have been ranked and organized. Each drive, Kant would insist, is other, outside the rest of the drives, heteronomous.[81] How can we get a unified and autonomous self out of a bundle of heteronomous drives? However we understand the subject, as the dominant drive, the regent, or as all the drives, the whole bundle, the self will be made up of heteronomous drives. The "I" will be made up of elements either that are simply not me or that at least are other than parts of me. If so, then how can I speak of an "I" that persists? How can I say that I am and remain myself throughout my life if I am nothing but a bundle of struggling, shifting, and changing drives dominated and organized merely to one degree or another?

For Nietzsche this is not a problem at all. We do not need the sort of autonomous self Kant would try to convince us we need. We were never able to experience such a self anyway. We do not *know* that it is there. All we experience is a flux of drives, feelings, images, and so forth. We do not experience a single, unified, autonomous self, and we do not actually experience any of our drives, feelings, or desires as heteronomous either. We only *infer* their heteronomy from the fact that they would be outside an autonomous self—and we assume there must be an autonomous self. But why make that assumption? A regent at the head of a communality gives us all the unity we need.

But still, Kant would insist, we have not explained how I can say that I am and remain myself throughout my life if I am just a bundle of struggling and shifting drives. The subject, as Nietzsche understands it, is nothing but a simplified and falsified flux of chaotic becoming. There is no explanation for how it remains the same over long periods of time. Regents, after all, can be weakened, forced to share power, even overthrown.[82] Kant insists that the only explanation possible requires the assumption of a unified transcendental self. Nietzsche has an alternative explanation—though we must prepare ourselves for it being a strange one. Nietzsche's doctrine of eternal recurrence is his explanation for how the self remains perfectly the same. But before we get to eternal recurrence, we must say a bit about will to power, which is designed to explain how unity can be achieved in a subject understood as a bundle of drives.

VII. Will to Power

Will to power is a theory designed to deal with chaos and to explain the possibility of a composite self. It explains how, given that reality is chaos, the appearance of order is possible. It explains how a composite self can be formed and held together. And thus it begins to explain how we can keep the horror of existence at bay through the consolidation of stable structures. If existence is horrible, if it must be hidden, then we must give an epistemological explanation of how we hide it. An ordinary realist epistemology would not find it easy, maybe not even possible, to explain how we systematically hide from ourselves, because we must, the truth about reality. Will to power is a theory of how we construct structures that hide chaos and the horror of existence.

Furthermore, as we will eventually see, will to power prepares the ground for eternal recurrence. Indeed, eternal recurrence might be seen as merely the highest expression of will to power, and eternal recurrence is Nietzsche's final answer to how stability and unity are possible in a world of chaos.

Will to power, as Magnus points out, implies no transcendent unity lurking behind the world—as, for example, did Schopenhauer's conception of will.[83] Nietzsche develops his doctrine of will to power as an alternative to traditional metaphysics. There are no substances, no things, no selves, no regularity, no laws—there are no unities in the traditional sense. All is isolated. Nevertheless, will to power gives us a radical principle of unity—a unity, however, compatible with chaos:

> My idea is that every specific body strives to become master over all space and to extend its force (—its will to power:) and to thrust back all that resists its extension. But it continually encounters similar efforts on the part of other bodies and ends by coming to an arrangement ("union") with those of them that are sufficiently related to it: thus they then conspire together for power. And the process goes on—[84]

> All "purposes," "aims," "meaning" are only modes of expression and metamorphoses of one will that is inherent in all events: the will to power.[85]

To view the world in terms of power, it generally seems helpful to break things down as far as possible and then try to understand how such elements combine to form complexes—that was certainly Hobbes's approach in *Leviathan*. For Nietzsche, reality consists of dynamic centers of force—pure drives or affects—each of which is related to all others in struggle. Each drive is a "kind of lust to rule," each "construes all the rest of the world from its own viewpoint, i.e., measures, feels, forms, according to its own force." Each drive has a "perspective that it would like to compel all the other drives to accept as a norm."[86]

Nietzsche rejects the traditional notion of a cause behind things. A quantum of force is nothing other than precisely a driving, willing, or effecting. There can be no separation into neat causes and effects, agents and results, doers and deeds. There is nothing but the acting. To posit a cause, agent, or doer is merely to project a fiction into the process much as the popular imagination separates lightening from its flash as if the former existed apart from and produced the latter. The being behind the deed is a mere fiction added to the deed.[87] Rather, for Nietzsche, the "essence" of any quantum of force lies in its "relation to all other quanta." Every quantum of force, every displacement of power, will be felt throughout the whole system. *"[N]othing exists apart from the whole!"* It is impossible to isolate a single cause or set of causes which produce an event. Every event ultimately is the outcome of all evolution, the result of eternity. To change anything that has occurred would mean changing everything in the past. Things are unable to be other than they are. The individual is "a piece of fate."[88]

For Nietzsche, there are no unified entities that are stable in themselves, merely changing configurations arising from the interaction and struggle of power quanta. This model applies in nature, in society or culture, and in individual consciousness—or, given that there is considerable disagreement on this matter, one can at least find texts and commentators which suggest that it applies in each of these areas.[89] Each configuration or structure seeks to discharge its strength and to reach its maximal power. Increases in power result from struggle between structures. One structure confronts another as an obstacle, overcomes it, and assimilates it. One drive dominates and organizes others. Higher levels of power require higher organization.[90]

In the realm of the mind, Nietzsche thinks, "our intellect is only the blind instrument" of one drive or another.[91] He says, "the thinking that rises to *consciousness* is only the smallest part . . . —the most superficial and worst part . . . ." of what goes on in us.[92] In this realm, higher levels of organization require discipline, restraint, and denial. For this reason, expressions of the ascetic ideal, like the self denial of the stoic and the saint, represent high levels of will to power. Higher spiritual power results from internalization, a directing of instincts or drives inward, a confronting of these internalized drives as obstacles, an overcoming of them, and a sublimation of their energy to higher levels.[93]

We should be careful to notice that while will to power does not rule out domination, and while domination is an important part of it,[94] nevertheless, what is most important about will to power is empowerment,[95] not domination. This will be key to understanding the *Übermensch,* as we will see in subsequent chapters.

At any rate, will to power is central to introducing meaning where there is only meaninglessness. We impose our own forms on the world.[96] As Nietzsche puts it in the *Genealogy of Morals:*

Whatever exists . . . is again and again reinterpreted to new ends, taken over, transformed, and redirected by some power superior to it; all events in the organic world are a subduing, a *becoming master,* and all subduing and becoming master involves a fresh interpretation, an adaptation through which any previous "meaning" and "purpose" are necessarily obscured or even obliterated. . . . [P]urposes and utilities are only *signs* that a will to power has become master of something less powerful and imposed upon it the character of a function; and the entire history of a "thing," an organ, a custom can in this way be a continuous sign-chain of ever new interpretations and adaptations whose causes do not even have to be related to one another.[97]

To keep the horror of existence at bay, to impose meaning upon a meaningless void, requires a high degree of will to power.

We must also say something of the relationship between will to power and truth. Nietzsche claims that the "criterion of truth resides in the enhancement of the feeling of power."[98] I think we must understand this in the sense that what gives us the greatest feeling of power is what we *take to be true.* Nietzsche says, what "gives the intellect the greatest feeling of power and security, that is most preferred, valued and consequently characterized as true."[99] In *Will to Power,* he also says:

Knowledge works as a tool of power. Hence it is plain that it increases with every increase of power—

The meaning of "knowledge": here . . . is to be regarded in a strict and narrow anthropocentric and biological sense. In order for a particular species to maintain itself and increase its power, its conception of reality must comprehend enough of the calculable and constant for it to base a scheme of behavior on it. The utility of preservation—not some abstract-theoretical need not to be deceived—stands as the motive behind the development of the organs of knowledge.[100]

All of this utility, preservation, increase of power, while determining what we *take to be true,* need not, Nietzsche tells us, have anything to do with *real truth:* "are they for that reason truths? What a conclusion! As if the preservation of man were a proof of truth!"[101] Nietzsche says, "The falseness of a judgment is for us not necessarily an objection to a judgment. . . . The question is to what extent it is life-promoting, life-preserving, species–preserving, perhaps even species-cultivating. And we are fundamentally inclined to claim that the falsest judgments . . . are the most indispensable for us."[102] Will to power is a process of constructing truths, that is, what we *take to be truth,* in other words, illusions that mask the *actual* truth. Will to power is the evolutionary development of the avoidance of truth, the masking of the horror of existence. Will to power seeks life, not truth.

Eternal recurrence, we will come to see, is the highest expression of will to power and at the same time its stabilization. If all is chaos, if there are nothing but conflicting drives, each seeking to dominate, absorb, and channel the others, if there is no subject except as a regent at the head of a bundle of drives, if there is really no object and no cause and effect, if there is just chaos, this is not really a problem if every single detail will return, return eternally, in exactly the same way, with exactly the same meaning.[103] Eternal recurrence allows chaos to remain chaos and will to power the configuration of chaos, yet provides them the highest possible order—eternal order.

VIII. Perspectivism

Will to power implies that all is an interpretation—a perspective. As Nietzsche put it in the *Genealogy of Morals*, "whatever exists . . . is again and again reinterpreted to new ends, taken over, transformed and redirected by some power superior to it. . . . A will to power has become master of something less powerful and imposed upon it the character of a function. . . ."[104] Against the view that there "are only *facts* . . . ," Nietzsche argues in *Will to Power*: "No, facts is precisely what there is not, only interpretations. . . . The world . . . has no meaning behind it, but countless meanings.—'Perspectivism.'"[105] He warns us to: "be on our guard against the hallowed philosophers' myth of a 'pure, will-less, painless, timeless knower.'" This presupposes "an eye such as no living being can imagine, an eye required to have no direction, to abrogate its active and interpretive powers—precisely those powers that alone make of seeing, seeing *something*. All seeing is essentially perspective, and so is all knowing."[106]

Perspectivism implies that "actions are always open to many interpretations, always unfathomable."[107] In *Will to Power*, Nietzsche claims that a thing "would be defined once all creatures had asked 'what is that?' and had answered their question. Supposing one single creature, with its own relationships and perspectives for all things, were missing, then the thing would not yet be 'defined.'"[108] But then he tells us that there is: "[n]o limit to the ways in which the world can be interpreted."[109] If there is no limit to the ways the world can be interpreted, if interpretations are infinite, then there will always be a perspective yet missing and the thing will never be defined.

But isn't this a problem? As Nietzsche puts it in *The Gay Science*:

> Our new "*infinite*."— How far the perspective character of existence extends or indeed whether existence has any other character than this; whether existence without interpretation, without "sense," does not become "nonsense"; whether, on the other hand, all existence is not essentially actively engaged in *interpretation*—that cannot be decided even by the most industrious and most scrupulously conscientious analysis and self-examination of the intellect; for in the course of this analysis the human intellect cannot avoid seeing itself in its own perspectives, and *only* in these. We cannot look around our own corner.[110]

If all is interpretation, isn't that claim itself merely interpretation? Isn't every last claim made by Nietzsche merely interpretation? Well, if so, it doesn't seem to bother him: "Supposing that this also is only interpretation—and you will be eager enough to make this objection?—well, so much the better."[111] Why doesn't it bother Nietzsche?

We must see that perspectivism is not at all incompatible with real truth.[112] It is not incompatible, in the first place, because it is crucially important to us that we be able to hide the real truth—the horror of existence. Thus it is quite fortunate for us that we can get absorbed in perspectives. Such perspectives, we have seen, can be of two kinds. They can be merely what we *take to be true,* that is, illusions. But they can also be *actual truths.* Both can absorb us and deflect us from the ultimate truth, the horror and meaninglessness of existence.[113]

But *can* we have *real* truth if all is perspective? Well, strictly speaking, to accept the horror of existence as the ultimate truth is to adopt a certain perspective toward existence. After all, it cannot be denied that the horror of existence *is* a perspective. From the perspective of individual-conscious-human beings, nature is threatening and terrifying. It produces meaningless suffering and does not care about us. From the perspective of some other being, or the perspective of the totality of things, or from our own perspective as biological-organic-natural beings, nature may not be horrible. We can even find our primordial unity with nature intoxicating and ecstasy producing.[114] So the truth of the horror of existence is perfectly compatible with perspectivism. It itself is a perspective and we need other perspectives to hide it.

But if it is just another perspective, how can we hold it to be *true?* Don't we have to dismiss it as just another perspective? This is the fundamental mistake that the anti-perspectivist continually makes. The fact that something is a perspective does not mean that it is to be dismissed. We *need* perspectives. We need *multiple* perspectives. We cannot live without them. If we had only one perspective, if we had nothing but the truth, if we saw nothing but the horror of existence, we would probably perish. Other perspectives can well be of higher value than the truth. If we dismissed perspectives, we could not hide the horror of existence.

Nietzsche says that Europeans interpreted the French Revolution for so long "that *the text finally disappeared under the interpretation.*" And he says that this might even happen with respect to our whole past "and in that way alone make it tolerable to look at."[115] If all is perspective, if all is interpretation, if the text even disappears under the interpretation, well so much the better. It might make things tolerable to look at, it might be the *only* way to make them tolerable—it might be the only way to mask the horror of existence.

Yes, but if all is taken to be perspective, even conceding the fact that we have no grounds for dismissing it, still, if it is a mere perspective, we have no better grounds for accepting it. This too involves a fundamental misconception on the part of the anti-perspectivist, that if something is a perspective it is a *mere* perspective, *nothing* but a perspective, no better than any other perspective, something with little or no import. That is a serious mistake. Some things, even if we decide they are nothing but perspectives, nevertheless carry real weight. As Ahern suggests, what distinguishes Nietzsche from deconstructionists is that he does not think all perspectives are equal. Nietzsche ranks perspectives.[116] As

Nehamas puts it, perspectivism is not relativism—it does not hold that one view is as good as any other.[117] For example, Nietzsche tells us: "If we sharpened or blunted our senses tenfold, we should perish."[118] Some perspectives are far worse and some far better than others. So also if our star threatens to cool and thus to kill off the human species as a whole, this perspective, I should think, would carry a *certain* weight even though it is *merely* a perspective, *nothing* but a perspective, no *less* a perspective than any other perspective.

We can conclude this chapter by saying that will to power involves a conflict of drives, each drive trying to dominate the others, so that what emerges is a subject which is like a regent at the head of a communality. All of this, which is will to power, is a process of simplifying reality, distorting it, imposing perspectives, making it calculable, making it livable. All of this is a process of avoiding truth so that it does not threaten us. Will to power seeks life, not truth. Will to power is the evolutionary development of the avoidance of truth.

Chapter Four

The *Übermensch* and Eternal Recurrence

I. Nihilism and the *Übermensch*

We have yet to draw out all the consequences of accepting the horror of existence. At *Genealogy of Morals,* III, §28, in discussing will to truth, which we find especially in science and in Christianity, Nietzsche says, as we have seen, that this will is leading to "an awe-inspiring *catastrophe,* the outcome of a two-thousand-year training in truthfulness, which finally forbids itself the *lie of belief in God.* . . . Christian truthfulness has drawn one conclusion after another, it finally draws its *strongest conclusion,* its conclusion *against* itself."[1] Nietzsche thinks this will to truth, in driving us toward truth over the course of the centuries, is finally about to arrive at the horror of existence. We are about to be plunged into nihilism.[2] Nietzsche tells us that nihilism means:

> "Everything lacks meaning" (the untenability of one interpretation of the world, upon which a tremendous amount of energy has been lavished, awakens the suspicion that *all* interpretations of the world are false).[3]

> What does nihilism mean? *That the highest values devaluate themselves.* . . . "[W]hy?" finds no answer. . . . Radical nihilism is the conviction of an absolute untenability of existence when it comes to the highest values one recognizes. . . . This realization is a consequence of the cultivation of "truthfulness."[4]

In order to mask the horror of existence, we have constructed truths, what we *take to be truths,* that is, illusions. "Now that the shabby origin of these values is becoming clear, the universe seems to have lost value, seems 'meaningless'."[5] Nihilism is a "psychological state" that we reach "when we have sought a 'meaning' in all events that is not there: so the seeker eventually becomes discouraged." One becomes, "ashamed in front of oneself, as if one had *deceived* oneself all too long.—"[6] As we approach the real truth, the horror of existence, the 'truths' we have constructed, the meaning and purpose we have made for ourselves, collapse. Thus we are plunged into a terrible void. An empty cosmos, meaningless suffering, the horror of existence are about to stare us in the face. We are headed for nihilism. And we are likely to perish.

What is needed is someone with the strength to face this horror without being paralyzed, someone with the ability to create a new veil, impose a new truth, construct a new meaning. As Nietzsche puts it:

> But some day, in a stronger age than this decaying, self-doubting present, he must yet come to us, the *redeeming* man of great love and contempt, the creative spirit whose compelling strength will not let him rest in any aloofness or any beyond. . . . This man of the future, who will redeem us not only from the hitherto reigning ideal but also from that which was bound to grow out of it, the great nausea, the will to nothingness, nihilism; this bell-stroke of noon and of the great decision that liberates the will again and restores its goal to the earth and his hope to man; this Antichrist and antinihilist; this victor over God and nothingness—*he must come one day.*—[7]

Nietzsche holds that the task of the true philosopher is to *"create values."* Genuine philosophers are: *"commanders and legislators:* they say, *'thus* it *shall* be!'* . . . With a creative hand they reach for the future, and all that is and has been becomes a means for them, an instrument, a hammer. Their 'knowing' is *creating,* their creating is a legislation, their will to truth is—*will to power."*[8] "Formerly," Nietzsche tells us, some philosophers "believed themselves capable of inventing new religions or of replacing old ones with their philosophical systems; nowadays they have lost all this old arrogance and are as a rule pious, timid and uncertain folk."[9] We must hope for new philosophers with the strength and originality to revalue existing values.[10]

At the center of Nietzsche's thought—at all periods of his thought—we find the great man.[11] In the *Birth of Tragedy,* the solution to the horror of existence was to revive Greek tragic culture through German music, especially the music of Wagner. In *On the Uses and Disadvantages of History for Life,* the goal of humanity was to be achieved by a few giants speaking to each other across the desert intervals of historical time:

> The time will come . . . when one will regard not the masses but individuals, who form a kind of bridge across the turbulent stream of becoming. These individuals do not carry forward any kind of process but live contemporaneously with one another; thanks to history, which permits such a collaboration, they live as that republic of genius of which Schopenhauer once spoke; one giant calls to another across the desert intervals of time and, undisturbed by the excited chattering dwarfs who creep about beneath them, the exalted spirit-dialogue goes on. It is the task of history to be the mediator between them and thus again and again to inspire and lend the strength for the production of the great [*Grossen*] man. No, the goal of humanity cannot lie in its end but only in its highest exemplars.[12]

In *Beyond Good and Evil,* Nietzsche says, "A people is a detour of nature to get to six or seven great men [*grossen Männern*]."[13] In some texts, most notably *Thus Spoke Zarathustra,* Nietzsche uses the term *'Übermensch'*[14] in discussing such great men, but that term rarely appears in later texts.[15]

In my opinion, the best example of the *Übermensch* appears in the *Genealogy of Morals*—though perhaps we should only say the best example of the *great man,* since Nietzsche does not use the term *'Übermensch'* here:

> The earliest philosophers knew how to endow their existence and appearance with a meaning. . . . As men of frightful ages, they did this by using frightful means: cruelty toward themselves, inventive self-castigation—this was the principal means these power-hungry hermits and innovators of ideas required to overcome the gods and tradition in themselves, so as to be able to *believe* in their own innovations. I recall the famous story of King Vishvamitra, who through millennia of self-torture acquired such a feeling of power and self-confidence that he endeavored to build a *new heaven*—the uncanny symbol of the most ancient and the most recent experience of philosophers on earth: whoever has at some time built a "new heaven" has found the power to do so only in his *own hell.*[16]

We need someone strong enough to face the threat of nihilism without being paralyzed, someone able to look into the void without perishing, someone who can finally overthrow Europe's old gods and their crumbling truths, someone with the creative power to construct a new heaven—that is, a new vision, a new *Weltanschauung,* a new meaning structure. To be an *Übermensch* or a great man, I suggest, one must have the power to accomplish what, in a horrific cosmos, is the most fundamental, the most important, and the most necessary task. One must have the power to create meaning, truths—that is, illusions. One must be able to mask the horror and meaninglessness of existence. The *Übermensch,* Zarathustra says, *"shall be* the meaning of the earth!"[17]

Christianity's will to truth, we have seen, is driving us toward the truth—the real truth. We are about to be pushed into the empty void. A meaningless cosmos and meaningless suffering are about to stare us in the face. We are headed for nihilism. We are at the edge of the abyss. We will perish if we are unable to stop this decline. We need an *Übermensch,* a great man, a Vishvamitra, to create a new heaven, a new myth, a new veil, a new meaning.

In short, I do not think we can understand the *Übermensch* as representing merely a certain attitude toward life, as Magnus argues.[18] The *Übermensch* must have more than an attitude, he must have an ability—a *power.* The *Übermensch* must be able to create—he must be able to create new meaning. Indeed, he must have the power to create a new worldview capable of masking the horror and emptiness of existence—as did the likes of Homer, Socrates, and Jesus. That, I suggest, is what is essential to being a great man or an *Übermensch:* "He who *determines* values and directs the will of [millennia] by giving direction to the highest natures is the *highest* man."[19]

II. Eternal Recurrence

Eternal Recurrence is both the test of the *Übermensch* and also the new heaven, the new *Weltanschauung*, constructed by the *Übermensch*. Nietzsche announces the doctrine of eternal recurrence for the first time at *Gay Science* §341:

> *The greatest weight.*—What, if some day or night a demon were to steal after you into your loneliest loneliness and say to you: "This life as you now live it and have lived it, you will have to live once more and innumerable times more; and there will be nothing new in it, but every pain and every joy and every thought and sigh and everything unutterably small or great in your life will have to return to you, all in the same succession and sequence—even this spider and this moonlight between the trees, and even this moment and I myself. The eternal hourglass of existence is turned upside down again and again, and you with it, speck of dust!"
>
> Would you not throw yourself down and gnash your teeth and curse the demon who spoke thus? Or have you once experienced a tremendous moment when you would have answered him: "You are a god and never have I heard anything more divine." If this thought gained possession of you, it would change you as you are or perhaps crush you. The question in each and every thing, "Do you desire this once more and innumerable times more?" would lie upon your actions as the greatest weight. Or how well disposed would you have to become to yourself and to life to *crave nothing more fervently* than this ultimate eternal confirmation and seal?[20]

It is not enough that eternal recurrence simply be believed. Nietzsche demands that it actually be loved. In *Ecce Homo,* he explains his doctrine of *amor fati:* "My formula for greatness in a human being is *amor fati:* that one wants nothing to be different, not forward, not backward, not in all eternity. Not merely bear what is necessary, still less conceal it . . . but *love* it."[21] In *Thus Spoke Zarathustra,* Zarathustra says: "'To redeem those who lived in the past and to recreate all 'it was' into a 'thus I willed it'—that alone should I call redemption."[22] To turn all "it was" into a "thus I willed it" is to accept fate fully. One would have it no other way, one wants everything eternally the same, one *wills* it the same: "Was *that* life? . . . 'Well then! Once more!'"[23]

How are we to understand these doctrines? We must start by getting clear about the basics of what they involve. We should notice first that eternal recurrence fits with, indeed, seems simply to be a further development of, Nietzsche's doctrine of internal relations. For Nietzsche, the essence of any quantum of force lies in its relation to all other quanta. *"[N]othing exists apart from the whole!"*[24] It is impossible to isolate a single cause or set of causes that produce an event. If this is so, Nietzsche insists, then every event would ultimately be the outcome of all evolution. To change anything that has occurred would mean changing everything in the past.[25] If every event is the outcome of all past evolution, if to change one detail would involve changing the whole past, then it would seem that if things ever returned to their original position, they would have to unfold in the same way as before, or all of the past and even all past pasts would have to be changed. Nietzsche holds that from any given state of the universe, all future states follow.[26] Thus from identical states, identical futures would follow.

We must also notice that there are two alternative versions of eternal recurrence. We might call them the great year theory and the dice game theory. All the published versions of eternal recurrence insist that everything returns just as it was in previous cycles—in the very same order down to the smallest detail. In *Thus Spoke Zarathustra,* perhaps echoing an ancient doctrine, Nietzsche refers to these recurrences as great years.[27]

We must take up some problems as we go along here. Magnus argues that eternal recurrence of the same is actually impossible. For there to be 'cycles' in the plural, two cycles, they would have to recur at *different* times, one after the other. Thus they would not be the *same;* they would *differ* temporally.[28]

Magnus attributes a meaning to the word 'same' that in my opinion Nietzsche did not intend. In the passage quoted above from *Gay Science* §341, and elsewhere, the message is clearly that the *same* returns at *different* times. Stambaugh helpfully points out that the German word, '*das Gleiche,*'

> does *not* express simple identity, and therefore does not, strictly speaking, mean the Same. It lies somewhere between the Same and the Similar, but means neither exactly. For example; If two women have the same hat on, they have, strictly speaking, one hat on at different times. (One borrowed or stole the other's hat.) If two woman have the "same" (in the sense of *gleich*) hat on at the same time, they have two hats which resemble each other so exactly that one could think that one woman had borrowed the other's hat, if one saw these women at different times. This is more than similarity, but it is not identity.[29]

Gay Science §341 is saying, I suggest, that the *only* difference that can be found in the recurrence of the spider and the moonlight is a *temporal* one, that is, that the *same* spider and the *same* moonlight will return at *different* times.

In a similar vein, Soll argues that eternal recurrence of the same would not crush us at all. If every detail of one recurrence were exactly the same as every detail of another, if they were radically indistinguishable, recurrence would not be terrifying. To be terrified, Soll thinks, we would have to be able to accumulate new experience from cycle to cycle, remember past recurrences, and tremble in anticipation of their return. If all recurrences were exactly the same, if new experience could not build and accumulate, recurrence would be a matter of complete indifference.[30] I think this view is mistaken. In the first place, people who lead a life of intense suffering often look forward to death as an escape from that suffering. Aeneas, for example, when he visited the underworld in Book VI of the *Aeneid,* expected just that. When he found that he would have to be reincarnated, he was appalled. His next reincarnated life, it was true, would not be exactly the same, as for Nietzschean eternal recurrence, but Aeneas seemed to expect it to be similar enough in its misery and suffering. And despite the fact that in his reincarnated life he would not remember his present life,

Aeneas was nevertheless horrified at the idea that he would have to go through it all again.[31]

Furthermore, while it is true that experience cannot build and accumulate from cycle to cycle, nevertheless, we must recognize that there are places in which Nietzsche suggests that it *is* possible to remember earlier recurrences.[32] Moreover, we can certainly be *aware* of other recurrences in the sense of *believe* in them—the demon *informs* us of these other recurrences. This raises no problems as long as the very same memory, awareness, and reaction recur in each and every cycle at the very same point—each and every cycle must be exactly the *same*. It is possible that Soll assumes that such memories, awarenesses, and reactions would necessarily make the cycles different because they would have to be absent in at least one cycle—the first.[33] But that would be a mistake. Nietzsche is quite clear. Time is infinite[34]—there is no *first* cycle. These memories, awarenesses, and reactions could occur in *all* cycles at exactly the same point in the sequence.

Still, Soll argues that it is "impossible for there to be among different recurrences of a person the kind of identity that seems to exist among the different states of consciousness of the same person within a particular recurrence. . . . Only by inappropriately construing the suffering of some future recurrence on the model of suffering later in this life does the question of eternal recurrence of one's pain weigh upon one with 'the greatest stress.'"[35] I think this too is mistaken. I can very well not want to live my life again even if in the next cycle I will not remember the pain of this cycle. If I am to love my life, not want to change the slightest detail, if I am to desire to live it again, it does not matter if in the future cycle I do not remember this cycle. If the demon *tells* me, if I *believe,* that the future cycle will be exactly the same, if I *know* that now, then it could be quite difficult, *right now,* to be positive enough about my existing painful life to wish to go through it again, even if when I do go through it again I will not remember it.

Soll's point gains whatever plausibility it has by looking back from a future life at our present life and denying that we could remember anything or tremble in anticipation of its return. But that is not the only perspective one can take on the matter and it is not the perspective Nietzsche wants to emphasize here. For Nietzsche the demon forces us to look over our present life, reflect upon it, test our attitude toward it, and assess the degree of positiveness we have toward it right now. We do that by asking how we feel about having to live it over again without the slightest change. What is relevant here is how we feel about our *present* life—right now at the *present* moment.

It is also irrelevant to suggest that there is insufficient identity for me to think that it will really be me in the next cycle. The point, for Nietzsche, is how I react to my *present* life—the threat of a future life is brought up to elicit this reaction. If I do not identify with the person who will live my next life, if I do not care about them, if I consider them an other, then I evade the question the demon put to me—and I avoid the heart of the issue. The question is whether I love my life, my present life—love it so completely that I would live it again? I am being asked if I would live my life again to see if I love my present life. If I insist on viewing the liver of my next life as an other, what I should do at the very least is ask myself whether I love my present life enough that I could wish it on another.

But it is not clear to me that we can treat that person in the next cycle as an other. If all things are essentially related to all other things, if a thing *is* its relations to all other things, if there is no fixed, unified, or transcendental self, if the self is a bundle of drives that, like all other things, is nothing but its relations, then, when that bundle of drives returns in a different cycle to the same exact set of relations, there would be as much identity between selves in the two cycles as there would be between the self at different moments of one cycle. On Nietzsche's theory of the self, I do not see how we could deny that selves in different cycles are the same.

In *Will to Power,* Nietzsche calls eternal recurrence "the most *scientific* of all possible hypotheses."[36] And in *Will to Power,* though not in any published texts, Nietzsche seems to try to prove the doctrine scientifically.[37] Indeed, Lou Salomé tells us that Nietzsche intended "to devote ten years of exclusive study to the natural sciences at the University of Vienna or Paris"[38] in order to prove the doctrine. There has been a good deal of disagreement over these proofs. Both Danto and Magnus argue that they will not hold up under analysis. Sterling, on the other hand, has tried to reconstruct and defend them.[39]

I do not think it would be helpful to rehash these issues in any detail. If we ask what science or scientific proof can amount to for Nietzsche, we quickly discover that it becomes quite problematic to hold that science can straightforwardly prove the truth of any hypothesis. I have already argued that science embodies a very powerful will to truth, and while it can ultimately get us to the real truth, the horror of existence, and thus plunge us into nihilism, in the meantime, whether science gets us real truth or simply what we take to be truth, it nevertheless functions to mask the horror of existence, the ultimate truth—it deceives. Thus, if science were used to try to prove the doctrine of eternal recurrence, we would have to ask ourselves whether science would be moving us toward the ultimate truth, or would be deceiving us and masking that truth, or would be doing a bit of both? And there is nothing about science or scientific method that will give us a simple guarantee that we have gotten one of these rather than the others.[40] In *Will to Power,* Nietzsche says of science (as well as of metaphysics, morality, and religion) that "these things merit consideration only as various forms of lies: with their help one can have *faith* in life."[41] Wood argues that in these proofs Nietzsche "is showing how eternal recurrence can be argued for even in terms that he did not himself endorse." He is giving scientific justification for something we might have other better reasons for believing.[42] However, there are even worse problems connected with Nietzsche's scientific proofs of eternal recurrence.

The scientific proofs, I want to argue, hold a second and very different theory of eternal recurrence—a dice game theory. Here, in order to make recurrence more plausible, Nietzsche argues that time is infinite and force (as well as the possible combinations of force) finite. Thus, in infinite time, *all possible* combinations of force would recur.[43]

Zuboff and Krueger point out that the result of this argument is that while one's life will recur over and over again, between those recurrences all possible combinations of one's life would also recur.[44] One would relive *many* different lives, if, that is, all of them could be called lives. One's life sequence would be scrambled in every *possible* way. Some of these scrambled lives would be meaningless, not just in Nietzsche's ordinary existential sense, they could not be meaningful in *any* sense. Such eternal recurrence would contradict *amor fati*. An *Übermensch* able to love his most recent fate, wish every detail eternally the same, and find such recurrence an ultimate confirmation, would not get his wish and would not be confirmed in each recurring life. He could not love these other fates, if only because it would be impossible to know what they would be.

Sterling, however, argues that eternal recurrence could still work for Nietzsche as long as each of the variations of one's life were themselves to recur eternally. But what Sterling seems to have in mind are very mild variations, for example, having a different job or living in a different place.[45] But "all possible combinations" would mean something far more radical—lives so scrambled they could not even be thought of as lives. Certainly, from the perspective of any one life, including the perspective of Nietzsche's life (the one we know about), it would be impossible to love these other lives (or non-lives, or scrambled lives) simply because it would be impossible to know what they were. And if somehow one could, in one's present life, love these other scrambled lives, that would in no way amount to an affirmation of one's present life because the scrambled lives would all be different from one's present life. Indeed, the only way I can imagine one loving these unknown scrambled lives would be if one had lived such a miserable life that one felt that *any* other life would be preferable. But that would *not* be to affirm one's present life and would thus be a rejection, not an acceptance, of eternal recurrence of the *same* as well as of *amor fati*.

What if, however, one were to hold that one must embrace *amor fati* within *each* of these different life series, that is, that one must in each life series desire the eternal return of that life. This would avoid the problem of not knowing about any of one's other life series. From within any particular life series one need not will anything with respect to another life series. This, however, will not help. It may even make things worse. One would never be able to know whether one had succeeded in loving one's life within all one's other life series. In some of them one might be insane, a moron, or in some other way unable to reflect on one's life in any significant sense. Even if one were able to love one's fate within one of one's life series, the fact that one could never be sure that one had done so in the rest of one's life series could weaken one's resolution within the life in which one was able to love one's fate.[46] It would certainly weaken any attempt to love one's life as a whole in all its series. I think we have to say that *amor fati* requires eternal recurrence of the *same*.

Furthermore, given Nietzsche's conception of the self sketched above, namely, that if a thing *is* its relations to all other things, if the self is a bundle of drives that is nothing but its relations, then any change in these relations, certainly of the radical sort implied by the dice game theory, means that we would have a different self. It would mean that I cannot hold another changed life series to be *my* life series. The person living my scrambled life would have to be understood as another person. I am only the person living my present life series. And thus again we collapse back into eternal recurrence of the *same*.

It is possible that Nietzsche saw these consequences and thus left such scientific arguments out of his published writings. At any rate, scientific arguments from chance combination lead to conclusions that contradict eternal recurrence of the *same* and thus cannot serve the purpose that eternal recurrence was designed to serve. Even if one were to conclude that the scientific proofs were intended to be proofs in the ordinary sense, the dice game theory would not lead to an *Übermensch*—it would crush him and make *amor fati* impossible. On the other hand, the great year theory, even as a mere assertion, a mere belief, could make the *Übermensch* possible.

Nietzsche claims that just thinking about the possibility of eternal recurrence can shatter and transform us.[47] In published works, eternal recurrence is presented as the teaching of a sage, the revelation of a demon, or as a thought that gains possession of one. At *Gay Science* §341, we must notice, eternal recurrence is not presented as a truth. Commentators frequently argue that it simply does not matter whether or not it is true; its importance lies in the effect it has on those who believe it.[48] Lou Salomé tells us:

> Even a cursory study of the problem soon showed [Nietzsche] that a scientific foundation for the recurrence teaching based on atomistic theory would not be tenable; and so he found that his fears about the fateful idea would not be validated nor be irrefutable. With all that, he seemed to be freed from his prophetic mission and from a fate he had anticipated with horror. But then, however, something characteristically strange stepped into the picture; far from being able to feel himself released through this gained insight, Nietzsche took an entirely opposite position toward it. From the moment when his frightening surmise became unprovable and untenable, it became hardened for him—as if through a magic formula—into an irrefutable conviction. What was to have become a scientifically proven truth assumed instead the character of a mystical revelation.[49]

Thus, if Soll were able to tell Nietzsche that he should not be concerned about eternal recurrence because it would not be him (Nietzsche) the next time around, Nietzsche, I think, would reject that interpretation. Indeed, if necessary, Nietzsche might even change his presentation of the doctrine. The whole point is to ask what attitude one will come to have toward one's life if one believes it will return eternally? Eternal recurrence does not seek to produce an attitude of indifference. That is not the point of eternal recurrence. If Soll could convince Nietzsche that indifference would be the logical response, Nietzsche, I suggest, would change his exposition of the doctrine.

We must also notice that there are two versions of the doctrine of *amor fati*. In *Thus Spoke Zarathustra,* Nietzsche says: "Have you ever said Yes to a single joy? . . . then you said Yes to *all* woe. All things are entangled, ensnared, enamored; if ever you wanted one thing twice, if ever you said, 'You please me, happiness! Abide, moment!' then you wanted *all* back."[50] In *Will to Power,* he says: "If we affirm one single moment, we thus affirm . . . all existence."[51] Here, all we need do is love one moment and that then requires us to accept all moments. All we need desire is the return of one peak experience, as Magnus puts it,[52] for which we must accept all the rest. This suggests that our attitude toward much of our life, even most of it, could be one of toleration, mere acceptance, or it could even be negative. All we need do is love one great moment. That is quite different, and much *easier,* than loving *all* moments of one's life—every single detail. The latter is the view of *Ecce Homo,* which says that *amor fati* means that one "wants *nothing* to be different" and that we "[n]ot merely *bear* what is necessary . . . but *love* it."[53] We want "a Yes-saying without reservation, even to suffering. . . . Nothing in existence may be subtracted, nothing is dispensable."[54]

Moreover, the first version of *amor fati* suggests that what would make us accept eternal recurrence is one single joy, one moment of *happiness.* That, I suggest, is not going to get Nietzsche were he wants to go. As I hope to show in Chapter 5, Nietzsche needs to hold the stronger and more difficult doctrine, that we must love every moment, even the ones that involve pain and suffering— *especially* the ones that involve pain and suffering.

III. Eternal Recurrence, Chaos, and the Self

We live in an empty and meaningless void—a chaos of sheer becoming. As we have seen in earlier chapters, Nietzsche wants to get as close to this truth as he possibly can without perishing.[55] Some veiling is necessary for life, but Nietzsche wants as little as possible. To turn all "it was" into a "thus I willed it," to accept the past *as if* you had chosen to make it that way, imposes subjective order and meaning on what in itself has no order or meaning. Chaos is no longer completely meaningless or valueless. Each moment passes, it cannot be held or made intelligible on its own, but if it will return eternally, then our feelings, interpretations, the value and significance we impose upon each moment, gain a peculiar absoluteness. They will accompany that moment forever. Eternal recurrence is as close as we get to being in a world of becoming.[56] We get as close as possible to the truth of becoming without being destroyed by it.

If all things are chaos, if we have nothing but conflicting drives, each seeking to dominate, absorb, and channel the others, if there is no subject except as a regent at the head of a bundle of drives, if there is really no object and no cause behind things, if there is just chaos, well so what, what difference does it make? This is not a problem at all—if every single detail of our lives will return, over and over again eternally, in the very same way, with exactly the same meaning, without the slightest change.[57] Eternal recurrence does not give us a beyond, a different world, a higher or better world. The only world we have is this one. But eternal recurrence gives us a unity and identity that we otherwise would lack. Eternal recurrence allows chaos to remain chaos and will to power the configuration of chaos, yet provides us the highest possible order—eternal order.

If I am just a bundle of struggling and shifting drives, how can I hold that I am and remain myself over time? If the subject is nothing but simplified and falsified chaos, how can we explain how it remains the same throughout its life? Eternal recurrence promises that I will remain the same, exactly and precisely the same, without the change of the slightest detail, not merely throughout this life, but for an eternity of lives, indeed, that I have already done so through an eternity of past lives. Eternal recurrence provides the highest possible order. Every image, every feeling, every representation, every detail of the temporal flux of inner sense is determined, is fated, is absolutely necessary, can be no other way than it is, and will repeat, has already repeated—for eternity. The self, for Nietzsche, is not just a radically unstable postmodern self. It is such a self, but it is not *simply* such a self. It also has a stability, sameness, and unity that go far beyond anything Kant ever imagined in his wildest dreams.[58]

It is true that a postmodern conception of the self alone would give us insufficient unity. It cannot explain how the self remains sufficiently the same for it to organize experience over long periods of time as the experience of a single self. I must remain myself. I cannot change into something else or some other self or the object of my experience would not be retained, reproduced, and remembered by me, thus would not be my experience, thus would not amount to experience. But a postmodern conception of the self *together* with a doctrine of eternal recurrence is quite capable of explaining how the self remains exactly and precisely the same—without the slightest change. Indeed, we might even say that Nietzsche's commitment to a postmodern conception of the self *requires* eternal recurrence if it is to be able to explain the possibility of organized experience over long periods of time.

Chapter Five

Eternal Recurrence Continued

I. Eternal Recurrence and the Horror of Existence

In *Will to Power,* Nietzsche writes: "Let us think this thought in its most terrible form: existence as it is, without meaning or aim, yet recurring inevitably . . . *'the eternal recurrence.'*"[1] This passage reminds us of an important point. The philosopher who introduces eternal recurrence, the philosopher who believes in *amor fati,* is also the very same philosopher who believes in the horror and meaninglessness of existence. This is a point that is never emphasized—indeed, it is hardly even noticed—by commentators.[2] Lou Salomé tells us that Nietzsche spoke to her of eternal recurrence only "with a quiet voice and with all signs of deepest horror. . . . Life, in fact, produced such suffering in him that the certainty of an eternal return of life had to mean something horrifying to him."[3]

Try to imagine yourself with a migraine. Imagine yourself in a feverish state experiencing nausea and vomiting. Imagine that this sort of thing has been going on for years and years, and that you have been unable to do anything about it. Extreme care with your diet, concern for climate, continuous experimenting with medicines, all accomplish nothing. You are unable to cure yourself. You have been unable even to improve your condition significantly.[4] You have no expectation of ever doing so. Suppose this state has led you to see, or perhaps merely confirmed your insight into, the horror and terror of existence. It has led you to suspect that perhaps Silenus was right. Best never to have been born. Second best, die as soon as possible. All you can expect is suffering, suffering for no reason at all, meaningless suffering. You have even thought of suicide.[5] Now imagine that at your worst moment, your loneliest loneliness, a demon appears to you, or you imagine a demon appearing to you. And this demon tells you that you will have to live your life over again, innumerable times more, and that everything, every last bit of pain and suffering, every last migraine, every last bout of nausea and vomiting, will return, exactly the same, over and over and over again.

What would your reaction be? If your reaction were to be negative, no one would bat an eye. But what if your reaction was, or came to be, positive? What if you were able to love your life so completely that you would not want to change a single moment—a single moment of suffering? What if you were to come to crave nothing more fervently than the eternal recurrence of every moment of your life? What if you were to see this as an ultimate confirmation and seal, nothing more divine? *How could you do this?* Why would you do this? Why wouldn't it be madness? What is going on here? How has this been overlooked by all the commentators? This cries out for explanation.

Eternal recurrence, I think we can say, illuminates the horror of existence. No matter what you say about your life, no matter how happy you claim to have been, no matter how bright a face you put on it, the threat of eternal recurrence brings out the basic horror in every life. Live it over again with nothing new? It is the 'nothing new' that does it. That is how we make it through our existing life. We hope for, we expect, something new, something different, some improvement, some progress, or at least some distraction, some hope.[6] If that is ruled out, if everything will be *exactly* the same in our next life, well that is a different story. If you find people who claim to be supremely happy with their lives, just see what happens if they start to think that they will have to live them over again.

Suppose that you can, as Aristotle suggested, look back over your life as a whole and feel that it was a good one—a happy one. Would that make you want to live it again? Would you at the moment in which you feel that your life was a happy one also *"crave nothing more fervently"* than to live it again? What if your life was a joyous life or a proud life? It is quite clear that you could have a very positive attitude toward your life, and not at all want to live it again. In fact, wouldn't the prospect of eternal repetition, if the idea grew upon you and gained possession of you, begin to sap even the best life of its attractiveness? Wouldn't the expectation of eternal repetition make anything less appealing?[7] Wouldn't it empty your life of its significance and meaning? Most commentators seem to assume that the only life we could expect anyone to want to live again would be a good life.[8] That makes no sense to me. On the other hand, most people would assume that a life of intense pain and suffering is not at all the sort of life it makes any sense to want to live again. I think Nietzsche was able to see that a life of intense pain and suffering is perhaps the only life it really makes sense to want to live again. Let me try to explain.

For years Nietzsche was ill, suffering intense migraines, nausea, and vomiting. Often he was unable to work and confined to bed. He fought this. He tried everything. He sought a better climate. He watched his diet fanatically. He experimented with medicines. Nothing worked. He could not improve his condition. His suffering was out of his control. It dominated his life and determined his every activity. He was overpowered by it. There was no freedom or dignity here. He became a slave to his illness. He was subjugated by it. What was he to do?

At the beginning of the essay, "Concerning the Sublime," Schiller wrote:

> Nothing is so beneath the dignity of a human being as to suffer violence. . . . Whoever cowardly suffers it, tosses his humanity aside. . . . Every human being finds himself in this position. He is surrounded by countless forces, all superior

to him and all playing the master over him. . . . If he can no longer oppose physical forces with a corresponding physical force, then nothing else remains for him to do to avoid suffering violence than *to do completely away with a relation* so deleterious to him and to *destroy conceptually* a brute force that he in fact must endure. However, to destroy a force conceptually means nothing other than to submit to it voluntarily.[9]

While Nietzsche does not go about it in the way Schiller had in mind, nevertheless, this is very much what Nietzsche does. What was he to do about his suffering? What was he to do about the fact that it came to dominate every moment of his life? What was he to do about the fact that it was robbing him of all freedom and dignity? What was he to do about this subjugation and slavery? He decided to submit to it voluntarily. He decided to accept it fully. He decided that he would not change one single detail of his life, not one moment of pain. He decided to love his fate. At the prospect of living his life over again, over again an infinite number of times, without the slightest change, with every detail of suffering and pain the same, he was ready to say, "'Well then! Once more!'"[10] He could not change his life anyway. But this way he broke the psychological stranglehold it had over him. He ended his subjugation. He put himself in charge. He turned all "it was" into a "thus *I* willed it." Everything that was going to happen in his life, he accepted, he chose, he willed. He became sovereign over his life. There was no way to overcome his illness except by embracing it. If you love your fate, you are free.

Eternal recurrence is a test, a test to see who counts as a candidate for the *Übermensch.* Nietzsche says: *"I assess the power of a will by how much resistance, pain, torture it endures and knows how to turn to its advantage; I do not account the evil and painful character of existence a reproach to it, but hope rather that it will one day be more evil and painful than hitherto—"*[11] "What does not kill me makes me stronger."[12] Thus:

> To those human beings who are of any concern to me I wish suffering, desolation, sickness, ill-treatment, indignities—I wish that they should not remain unfamiliar with profound self-contempt, the torture of self-mistrust, the wretchedness of the vanquished; I have no pity for them, because I wish them the only thing that can prove today whether one is worth anything or not—that one endures.[13]

Drives become more powerful by facing obstacles and overcoming them. The greater the obstacle overcome, the greater the power of the drive.[14] What is the greatest obstacle? Eternal recurrence of the horror of existence. To face as much truth as we can bear,[15] to look into the meaningless void, to intensify our suffering by making it eternal, and to love every moment,[16] that is the test of real power, that is the test of the highest power, that is the test of the *Übermensch.* It was through millennia of such self-torture, after all, that King Vishvamitra acquired enough "power and self-confidence that he endeavored to build a *new heaven.*" Moreover, "whoever has at some time built a 'new heaven' has found the power to do so only in his *own hell.*"[17]

II. Loving Every Moment

I think we are now in a position to see that for eternal recurrence to work, for it to have the effect that it must have for Nietzsche, we must accept without qualification, we must love, *every* single moment of our lives, *every* single moment of suffering. We cannot allow ourselves to be tempted by what might at first sight seem to be a much more appealing version of eternal recurrence, that is, a recurring life that would include the desirable aspects of our present life while leaving out the undesirable ones. To give in to such temptation would be to risk losing everything that has been gained. To give in to such temptation, I suggest, would allow the suffering in our present life to begin to reassert its psychological stranglehold. We would start to slip back into subjugation. We would again come to be dominated by our pain. We would spend our time trying to minimize it, or avoid it, or ameliorate it, or cure it. We would again become slaves to it.

For the same reason, I do not think it will work for us to accept eternal recurrence merely because of one or a few grand moments. Magnus, we have seen, holds that all we need desire is the return of one peak experience.[18] This suggests that our attitude toward the rest of our life could be one of toleration, acceptance, or indifference—it could even be negative. All we need do is love one great moment and, since all moments are interconnected,[19] that then will require us to accept all moments. This would be much easier than actually loving *every* moment of one's life—every single detail. The latter is what is demanded in *Ecce Homo,* which says that *amor fati* means that one "wants *nothing* to be different" and that we "[n]ot merely *bear* what is necessary . . . but *love* it."[20] We want "a Yes-saying without reservation, even to suffering. . . . *Nothing* in existence may be subtracted, *nothing* is dispensable."[21] If we do not love *every* moment of our present life for its own sake, those moments we do not love, those moments we accept for the sake of one grand moment, I suggest, will begin to wear on us.[22] We will begin to wish we did not have to suffer through so many of them, we will try to develop strategies for coping with them, we will worry about them, they will start to reassert themselves, they will slowly begin to dominate us, and pretty soon we will again be enslaved by them. Our attitude toward any moment cannot be a desire to avoid it, change it, reduce it—or it will again begin to dominate us. Indeed, in *Ecce Homo,* Nietzsche says that he had to display a "'Russian fatalism.'" He did so by

> tenaciously clinging for years to all but intolerable situations, places, apartments, and society, merely because they happened to be given by accident: it was better than changing them, than *feeling* that they could be changed—than rebelling against them.

Any attempt to disturb me in this fatalism, to awaken me by force, used to annoy me mortally—and it actually was mortally dangerous every time.

Accepting oneself as if fated, not wishing oneself "different"—that is in such cases *great reason* itself.[23]

Eternal recurrence is an attempt to deal with meaningless suffering. It is an attempt to do so which completely rejects an approach to suffering that says let us improve the world, let us change things, let us work step by step to remove suffering and produce happiness—the view of liberals, socialists, and feminists whom Nietzsche so often rails against. If it is impossible to significantly reduce suffering in the world, as Nietzsche thinks it is, then to make it your goal to try to do so would be to enslave yourself to that suffering. Instead, we must face our suffering, accept it, even increase it. We need to toughen ourselves. Eternal recurrence serves this purpose.

Before closing this section, we must consider a possible objection. I have argued that it makes little sense to expect anyone to want to relive a life of happiness or of great moments. The prospect of reliving such moments an infinite number of times would sap those moments of their meaning and significance. We must see that the same sort of objection would have no effect at all against the alternative claim that the only life it really makes sense to want to live again would be a life of pain and suffering? Why would this be the case? Why would this alternative claim hold up any better? What would make its appeal more lasting?

To answer these questions, imagine yourself reflecting on the idea of eternal recurrence. Imagine going through all the best moments of your life. Now run through them all again. Then again. And again. Sooner or later all those great moments would begin to pale. They would become boring. They would be sapped of their greatness. Repetition deadens them.[24] And sooner or later the idea of eternal recurrence would begin to weigh on you and to crush you.

On the other hand, imagine yourself reviewing all the worst moments of your life—moments of meaningless pain and suffering. Then imagine going through them all again. And again. Now imagine that you are somehow able to say to yourself that you would not change any one of those moments—that you would not change the slightest detail. Imagine that you are able to turn all "it was" into a "thus I willed it." If you are able to face the pain in your life and say, "Well then! Once more!", you would begin to break the stranglehold this pain has had over you. You would begin to build up greater strength. You would begin to increase your power. It makes no sense to say that eternal recurrence would sap a life of meaningless pain and suffering of its meaning. It had no meaning to begin with. It has no meaning to sap. Rather eternal recurrence would *give* it meaning. Embracing eternal recurrence, willing it so, loving one's fate, would turn one's pain and suffering into a discipline—a discipline that would increase one's power. Eternal repetition would sap great moments of their meaning, but it would turn moments of pain and suffering into moments of empowerment and thus give them a meaning. One would not tire of such moments—one could even relish their repetition. One might even create a new heaven out of one's hell. Repetition might sap moments of pain of their painfulness—and that would be a plus. But repetition would not sap moments of empowerment of their power—it would increase that power.

III. Innocence and Redemption

As we saw above in Section I of Chapter 3, since meaningless suffering is unbearable, we give it a meaning. We make it a punishment and inflict it ourselves. We thus keep meaningless suffering, the horror of existence, at bay. It is true that thereby the amount of suffering in the world is increased, but that seems to be worth it as the price of removing meaningless suffering. And we go even further. We inflict suffering upon ourselves. We create guilt. We give all suffering a meaning.

We must see that eternal recurrence continues this same strategy. It does not try to avoid suffering or escape it. It turns all suffering into a "thus I willed it." It imposes it, endorses it, loves it, would not change the slightest detail.[25] As Nietzsche put it in the passage quoted earlier concerning King Vishvamitra: "As men of frightful ages, they did this by using frightful means: cruelty toward themselves, inventive self-castigation. . . . Whoever has at some time built a 'new heaven' has found the power to do so only in his *own hell.*"[26]

Yet at the same time, while noticing that eternal recurrence continues to impose suffering, we must also notice that it does not impose it as punishment or guilt—that is not the meaning it seeks to impose. It seeks instead to create the *innocence* of existence.

If our acts repeat eternally, if they *must* repeat eternally, if they are not something we can change, if they are destined, then how could we be held responsible for them, how could we be held accountable, how could we be guilty of anything? It can make no sense to see our suffering as punishment. Our suffering is not a retribution. It is completely external. It is fated. It is like gravity. It just happens. And thus we are redeemed from guilt. We are innocent. Fate, necessity, eternal recurrence make us innocent.

In *The Anti-Christ,* Nietzsche says of Buddhism that it did not need "to make its suffering and capacity for pain *decent* to itself by interpreting it as sin—it merely says what it feels: 'I suffer.'"[27] Eternal recurrence, likewise, reduces our suffering just to the suffering. There are no psychological surpluses or increases.

In the past, we gave suffering a meaning—since meaningless suffering would have been unbearable. We created an illusion. We took suffering to be punishment for sin. We made ourselves guilty. We increased our suffering to avoid the horror of meaningless suffering. Eternal recurrence redeems us from this increased suffering. In *Daybreak,* Nietzsche says, we must "take the concept of punishment which has overrun the whole world and root it out!" It has "robbed of its innocence the whole purely chance character of events."[28]

But doesn't this mean that eternal recurrence returns us to, plunges us back into, *meaningless* suffering?[29] It rejects any concept of punishment. It rejects any concept of guilt. It rejects any concept of sin. It implies that suffering just happens. It just repeats eternally. It is just fated. There is no plan, no purpose, no *reason* for it. Doesn't eternal recurrence rub our noses in meaningless suffering?

In one sense this is perfectly correct. And Nietzsche does want to accept as much meaninglessness and suffering as he can bear.[30] Nevertheless, we must see that there *is* meaning here—in fact, it lies *precisely* in the meaninglessness. Embracing eternal recurrence means imposing suffering on oneself, meaningless suffering, suffering that just happens, suffering for no reason at all. But at the very same time, this creates the *innocence* of existence. The meaninglessness of suffering *means* the innocence of suffering. That is the new meaning that suffering is given. Suffering no longer has its old meaning. Suffering no longer has the meaning Christianity gave to it. Suffering can no longer be seen as punishment. There is no longer any guilt. There is no longer any sin. One is no longer accountable.[31] If suffering just returns eternally, if even the slightest change is impossible, how can one be to blame for it? How can one be responsible? It is none of our doing. We are innocent. The spirit of revenge is broken. This itself could explain why one would be able to embrace eternal recurrence, love every detail of one's life, not wish to change a single moment of suffering. One would be embracing one's own innocence. One would be loving one's own redemption from sin and guilt.

Eternal recurrence brings the great man or the *Übermensch* as close as possible to the real truth, meaninglessness, the void, the horror of existence, but it does not go all the way, or it would crush even the *Übermensch*. Eternal recurrence gives the *Übermensch* meaning. It eliminates emptiness. It fills the void. With what? It fills it with something entirely familiar and completely known, with something that is in no way new, different, or strange, with something that is not at all frightening. It fills the void with one's *own* life—repeated eternally. It is true that this life is a life of suffering, but (given the horror of existence) suffering cannot be avoided anyway, and at least suffering has been stripped of any surplus suffering brought about by concepts of sin, punishment, or guilt. It has been reduced to a life of innocence. The spirit of revenge has been eliminated. Moreover, as Nietzsche has said, it is only meaningless suffering that is the problem. If given a meaning, suffering even becomes something we can seek.[32] Eternal recurrence, the fatedness of suffering, its meaningless repetition, makes our suffering innocent. That might well be reason enough to embrace it. If we understand eternal recurrence adequately, I think we see that it is not at all a matter of indifference as Soll suggests. Indeed, while *we* may not be able to embrace it ourselves, I think we can at least see why Nietzsche might—and even why it might *actually make sense* for him to do so.

Nietzsche tells us that he has thought "pessimism through to its depths" and has arrived at the most "world-affirming human being who has not only come to terms . . . with whatever was and is, but who wants to have *what was and is* repeated into all eternity, shouting insatiably *da capo.*"[33] Eternal recurrence does not eliminate terror and suffering. It embraces it. It loves it. And this produces joy. Not joy instead of terror, not joy replacing terror, but joy *together* with terror. How is that possible? The innocence of existence makes it possible. You suffer, but you have been redeemed—relieved of sin and guilt. You have broken the psychological stranglehold of your suffering. You have made it your own. You will it. You love it. But, it is still terrible suffering.[34]

Here we begin to see how the doctrine of eternal recurrence resembles the tragic ideal of the *Birth of Tragedy*. In Greek tragedy, the Apollonian gave us enough distance, enough of a veil, that we could feel the Dionysian suffering of the tragic hero as powerful and creative—without being annihilated by it.[35] Similarly, eternal recurrence gives us enough distance, enough perspective, that we can experience the horror of our life without being annihilated by it—and, indeed, while being strengthened by it.

IV. Discipline and Pity

Eternal recurrence also gives suffering another meaning. If one is able to embrace eternal recurrence, if one is able to turn all "it was" into a "thus I willed it," then one not only reduces suffering to physical suffering, breaks its psychological stranglehold, and eliminates surplus suffering due to sin and guilt, but one may even in a sense reduce suffering below the level of physical suffering. One does not do this as the liberal, socialist, or Christian would, by changing the world to reduce suffering. In Nietzsche's opinion that is impossible, and, indeed, eternal recurrence of the same rules it out—at least as any sort of final achievement.[36] Rather, physical suffering is reduced by treating it as a test, a discipline, a training, which brings one greater power. One might think of an athlete who engages in increasingly strenuous exercise, accepts greater and greater pain, handles it better and better, and sees this as a sign of greater strength, as a sign of increased ability. Pain and suffering are turned into discipline. Indeed, it is possible to love such suffering as a sign of empowerment. One craves pain, "'*more* pain! *more* pain!'"[37] And the more suffering one can bear, the stronger one becomes. After all, through millennia of this kind of self-torture, King Vishvamitra acquired such a feeling of power and self-confidence that he endeavored to build a new heaven.[38] Eternal recurrence is the ultimate suffering, eternal suffering, which makes possible the greatest power.

If suffering is self-imposed, if the point is to break the psychological stranglehold it has over you, if the point is to turn suffering into empowerment, use it as a discipline to gain greater strength, then it would be entirely inappropriate for us to feel sorry for the sufferer. To take pity on the sufferer would demonstrate either an ignorance of the process the sufferer is engaged in, what the sufferer is attempting to accomplish through suffering, or it would show a lack of respect for the sufferer's suffering.[39] To pity the sufferer, to wish the sufferer did not have to go through such suffering, would demean the sufferer and the whole process of attempting to gain greater strength through such suffering.[40]

If we go further, if we decide that pity and compassion are the proper response to suffering in general, if we seek to make that a principle of public policy, as liberals, socialists, Christians, and feminists do, then, Nietzsche thinks, we make the struggle of the great man or the *Übermensch* even more difficult, we make it harder for him to adopt the right attitude toward suffering, to desire it, to want more of it. We subvert the courage he needs to empower himself.

Let us try to put ourselves in Nietzsche's place. He has suffered for years. He has suffered *intensely* for years. He has come to realize that he cannot end this suffering. He cannot even reduce it significantly. But he has finally been able to break the psychological stranglehold it has had over him. He is able to accept it. He wills it. He would not change the slightest detail. He is able to love it. And this increases his strength. How, then, would he respond to our pity? Very likely, he would be offended. He would think we were patronizing him. He would not want us around. He would perceive us as trying to rob him of the strength he had achieved, subjugate him again to his suffering, strip him of his dignity. He would be disgusted with our trying to be do-gooders, our attempt to impose our *own* meaning on his suffering (treating it as something to pity and to lessen) in opposition to the meaning he has succeeded in imposing on it.[41] He says to us: "To those . . . who are of any concern to me I wish suffering . . . I have no pity for them . . . I wish them the only thing that can prove today whether one is worth anything."[42]

Nietzsche has wagered a lot on his commitment to the notion that suffering cannot be significantly reduced in the world. Because if it can, then pity and compassion would be most important to motivate its reduction. Nietzsche is so committed to the value of suffering that he is willing to remove, or at least radically devalue, pity and compassion.

To appreciate how committed he is, suppose we are incorrigible do-gooders—liberals, socialists, or Christians. We just cannot bear to see anyone suffer. Suppose we find a researcher who is working on a cure for Nietzsche's disease. This researcher thinks that within a few years a drug can be produced to eliminate the disease. Suppose the researcher is right. And suppose that just as Nietzsche solidly commits to eternal recurrence, just as he is able to love his fate, just as he has decided he would not change the slightest detail of his life, we tell him about this cure.

How would Nietzsche respond? Would he give up his hard won attitude of accepting his migraines, nausea, and vomiting, of refusing to desire any change? Would he revert to his old attitude of hoping to reduce his suffering, trying out whatever might accomplish this? Would he give his illness a chance to reassert its psychological stranglehold? We must remember that our supposition is that he would *actually* be cured in a few years? But he would also forgo the discipline, the strengthening, the empowerment, that a commitment to eternal recurrence and *amor fati* would have made possible. While his illness would eventually be cured, he would not have developed the wherewithal to deal with any other suffering—*in a world characterized by the horror of existence.* We cannot know whether Nietzsche would finally decide to take the cure or not. What we can be sure of is that if he did he would not be the Nietzsche we know.

Kierkegaard retells the story of Abraham and Isaac. God commands Abraham to take his only son to Mount Moriah and to sacrifice him there as a burnt offering. Faithful Abraham sets off to obey God's will. But just as he arrives, just as he has drawn his knife, just as he is about to offer his son, he is told instead to sacrifice the ram which God has prepared. Kierkegaard suggests that if he had been in Abraham's position, if he had had sufficient faith in God and had obeyed him as Abraham did, if he had been able to summon the same courage, then, when he got Isaac back again he would have been embarrassed. Abraham, he thinks, was not embarrassed. He was not embarrassed because he believed all along, by virtue of the absurd, that God would not require Isaac.[43] Abraham was a knight of faith. The highest level Kierkegaard could have achieved, he says, would have been that of a tragic hero.[44]

What about Nietzsche? Let us assume that Nietzsche has fully committed to eternal recurrence and *amor fati,* that he has come to love his fate, that he has decided he would not change the slightest detail. Moreover, he has announced this to the world in his writings. Let us assume that over the years this commitment has empowered him, given him greater strength. We do-gooders now inform him that we can cure his disease and eliminate his suffering. Even further, suppose we were able to prove to him that eternal recurrence is impossible. Would Nietzsche be embarrassed?

Maybe. But it is not absolutely certain that he would be. He might respond that believing in eternal recurrence—perhaps even by virtue of the absurd— allowed him to face the horror of existence. He might respond that it does not really matter whether his life will *actually* return. The only thing that matters is the attitude he was able to develop toward his present life. He might respond that it does not really matter that it has become possible to cure his particular illness, there is still plenty of other suffering to be faced given the horror of existence. He might respond that what matters is the strength he was able to gain from believing in eternal recurrence and loving his fate, not whether eternal recurrence is actually true.[45]

V. Eternal Recurrence and Others

On the other hand, we must also notice that if we accept eternal recurrence and *amor fati,* if we reject change, if we rule out even the desire for change, if we must love every moment, then, as Magnus, Clark, and Owen point out, we end up with ghastly consequences.[46] We would have to love—we would have to *welcome* the return of—even things like the atrocities of Hitler.

Frankly, I do not think this would drive Nietzsche to abandon his doctrine. He must love every last detail. If he falters, if he decides only to love the whole process enough so that he is willing also to relive those parts that cannot be loved, as Clark puts it,[47] then the meaningless suffering that fills the world, the horror of existence, will begin to reassert its stranglehold. It will again come to dominate and he will again be enslaved. Nietzsche must look all suffering straight in the eye and love it. I do not think he need love Hitler, the holocaust, and other such horrific examples of suffering the way Christians are supposed to love their enemies, but he must love them in the way *warriors* love their enemies—that is, as a mark of distinction and an occasion for triumphing over them in battle.[48]

At any rate, what is at issue here in the doctrine of *amor fati,* it is quite clear, is not merely whether I am able to will to live my life over again—repeat my suffering and pain. At issue also is whether I can will on others the repetition of their suffering and pain. Perhaps I can accept my own suffering. Perhaps I can break its stranglehold by accepting it—since I cannot change it anyway. But what about others? Is it acceptable that I will that they relive their suffering eternally? Is it acceptable that I will their suffering in order to break the stranglehold that suffering has over me? Does it matter that I cannot change this anyway? We might not approve it, we might find it highly objectionable, but I see no reason to think that Nietzsche would balk at willing the suffering of others. Consider the following passage from *The Gay Science*:

> Who will attain anything great if he does not find in himself the strength and the will to *inflict* great suffering? Being able to suffer is the least thing; weak women and even slaves often achieve virtuosity in that. But not to perish of internal distress and uncertainty when one inflicts great suffering and hears the cry of this suffering—that is great, that belongs to greatness.[49]

In *Will to Power,* Nietzsche also says:

> To those human beings who are of any concern to me I wish suffering, desolation, sickness, ill-treatment, indignities. . . . I have no pity for them, because I wish them the only thing that can prove today whether one is worth anything or not—that one endures.[50]

> *I assess the power of a will by how much resistance, pain, torture it endures and knows how to turn to its advantage; I do not account the evil and painful character of existence a reproach to it, but hope rather that it will one day be more evil and painful than hitherto—*[51]

Indeed, in *Beyond Good and Evil,* Nietzsche also says:

> The Jews . . . are beyond any doubt the strongest, toughest, and purest race now living in Europe; they know how to prevail even under the worst conditions (even better than under favorable conditions).[52]

I do not think Nietzsche would be swayed by the concerns of Magnus, Clark, and Owen. Indeed, if one takes the last few quotations seriously, it follows for Nietzsche that things like Hitler and the holocaust are the very sorts of things that one must *especially* want to be repeated. The *worst* things must *especially* be loved—or they will continue to subjugate, consume, and destroy us.

One might think this outrageous. Magnus asks us, "How can eternal recurrence be willed after Dachau . . . ?"[53] One might even claim that Auschwitz makes Nietzschean *amor fati* historically impossible.[54] One might argue that the atrocities of the twentieth century make *amor fati* completely untenable. Let me say that I have no desire to defend Nietzsche. But I do want to try to explain him. While his position is filled with tension[55]—indeed, about to explode from it—more can be said by way of explanation. In *The Gay Science*, Nietzsche claims:

> Anyone who manages to experience the history of humanity as a whole as *his own history* will feel in an enormously generalized way all the grief of an invalid who thinks of health. . . . But if one endured, if one *could* endure this immense sum of grief of all kinds while yet being the hero who, as the second day of battle breaks, welcomes the dawn and his fortune, being a person whose horizon encompasses thousands of years past and future . . . if one could burden one's soul with all of this—the oldest, the newest, losses, hopes, conquests, and the victories of humanity; if one could finally contain all this in one soul and crowd it into a single feeling—this would surely have to result in a happiness that humanity has not known so far: the happiness of a god full of power and love, full of tears and laughter.[56]

If one can come to feel the whole history of human suffering as one's own, if one can endure this and want it to continue (and obviously all the more so if one could will it to return eternally), one could experience the joy and power of a god. That is Nietzsche's claim.

I have placed very heavy emphasis on the centrality for Nietzsche of the horror of existence. It is also quite clear, though, that Nietzsche frequently speaks of joy and joyousness.[57] The possibility of such joy must be explained. I think the passage just quoted from *The Gay Science* begins to make clear how horror and joy are compatible. The sort of joy Nietzsche has in mind is like the joy of triumph in battle. The battle involves great suffering for yourself and also for others, but you endure it, you welcome it, you take joy in getting through the pain and suffering, you take joy in triumphing over it. So also, if you can look back over your life, a life of suffering and misery, a life of suffering and misery for yourself and also for others, if you can break the stranglehold this suffering has had over you, if you can still look forward to life, if you can accept eternal recurrence, if you can love your fate, then you can experience a godlike joy. The joy does not replace the suffering. It does not eliminate the suffering. You suffer *and* you experience joy.[58] Indeed, without the suffering you could not experience this sort of joy.

Nietzsche could even argue that the more terrible the suffering, the greater the joy. This must be explained. If, by way of contrast, we were to think that we live in a designed cosmos (or even in a perfectible one that has been reasonably perfected), then, Nietzsche might hold, it would be as if our happiness had just been handed to us, something we could complacently expect, like cows in the pasture. It would be, as he puts it in *Beyond Good and Evil,* like the "green-pasture happiness of the herd."[59] But if existence is terrible, if it is filled with meaningless pain and suffering, suffering for yourself and for others, and if you have been able to endure it, if you have been able to triumph over it, if you have broken its stranglehold, if you can welcome it, if you can will every moment of it, if you have given it new meaning, if you have redeemed it from guilt, if you have made it innocent, if like a god you have succeeded in so transforming existence, then your joy, your exuberance, your yes-saying, would be of quite a different order than that of the herd-like creature grazing in its green-pasture happiness. That is Nietzsche's vision as best I can explain it.

VI. Eternal Recurrence and the Categorical Imperative

Some commentators raise the question of whether Nietzsche intends eternal recurrence to be like a categorical imperative.[60] At *Gay Science* §341, we have seen, Nietzsche said: "The question in each and every thing, 'Do you desire this once more and innumerable times more?' would lie upon your actions as the greatest weight." In the *Nachlass,* he also writes: "My doctrine declares: the task is to live in such a way that you must wish to live again—you will anyway."[61]

On the other hand, though, in *Twilight of the Idols,* Nietzsche says:

> Let us consider finally what naïvety it is to say 'man *ought* to be thus and thus!'
> . . . The individual is, in his future and in his past, a piece of fate. . . . To say to
> him 'change yourself' means to demand that everything should change, even in
> the past.[62]

The obvious objection to understanding eternal recurrence as like a categorical imperative, it would seem, is that for a categorical imperative to make any sense, for moral obligation to make any sense, it must be possible for individuals to *change themselves.* And Nietzsche denies that individuals can change themselves. Magnus thinks the determinism "implicit in the doctrine of the eternal recurrence of the same renders any imperative impotent. . . . How can one *will* what must happen in any case?"[63] Eternal recurrence seems to deny that an *ought* can make any sense at all.

At the other end of the spectrum, those who do hold that eternal recurrence is like a categorical imperative, for their part, tend to ignore or deny that eternal recurrence is eternal recurrence of the same, that is, they ignore the determinism involved in eternal recurrence.[64] In this section, then, I want to explore the extent to which it can be claimed that eternal recurrence is like a categorical imperative without downplaying Nietzsche's commitment to determinism.

We must be careful to remember, then, that eternal recurrence is eternal recurrence of the *same.*[65] It is impossible to do anything in our present life that we have not done in our previous lives. Nothing new or different can occur. Nevertheless, the only thing that follows from this, the only thing we can deduce from what has gone on up to the present point in our current life is that every detail must have been repeated in our past lives (assuming, of course, that eternal recurrence is true). We do not know yet, in our present life, what we are going to do during the rest of our life. And eternal recurrence is able to tell us nothing at all about that. Eternal recurrence gives me no information ahead of time about what I can or cannot do in the rest of my present life. It is merely the case, rather, that whatever I do end up doing tells me what I must have done over and over in past lives and will do again in future lives.

If I believe the truth of eternal recurrence, then I believe that in my present life I cannot change anything from my past lives, but I also realize that I cannot know ahead of time what I am about to do, that is, what it is I *must* do in my present life. The fact that I take whatever I will do in the future to be strictly determined, the fact that it is fated, does not give me any information whatsoever about what it is that is fated. It does not tell me that I must do this rather than that. It gives me no information whatsoever about the details of my fate. Only once I do whatever I do can I know that it was the outcome of the whole past and of all past pasts. In short, all this determinism, rigid as it is, tells me nothing ahead of time of what I am going to do in my present life.

What, then, is the point of all the emphasis Nietzsche puts on determinism, if it gives us no guidelines concerning future action in this life? The point, I suggest, is merely to generate a certain attitude toward whatever it is we end up doing. This is what Nietzsche means, I think, when he says you should "live in such a way that you must wish to live again," and immediately adds, "you will anyway." He is not suggesting that we do something different from our last recurrence, nor something that is not the fated outcome of all past history. That, he thinks, is impossible. He is merely suggesting a certain attitude toward whatever it is we finally do.

But still, isn't it impossible for *attitudes* to change from life to life? Aren't they too the outcome of all past history? At *Gay Science* §341, Nietzsche said that if the thought of eternal recurrence "gained possession of you, it would change you as you are or perhaps crush you."[66] This might seem to suggest that attitudes can change. The claim that the thought of eternal recurrence "would change you as you are" suggests that in some sense you change, though also it suggests that in some sense you do not. Eternal recurrence "would change you," yet you would remain "as you are." We might be tempted to understand this as implying that attitudes can change in the sense that attitudes can arise that were not the outcome of past history.[67] But I do not think it necessary for us to assume that this is what Nietzsche means. We should not weaken his determinism without good textual warrant for doing so.

It is quite possible to stick with the interpretation that all things, even attitudes, are the outcome of past history and still make sense of changes in attitude. The basic characteristic of past history, its strict determinism, plus the fact that our life must be lived again and again, if we were to reflect upon this, if "this thought gained possession of" us, could easily cause (in perfect compatibility with the strictest determinism) a certain attitude in us, the attitude that we should accept this determinism and go along with it, or, as Nietzsche chooses to put it, the attitude that we should "live in such a way that [we] must wish to live again—[we] will anyway." Thus, it can make perfect sense to say that reflecting on the determinism of past history (together with the fact that it will return eternally) could change us as we are. This explanation of change is not at all incompatible with the determinism Nietzsche subscribes to, indeed, it is simply a *result* of it. It is perfectly acceptable to hold that past history contains processes that produce changes from one historical moment to the next, it is just that once we see what those changes in fact are we must take them to have been fated, strictly determined, and thus we must accept that it would be impossible to change them from the way they have actually been determined by past history (as well as by past cycles).

So also, reflecting upon such determinism, upon the fact that nothing can be changed, upon the fact that all is fated, might cause a further attitude, the attitude that: 'Fine, I wouldn't change it anyway!' And if such an attitude were produced in us, then when we hear about eternal recurrence it might strike us as divine. When we hear about our fate, we might love it. We might even be able to turn all "it was" into a "thus I willed it." When we hear about all this rigid determinism, we could conceivably "*crave nothing more fervently* than this ultimate eternal confirmation and seal."

So far, then, we have explained the sense in which change is possible for Nietzsche. The question is whether this is enough to allow us to say that eternal recurrence is like a categorical imperative?

I think we *can* say that eternal recurrence gives us an imperative. In *Thus Spoke Zarathustra,* Nietzsche himself writes: "Once man believed in soothsayers and stargazers, and therefore believed: 'All is destiny: you ought to, for you must.'"[68] This is to say that all our actions are fated, determined, they cannot be changed, and thus we "must." But it is also to say that we should have a certain attitude toward this fate, that we accept it, will it, love it, that we "ought." In short, the imperative is that we ought to "live in such a way that [we] must wish to live again—[we] will anyway."

Once we adopt this attitude, but not before, we can be sure that we adopted it in all past lives. Only then can we be sure that this attitude has been fated— that we had no choice but to adopt it. But until we adopt this attitude, we do not know whether or not we are fated to do so. We cannot know ahead of time what our reaction will be when we finally realize that all is fated. Our reaction could be one of horror—we could be crushed by the fatedness of our actions. Or the fact that all is fated, once "this thought gained possession of" us, might cause an attitude of acceptance. Furthermore, Nietzsche's urging us to "live in such a way that [we] must wish to live again—[we] will anyway," together with his further reflections on eternal recurrence and *amor fati,* might just be the factors that tip us in the right direction. Thus it seems to me quite legitimate to understand Nietzsche's urging as an imperative.

We can also say, I think, that the imperative which eternal recurrence gives us involves universalization—indeed, the ultimate universalization. Borrowing Kant's language, we could say that Nietzsche wants us to act on those maxims we could will be repeated eternally—we will anyway.[69]

Nevertheless, there are enormous differences between Kant and Nietzsche that we must attend to. Perhaps the most important is that the *Übermensch* can will that *anything* be repeated eternally.[70] After all, he turns *all* "it was" into a "thus I willed it." He loves every detail of his life no matter what it is. Suppose we consider an action like telling a lie. For Kant, we cannot universalize telling a lie and thus we should not tell one. Nietzsche, of course, does not think that discovering whether or not a maxim is universalizable will or should determine our behavior one way or the other. After all, whether we lie or not is determined by all past history and its eternal recurrence—it is fated. It cannot be determined by the rational analysis of maxims alone. Unlike the categorical imperative, then, eternal recurrence has nothing to do with the moral rightness of actions.

Nietzsche is not concerned with whether or not we tell a lie. He is concerned with the *attitude* we adopt toward whatever action we do take. He wants us to love every detail of our lives—whether we told a lie or not. What matters is not whether we lied, but whether we love our actions. Eternal recurrence is not concerned with *what* is affirmed, only with *affirmation*. The *Übermensch* can act so as to violate the moral law in the most objectionable way, and yet still love every detail of his life. The categorical imperative commands ethical content; eternal recurrence does not.

Nietzsche, then, cannot live up to the demands of the Kantian form of universalization. We might also ask, though, whether Kant could live up to the demands of the Nietzschean form of universalization? Can Kant fulfill the Nietzschean demand that he act only on that maxim he could will be repeated eternally? Could Kant live in such a way that he must wish to live again—he will anyway? Suppose that you have led a moral life in the Kantian sense, acting for the sake of the categorical imperative at every step—or that you have come as close to this as would be possible for a human being. Would you therefore be willing to live your life again—would you be willing to live it again an infinite number of times? Could the Kantian categorical imperative be expected to produce *amor fati*? The moral law, Kant says, does produce in us a feeling of respect—a feeling self-wrought by a rational concept.[71] It would produce in us respect for the moral law and presumably even more so for a moral law that had succeeded in (or come close to) regulating an entire life. Well then, could we expect that a life so regulated by the moral law would engender in us sufficient respect that we should be willing to live that life again? To put it in shorthand, could the Kantian categorical imperative lead to *amor fati*—the embracing of Nietzschean eternal recurrence?

A much more likely reaction, to be honest, would be that of Aeneas, the most *pious* of men, who nevertheless was appalled when he discovered that he would have to live his life again.[72] If there is anything about a moral life that should make one want to live it again, an infinite number of times, I do not see what it would be.[73]

Indeed, I think that the prospect of living one's life over and over again an infinite number of times, once "this thought gained possession of you," would sap the Kantian moral life of its very significance. Whatever appeal a moral life might have would be undermined by the prospect of repeating it infinitely. Eternal recurrence obviously implies that there is no noumenal realm, no transcendental self, no freedom of the Kantian sort. Every action, every thought, every reflection returns eternally and exactly the same. We have determinism, causality, heteronomy—all the way down. While acting autonomously on the moral law would produce in us a sense of dignity,[74] for Kant, the prospect of being fated to repeat that same exact action an infinite number of times, far from producing an increased sense of dignity, would *eliminate* autonomy and thus subvert any dignity.

Thus, while actions are universalizable for Nietzsche, they are not universalizable in Kant's sense. We might say that for Nietzsche they are subjectively universalizable. Whether one is able to universalize them depends upon one's subjectivity—one's attitude. Such universalization is not something objective, something we can expect of all rational beings. The *Übermensch* can will to universalize every detail of his life—will to repeat it eternally—but this is clearly not the case for everyone. Most people, in fact, would be crushed by the idea of eternal recurrence. Moreover, the *Übermensch* is able to universalize what for Kant is not universalizable. We have already seen that the *Übermensch* can will the eternal return of the holocaust, which would obviously violate Kant's categorical imperative in the grossest way. On the other hand, Kant would not be able to live up to the demands of Nietzschean universalization—he could not accept eternal recurrence.

In comparing eternal recurrence and the categorical imperative, then, we have major differences between Nietzsche and Kant. And one of the main differences is that Nietzsche's views on eternal recurrence seem to have little to do with morality. We must begin to explain, then, the way in which Nietzsche's views on eternal recurrence are connected with moral matters. Nietzsche says that we should live in such a way that we must wish to live again—we will anyway. This means that we should act as if our acts were all fated—they are anyway. The consequence of this, we have seen, is that we should act as if our acts were all *innocent*—they are anyway. Eternal recurrence, Nietzsche thinks, redeems us from guilt and makes us innocent. Nietzsche wants to restore the innocence of existence. He wants to rid the world of guilt, sin, punishment, and the spirit of revenge.

As we have seen, Nietzsche's position is that because we cannot accept meaningless suffering, we have given it a meaning—as punishment. We inflict punishment ourselves to invest it with a meaning. In fact, we go even further, we inflict suffering on ourselves internally—we invent guilt. We also invent a will and thus responsibility so that we can be held guilty and so that God can have a right to inflict punishment.[75] Nietzsche wants to reject this whole set of meanings that have been given to suffering, return us to the innocence of existence, and construct a different meaning for suffering. Eternal recurrence reduces our suffering just to the suffering. There are no psychological surpluses or increases.

If our actions repeat eternally, if they *must* repeat eternally, if they are not something we can change, if they are fated, then we cannot be held responsible for them, we cannot be guilty of anything. It makes no sense to see our suffering as punishment. We are innocent. Our suffering is not a retribution. It just happens. One is no longer accountable.[76] We are redeemed from sin and from guilt.[77] Nietzsche says, we must "take the concept of punishment which has overrun the whole world and root it out!" It has "robbed of its innocence the whole purely chance character of events."[78] Fate, necessity, eternal recurrence restore the innocence of existence.

To conclude this section, then, I think we can say that despite Nietzsche's commitment to an extreme form of determinism, there is no problem in his advocating that we live in such a way that we must wish to live again—we will anyway. Moreover, it is not unreasonable to describe this as an imperative. Furthermore, this imperative urges us to act as if our acts were all *innocent*—they are anyway. None of this requires us to act any differently. It certainly does not require changing the past—let alone the whole of past history or our past lives. It simply tries to cause a change in the way we view our actions. It tries to redeem them. It tries to redeem them from sin and guilt. And thus it does not seem to me unreasonable to describe what we have here as in some sense a *moral* imperative. And since this moral imperative has a certain universal and necessary quality to it, I can see nothing wrong with calling it a *categorical* imperative. Though, again, we must be careful to remember all of the deep differences that exist between Nietzsche's categorical imperative and Kant's.

VII. Abolition of the True World and the Affirmation of Life

Historically, our response to the horror of existence, our attempt to conceal it, our attempt to give otherwise meaningless suffering a meaning, Nietzsche thinks, involved the construction of a beyond, a better world, a *true* or a *real* world:

> Man seeks . . . a world that is not self-contradictory, not deceptive, does not change, a *true* [*wahre*] world—a world in which one does not suffer.[79]

> [A]n escape remains: to pass sentence on this whole world of becoming as a deception and to invent a world beyond it, a *true* [*wahre*] world. But as soon as man finds out how that world is fabricated solely from psychological needs, and how he has absolutely no right to it, the last form of nihilism comes into being: it includes disbelief in any metaphysical world and forbids itself any belief in a *true* world.[80]

In *Twilight of the Idols,* in the chapter entitled "How the 'Real World' at last Became a Myth," Nietzsche charts the history of this error as follows:

1. The real [*wahre*] world, attainable to the wise, the pious, the virtuous man—he dwells in it, *he is it.* . . . 'I, Plato, *am* the truth.' . . .
2. The real world, unattainable for the moment, but promised to the wise, the pious, the virtuous man ('to the sinner who repents'). . . . —*it becomes a woman,* it becomes Christian. . . .
3. The real world, unattainable, undemonstrable, cannot be promised, but even when merely thought of a consolation, a duty, an imperative . . . the same old sun, but shining through mist and scepticism; the idea grown . . . Königsbergian. . . .
4. The real world—unattainable? Unattained, at any rate. And if unattained also *unknown.* Consequently also no consolation, no redemption, no duty: how could we have a duty towards something unknown? . . . Cockcrow of positivism. . . .
5. The 'real world'—an idea no longer of any use, not even a duty any longer—an idea grown useless, superfluous, *consequently* a refuted idea: let us abolish it! . . . Plato blushes for shame; all free spirits run riot. . . .
6. We have abolished the real world, what world is left? the apparent world perhaps? . . . But no! *with the real world we have also abolished the apparent world!* . . . end of the longest error; zenith of mankind; INCIPIT ZARATHUSTRA.[81]

Eternal recurrence is certainly not a beyond, a different world, a better world, a *true* or a *real* world. It is just this one, repeated over and over. Moreover, this world is a world of horror and terror. Eternal recurrence repeats the horror of existence over and over and over again. A cynic might suspect Nietzsche of working up the notion of eternal recurrence to knock the concept of a true world flat—a sort of doomsday weapon that in order to destroy the enemy destroys everything.

Nietzsche, however, wants to insist that it is not him but the proponents of the *true* world that have devalued and destroyed this one: "The concept of the 'beyond,' the 'true world' invented in order to devaluate the only world there is."[82] They turn this world into a mere means to the beyond: "Religion has debased the concept 'man'; its ultimate consequence is that everything good, great, true is superhuman."[83] "It is of cardinal importance that one should abolish the *true* world. It is the great inspirer of doubt and devaluator in respect of the world *we are.*"[84] "All the beauty and sublimity we have bestowed upon real and imaginary things I will reclaim as the property and product of man . . . with what regal liberality he has lavished gifts upon things so as to impoverish himself. . . . His most unselfish act hitherto has been to admire and worship and to know how to conceal from himself that it was he who created what he admired.—"[85]

All systems of thought must seek to conceal the horror of existence. They must create meaning in order to make life possible. The traditional way of doing this has been to construct another world, a better world, a higher world. Without a doubt this has made life possible, but at the same time it devalued life. Nietzsche, too, thinks we cannot fully face the horror of existence. The *Übermensch* tries to bear as much as he can. But he must still create some meaning in a meaningless cosmos. For Nietzsche, though, this must be done without devaluing life. The *Übermensch* must affirm life. He must embrace it, love it, refuse to change the slightest detail.

Eternal recurrence gives suffering a very different kind of meaning, one which excludes any relation to a beyond. Eternal recurrence is not a test to see if we merit a higher world. It is not punishment, not atonement, necessary to reach a better world. Eternal recurrence rejects all of that. Suffering is just suffering. It just happens—and it returns eternally. We are innocent.[86] We shed the psychological burden of any surplus suffering. We break the spirit of revenge. And we are encouraged to love our fate, love every moment of suffering as a discipline, as a way of strengthening ourselves, as an empowerment. Suffering should be appreciated as an essential part of life, not something merely to be borne for the sake of a higher life.

Eternal recurrence rejects any notion that one's life can have an end, purpose, or goal above, beyond, or outside itself. We certainly cannot achieve any goal that has not already been repeated in all past cycles. It is quite true that we can seek to accomplish this or that, but how much significance can realizing such purposes have if we know we will lose it all, if we will have to start over again, if we are thrown back to the beginning, in every recurring life? Eternal recurrence saps all meaning from any notion of progress, realizing an end, or accomplishing a goal. How could one interest oneself in such things, if, as for Sisyphus, the boulder will roll back down and one must push it back to the summit again and again, life after life, for eternity? Eternal recurrence flattens any liberal, socialist, or feminist attempt to engage people in meaningfully and lastingly improving the world.

Eternal recurrence affirms only the moment. Each moment is worthy of return,[87] not something to be gotten beyond, not a step to another world. The moment must not be wasted by using it for the sake of a future.[88] In *Will to Power,* Nietzsche puts it as follows: "becoming must appear justified at every moment . . . the present must absolutely not be justified by reference to a future, nor the past by reference to the present."[89] Yovel puts it well. Eternal recurrence recognizes "the closed horizon of immanence as the totality of existence . . . ", and *amor fati* transforms "this recognition from a burden to a celebration. It is not resignation, but the active joy of the self-created man, liberated from the external yoke of transcendent religion, morality, utopia, or metaphysics. . . . What I wish to be endlessly repeated is not only the content of every moment but its very momentariness."[90]

As Magnus suggests, eternal recurrence also subverts Christianity. The creation, the incarnation, the resurrection, the last judgment cannot be unique and unrepeatable events.[91] And what would happen to the Christian afterlife if it had to be interrupted for us to be reborn in each recurrence? Eternal recurrence subverts the Christian notion of a life in a higher world. But eternal recurrence *does* promise an *after*life—indeed, an infinite number of lives after this one. Some of the appeal of Christianity is preserved. But this *after*life is not a higher life and does not demean this one. It is nothing but this life over and over again. Eternal recurrence fills the void with something completely familiar, completely known, nothing you have not already faced before.

What is objectionable for Nietzsche about Christianity is that it requires subordination and humility. One must admit to sin, to weakness, to guilt. One must repudiate one's actions and try to change oneself. Eternal recurrence requires none of that. Nothing you can do can affect your next life.[92] Nothing you can do can change this life from past lives. You live your life over again and again without the slightest change. You return from death without having to beg, submit, humiliate yourself, or feel guilty. One is redeemed from all that. One is made innocent. One's dignity is affirmed eternally. One gets the Christian promise, Nietzsche might say, without Christian groveling.

Chapter Six

Masters, Slaves, and *Übermenschen*

I. Masters and Slaves

Eternal recurrence, we have seen, is a new heaven—that is, a new meaning structure, a new worldview. It takes a great man or an *Übermensch* to impose such a vision. It takes an individual able to muster the greatest creative power in the face of the greatest obstacle, the greatest suffering—eternalized suffering. To understand this great man or *Übermensch,* we have a good deal more to do. Where does he come from? How is he produced? What is his character?

In the *Genealogy of Morals,* Nietzsche gives us an extended discussion of master morality, which he sharply contrasts to slave morality. It is considered simply obvious by most commentators that the great man or the *Übermensch* develops out of, or on the model of, the master and master morality—certainly not the slave and slave morality.[1] The understanding we have gained of the horror of existence, however, makes that interpretation untenable—and I will argue against it. Contrary to Nehamas, Deleuze, Danto, and many others, I want to argue that Nietzsche does not simply embrace master morality and spurn slave morality.[2]

To help make the case for all of this, I want, at least briefly, to examine the relationship between Hegel's master-slave dialectic and the conflict Nietzsche sets out between master morality and slave morality. I find it difficult to believe that Nietzsche did not intend his readers to recall the famous master-slave dialectic of Hegel's *Phenomenology of Spirit* as they read the *Genealogy of Morals.* Yet very few commentators ever notice, let alone explore, this connection. Those who do, like Deleuze, Greene, and Houlgate, think that Nietzsche, in direct opposition to Hegel, simply sides with the master, not the slave, and that Nietzschean genealogy renounces all Hegelian dialectic—or any sort of Hegelian developmental view of history.[3] I do not think any of these views are correct and I will argue against them.

In the first essay of the *Genealogy of Morals,* Nietzsche holds (very much in opposition to most other modern theorists) that morality originally had nothing to do with what benefited others, with what was non-egoistic or non-selfish, or even with what was useful to others.[4] It was not even concerned with what was done to *others,* but rather *who* did it, the character of the doers—the good ones themselves. 'Good' originally meant noble, aristocratic, powerful, true, the truthful ones. *We* are the good ones! It was a concept inextricably connected with class—the upper and superior class, the good people—their estimation and affirmation of themselves. Master morality was a triumphant affirmation of self.[5]

And 'bad' meant the opposite—the low, the plebeian, the base. This concept, too, was established by the aristocrats, not the slaves. It was established by those who "seized the right to create values . . . [t]he lordly right of giving names . . . they say 'this *is* this and this,' . . . and, as it were, take possession of it."[6] The bad were the *others,* the ones not like us good ones. Etymologically, Nietzsche claims, the word 'good' in all languages originally meant noble, aristocratic, great, excellent; and 'bad' meant base, common, plebeian.[7]

Slave morality is the very opposite of master morality. It is not self-affirming. Slaves do not first look to themselves and say we are good. Slave morality is reactive. It first looks to the other—the nasty, vicious, brutal masters. And it says they are evil. It is filled with *ressentiment.* Only secondly does it look to itself and affirm weakness, humility, subservience, not strength and power. This is the morality of priests, slaves, subordinates.[8]

Nietzsche thinks we find master morality in Homer, in Rome, in the Renaissance, and for a last brief moment in Napoleon before it disappears in the modern world. It has been defeated by slave morality. We find slave morality among the Jews, in Christianity, in the Reformation, in the French Revolution,[9] in democracy, in socialism, and in feminism—all of which are committed to the weak, the poor, and the powerless.

It is nearly impossible, as I have already suggested, to read the first essay of the *Genealogy of Morals* without recalling Hegel's master-slave dialectic. There we met two self-consciousnesses, each seeking the confirmation of their own reality. Each demanded the recognition—to the point of total submission—of the other. They engaged in a life and death struggle. One of them won and became master. The other lost and was made a slave. The first seemed to be established as a powerful, independent, autonomous consciousness, who then imposed his will upon the other and satisfied his desires—he put the slave to work and enjoyed life in a way he could not before. The slave, on the other hand, was established as a dependent consciousness, one who works and serves—a mere thing whose very reality was defined by-and-for-the-master.[10]

Then there occurred the profound reversal that makes the master-slave dialectic so classic. The master, we begin to see, is not really so independent. In fact, he is quite dependent. He depends upon the slave not only for work and the satisfaction of his desires, but for recognition as well.[11] On the other hand, for his part, the slave through fear and work begins to overcome his thing-like dependence. Daily fear for his life before the master forces the slave to become self-referent, self-conscious, aware of his own self-importance, and to do so in a way that deepens and interiorizes the slave far more than occurs for the master. And through work the slave transcends his dependence and develops the power to accomplish something of value. Work requires that desire be delayed and disciplined if one is to develop an ability to control nature and to create an object that can meaningfully satisfy human need and desire.[12]

Thus, the demands of the master, which begin as an external and repressive force, are internalized by the slave. They become a discipline which deepens and spiritualizes the slave. They push him to work and allow him to create something of significance. The same general model can be found at all levels of Hegel's thought, and ultimately it explains the construction of our whole reality. In particular, historical development, for Hegel, very much follows the model of the slave. In the *Philosophy of History,* Hegel writes:

> The two iron rods which were the instruments of this discipline were the Church and serfdom. The Church drove the "Heart" . . . to desperation—made Spirit pass through the severest bondage. . . . In the same way serfdom, which made a man's body not his own, but the property of another, dragged humanity through all the barbarism of slavery. . . . It was not so much *from* slavery as *through* slavery that humanity was emancipated. . . . It is from this intemperate and ungovernable state of volition that the discipline in question emancipated him.[13]

In the *Philosophy of Right,* Hegel puts it in more general terms:

> Mind attains its actuality only by creating a dualism within itself, by submitting itself to physical needs and the chain of these external necessities, and so imposing on itself this barrier and this finitude, and finally by maturing [*bildet*] itself inwardly even when under this barrier until it overcomes it and attains its objective reality in the finite.[14]

History is a process that involves external repression, which is accepted as a discipline, which is internalized and sublimated, which produces greater spiritual depth, and which allows one to create by transforming the world and oneself. In the *Phenomenology,* for Hegel, consciousness, which begins simply as a desiring consciousness, quickly becomes an ascetic, self-denying consciousness, and in the sphere of religion, at the stage which Hegel calls "Unhappy Consciousness," consciousness projects from itself, imaginatively creates, all of reality—though it takes this reality to be an other, a beyond, an ideal, not itself or its own doing.[15]

At any rate, while Hegel and Nietzsche agree that slaves in fact have won out over masters, nevertheless, Nietzsche seems to reject with contempt the Hegelian slave and Hegelian history, certainly as having anything to do with the emergence of an *Übermensch.* Instead, Nietzsche seems to side with the master and with genealogy as opposed to history.

For Nietzsche, the past is understood as the result of a meaning, a direction, an interpretation imposed upon things by those with the power to do so—by those with the "lordly right of giving names . . . they say 'this *is* this and this,' . . . and . . . take possession of it."[16] Whatever exists, Nietzsche says:

is again and again reinterpreted to new ends, taken over, transformed, and redirected by some power superior to it; all events in the organic world are a subduing, a *becoming master,* and all subduing and becoming master involves a fresh interpretation, an adaptation through which any previous "meaning" and "purpose" are necessarily obscured or even obliterated. . . . [P]urposes and utilities are only *signs* that a will to power has become master of something less powerful and imposed upon it the character of a function; and the entire history of a "thing," an organ, a custom can in this way be a continuous sign-chain of ever new interpretations and adaptations whose causes do not even have to be related to one another.[17]

The best example of this can be found in the second essay of the *Genealogy of Morals,* where Nietzsche explores the meaning of punishment. He says:

The concept "punishment" possesses in fact not *one* meaning but a whole synthesis of "meanings": the previous history of punishment in general, the history of its employment for the most various purposes, finally crystallizes into a kind of unity that is hard to disentangle, hard to analyze. . . . Today it is impossible to say for certain *why* people are really punished: all concepts in which an entire process is semiotically concentrated elude definition.[18]

The meaning of punishment is variable, accidental, plural. It has meant many very different things: rendering harmless, preventing further harm, inspiring fear, repayment, expulsion, preserving purity, a festival to mock a defeated enemy, and many other things.[19] As Deleuze puts it, the history of anything is the succession of forces that take possession of it or struggle for its possession. The same thing changes sense depending upon the forces that appropriate it. There is thus always a plurality of senses to anything.[20]

It would seem to be clear from this that history, for Nietzsche, cannot be going anywhere; it certainly cannot be progressing or developing in a Hegelian sense. There is no goal to history, nor even any goals within history. There is certainly no 'logic' to history. There is not even a single, coherent 'flow' of history. It is a random series of seizures by different forces. Looking back on it, we who study it can dig up a series of layers, geological strata, or, perhaps better, we find a palimpsest, one text written over another. There is as much logic, connection, development, goal-directedness, or necessity between different stages of history as there is between different layers of text in a palimpsest.

For this reason we need genealogy rather than Hegelian history. Genealogy, as Shapiro puts it, has to do "with the ascertaining of actual family lineages to determine rights to titles, honors, and inheritances."[21] These lineages are not at all necessarily the result of steady Hegelian growth like the interest in a bank account, but could well be the result of ruthless conflicts, reversals, accidents, victories, seizures. Where Hegelian history builds to, culminates in, and reinforces the present, genealogy, much more so than Hegelian history, has a powerful tendency to undermine the present. It can show us that things were radically different in the past, that despite our present condition our ancestors were great and grand and noble—or it may show us that they were small, ugly, and embarrassing. In *The Gay Science*, for example, Nietzsche tells us that an understanding of how moral judgments originated can spoil them for us.[22]

History is not, it would seem, a slave-like development, a discipline, a deepening, a working toward some end. In *On the Uses and Disadvantages of History for Life*, Nietzsche ridicules Hegel's notion that we have reached our zenith through world history, a view that "transforms every moment into a naked admiration for success and leads to an idolatry of the factual."[23] Nietzsche rejects this conservative aspect of Hegel's thought. Nietzsche wants to radically subvert the present. He uses genealogy to undermine the actual and hopefully to go beyond it. For Nietzsche we must look selectively to the past in order to create the future. But we can understand the past only "by what is most powerful in the present." Only by straining our noblest qualities to their highest power can we find what is greatest in the past.[24] It would seem that it would take a master, a great man, an *Übermensch*, to interpret the past, to grasp its greatest meaning—otherwise one would draw it down to one's own level. And what this master grasps then must be coined into something never heard before and used to create a new cultural vision—to impose and construct a future.[25] This is not the slave who suffers and labors. This is the master who names and imposes—who seizes, reinterprets, and projects a new vision. It would seem that Nietzsche rejects the slave and Hegelian history. It would seem that Nietzsche embraces the master and genealogy. And it would seem that the great man or the *Übermensch* is connected with the latter, not the former. It would seem so. That is the reading of almost all the commentators. Nevertheless, it is not, finally, Nietzsche's view. That is what I want to argue.

II. The Slave and the *Übermensch*

Even in the first essay of the *Genealogy*, if we look for them, there are passages that disturb the easy and seemingly obvious assumption that Nietzsche simply approves of the masters and not the slaves or priests. For example, he says that only with the priestly form of existence did man first become *"an interesting animal,* that only here did the human soul in a higher sense acquire *depth* and become *evil*—and these are the two basic respects in which man has hitherto been superior to the other beasts!"[26] He says that "history would be altogether too stupid a thing without the spirit that the impotent have introduced into it."[27] It is Nietzsche's view, I think, that the masters are not really very bright: "When the noble mode of valuation blunders and sins against reality, it does so in respect to the sphere with which it is *not* sufficiently familiar, against a real knowledge of which it has indeed inflexibly guarded itself: in some circumstances it misunderstands the sphere it despises, that of the common man, of the lower orders."[28] At any rate, it is quite clear that priests are much more intelligent than the masters: "A race of such men of *ressentiment* is bound to become eventually *cleverer* than any noble race."[29] This is hardly a flattering picture of the masters and it is far from a negative picture of the priests. The masters are quite stupid. They are beasts, not just in the sense of *wild* and *vicious* beasts, but also in the sense of *dumb* beasts. With masters alone, without priests, humans would not even have risen above the animals. What can we have been doing when we thought that Nietzsche simply idolized the masters and was repelled by the priests? That is just not his view:

> 'The masters' have been disposed of; the morality of the common man has won. One may conceive of this victory as at the same time a blood-poisoning. . . . The progress of this poison through the entire body of mankind seems irresistible. . . . To this end, does the church today still have any *necessary* role to play? . . . Which of us would be a free spirit if the church did not exist? It is the church, and not its poison, that repels us.— Apart from the church, we, too, love the poison.—[30]

Such passages, even if they do not yet convince us, should unsettle us, should make us very uneasy about the normal interpretation of the *Genealogy*.

In the second essay, Nietzsche continues his genealogy of morals, and the first question he takes up is how an individual with the ability to make promises—how responsibility—originally developed? This raises a problem for Nietzsche because he believes that we all have a natural tendency to forgetfulness. As we have seen in earlier chapters, for Nietzsche, it is absolutely essential to forget if we are to have any peace, and thus be able to act.[31] If we remembered everything, all the infinite detail we are constantly bombarded with, we would be overwhelmed; we would lose ourselves in the "stream of becoming."[32] Thus, if we are to breed an individual with responsibility, we must breed an ability to overcome forgetfulness and to keep promises. For Nietzsche, this required brutal torture and cruel punishment. A memory had to be *burned* into the individual:

> Man could never do without blood, torture, and sacrifices when he felt the need to create a memory for himself; the most dreadful sacrifices and pledges (sacrifices of the first-born among them), the most repulsive mutilations (castration, for example), the cruelest rites of all the religious cults (and all religions are at the deepest level systems of cruelties)—all this has its origin in the instinct that realized that pain is the most powerful aid to mnemonics.[33]

The important question that we must ask here is *who* this memory had to be burned into? One's immediate impression after reading the first essay and from some of the language at the beginning of the second essay, including the passage just cited, is that memory had to be burned into the slave, certainly not the master. This also seems to be the view of Deleuze, Danto, and Warren.[34] The notion of being subject to punishment and torture does not fit well with our image of a powerful, independent, and autonomous master. It would seem rather slave-like. But this is because we have been led astray in our understanding of Nietzsche's conception of masters and slaves. It is most certainly Nietzsche's view that memory, responsibility, truthfulness had to be burned into the masters. In describing the sovereign individual, Nietzsche clearly has the masters in mind:

> This precisely is the long story of how *responsibility* originated. The task of breeding an animal with the right to make promises. . . . [T]he labor performed by man upon himself during the greater part of the existence of the human race, his entire *prehistoric* labor, finds in this its meaning. . . . If we place ourselves at the end of this tremendous process . . . then we discover that the ripest fruit is the *sovereign individual* . . . the man who has his own independent, protracted will and the *right to make promises*—and in him a proud consciousness, quivering in every muscle, of *what* has at length been achieved and become flesh in him, a consciousness of his own power and freedom. . . . This emancipated individual, with the actual *right* to make promises, this master of a *free* will, this sovereign man—how should he not be aware of his superiority over all those who lack the right to make promises and stand as their own guarantors, of how much trust, how much fear, how much reverence he arouses—he *"deserves"* all three—and of how this mastery over himself also necessarily gives him mastery over circumstances, over nature, and over all more short-willed and unreliable creatures?[35]

The masters of the first essay are clearly examples of such sovereign individuals. The masters were the truthful ones, as opposed to "the *lying* common man."[36] It is, then, *especially* the masters that must have a memory burned into them—*more so* than the slaves.

What we must see here is that the second essay does not just continue on historically from the point reached at the end of the first essay. It does not just continue on discussing the historical development of masters and slaves. Rather, the second essay digs deeper genealogically; it goes back in time *before* the issues discussed in the first essay. It goes back before masters existed and tries to explain the origin of masters. And perhaps like all genealogy which *undermines,* the second essay begins to undermine our first impression of the master, the impression that we had at the end of the first essay. At any rate, these masters must have a memory burned into them through a discipline that is very much like that of Hegel's slave.

Moreover, if we begin to look for it, we can find other evidence, even in the first essay, that the society of the masters is one that involves repression, discipline, and coercion:

> The same men who are held so sternly in check *inter pares* by custom, respect, usage, gratitude, and even more by mutual suspicion and jealousy, and who on the other hand in their relations with one another show themselves so resourceful in consideration, self-control, delicacy, loyalty, pride, and friendship—once they go outside, where the strange, the *stranger* is found, they are not much better than uncaged beasts of prey. There they savor a freedom from all social constraints, they compensate themselves in the wilderness for the tension engendered by protracted confinement and enclosure within the peace of society, they go *back* to the innocent conscience of the beast of prey, as triumphant

monsters who perhaps emerge from a disgusting procession of murder, arson, rape, and torture, exhilarated and undisturbed of soul, as if it were no more than a students' prank.[37]

We tend to remember the ugly brutality of the last part of this passage rather than the emphasis on constraint, repression, and self-discipline of the first part. A good example of masters would be the ancient Spartans, vicious to their enemies, but whose life at home was one of barracks-room discipline, a discipline perhaps more rigorous and difficult even than that imposed upon their slaves. At any rate, the masters, as much as, or more than, the slaves, must develop the ability to keep promises, and for this to occur they must go through a discipline of torture and punishment.

Even further, there is no way to avoid seeing, once we start to look for it, that for Nietzsche this slave-like discipline produces spiritual depth, sublimation, creativity, and indeed that for Nietzsche this is the way that we must ultimately come to understand power. In the first essay, power often seemed to mean the ordinary power of the master—military power or political power. In the second essay that becomes a very secondary type of power. It is there. A memory is burned into us through punishment and torture. It is even Nietzsche's view that the state closes in on us and makes us direct our cruelty inward against ourselves.[38] But what we must see—the important point here—is that this external repression causes us to develop a power *within* ourselves. It brings about an internalization, a discipline, an *empowering*—and this is the form of power that Nietzsche is after. This is what power primarily and ultimately means for him. We begin to notice a shift in this direction when he tells us that what is most interesting about civil laws is not that they impose the will, say, of a ruler or master, but that they "constitute a partial restriction of the will of life" which serves "as a means of creating *greater* units of power."[39] Repression, very much in Hegelian fashion, produces a discipline, an overcoming, the development of greater power. Nietzsche nowhere sounds more like Hegel than in the following passage from *Beyond Good and Evil:*

> The discipline of suffering, of *great* suffering—do you not know that only *this* discipline has created all enhancements of man so far? That tension of the soul in unhappiness which cultivates its strength, its shudders face to face with great ruin, its inventiveness and courage in enduring, persevering, interpreting, and exploiting suffering, and whatever has been granted to it of profundity, secret, mask, spirit, cunning, greatness—was it not granted to it through suffering, through the discipline of great suffering?[40]

The power Nietzsche is after has little to do with the repression of others. It has much more to do with accepting repression oneself, turning it into a discipline that can produce sublimation and self-overcoming: the "self-overcoming of justice: one knows the beautiful name it has given itself—*mercy;* it goes without saying that mercy remains the privilege of the most powerful man, or better, his—beyond the law."[41] Moreover, this sort of power, it becomes clearer and clearer the further we proceed in the *Genealogy,* has little to do with the master of the first essay. By the time we reach the beginning of the third essay it has become quite evident that the main contenders for the sort of power Nietzsche is after are the poet, the priest, and the philosopher. Nietzsche even says that "a Homer would not have created an Achilles nor a Goethe a Faust if Homer had been an Achilles or Goethe a Faust."[42] It is not Achilles—a perfect example of the master of the first essay—that Nietzsche is after. He is after Homer—poor, *blind* Homer. Homer's accomplishment is far greater than Achilles'. The best example of the sort of power Nietzsche is after, the best example of the great man or the *Übermensch,* I have already suggested, is King Vishvamitra, "who through millennia of self-torture acquired such a feeling of power and self-confidence that he endeavored to build a *new heaven.*"[43]

In the *Nachlass,* Nietzsche tells us plainly: "The highest individuals are the creative human beings . . . the purest types and the improvers of humankind." He adds, however, that people often have "a false idea about who the highest specimens" are. They often think they are "the conquerors, etc., hereditary rulers."[44] We must notice that King Vishvamitra is not the master of the first essay. He is much more like Hegel's slave who develops internally, who deepens, who becomes more spiritual, who does so through discipline, torture, suffering, and who goes beyond the master, the old order, the old gods, by creating something new, a new religion, a new meaning structure, a new heaven.[45] Nietzsche even says in *Beyond Good and Evil* that: "Slavery is . . . both in the cruder and in the more subtle sense, the indispensable means of spiritual discipline and cultivation."[46]

However, King Vishvamitra is most interesting not because he represents just the slave principle, but because he represents a *linking* of the slave principle with the master principle,[47] and thus of history with genealogy. This must be explained.

Self-discipline, self-torture, going through one's own hell is necessary to build up power. And power is understood as the power to create a new vision. Just as for Hegel, the slave does not confront the master militarily or politically. The slave deepens, sublimates, overcomes by overthrowing the old gods and building a new heaven. The slave undermines old values and creates new ones. All quite slave-like, certainly, but nevertheless we must also see that there is something of the master here also. Vishvamitra imposes a new vision, revalues things radically, names them differently. He says "this *is* this and this," and "take[s] possession of it."[48] This imposition, this creation of a new reality, clearly requires a master-like power. To impose a new heaven you must have the power to do so—the power of an *Übermensch.* And at the point where this new vision is expressed there occurs a historical break. The new values imposed will be radically different from the old—conceptually and substantially different. The new meaning created will not evolve out of the old and in continuity with it. The *Übermensch* imposes a radically new and different creative vision. It short-circuits historical development. We get a new paradigm. A revaluation of all values. A new *Weltanschauung.* A new force takes possession of things and wrenches their meaning in a new direction.

At the same time, though, the power to set in motion this genealogical break was built up on the Hegelian slave model. It grew out of the slave morality of the Jewish and Christian herd. And so, for Nietzsche, I think we must say that whole stretches of history operate on the Hegelian developmental model of discipline, interiorization, and sublimation. This build-up can even last for centuries before an *Übermensch* comes along with the power to build a new heaven. In fact, it would seem that in large part the whole Jewish and Christian era up to the present, and perhaps also a good part of the tradition back to Socrates and Homer, in other words, much of Hegel's *Philosophy of History,* could be accepted roughly as it stands,[49] except that, for Nietzsche, it is not realizing the Absolute, but rather empowering a Vishvamitra who will finally overthrow it all and create a new worldview. Foucault is wrong, then, when he says that Nietzsche rejects ideal continuity and teleological movement.[50] It is true that history as a whole is not continuous and teleological. *Übermenschen* introduce breaks into it. But long segments can be continuous and teleological. And they are necessary to lead up to, and make possible, the *Übermenschen* who introduce these breaks.

If we now glance back at the first essay, we can begin to see how far we have come from the normal interpretation of the *Genealogy of Morals.* If we look back at the slaves, the herd, the Jews of the first essay, one of the questions we want to ask is how they differ from Vishvamitra—how they differ from the great man or the *Übermensch?* Don't we have to admit that there is a great deal of resemblance between the Jews and Vishvamitra? Isn't it difficult to find much difference? Don't the Jews as much as Vishvamitra overthrow the old gods and build a new heaven?[51] Don't they both revalue all values?

> It was the Jews who . . . dared to invert the aristocratic value-equation (good = noble = powerful = beautiful = happy = beloved of God) . . . saying "the wretched alone are the good; the poor, impotent, lowly alone are the good; the suffering, deprived, sick, ugly alone are pious, alone are blessed by God, blessedness is for them alone—and you, the powerful and noble, are on the contrary the evil. . . ." In connection with the tremendous and immeasurably fateful initiative provided by the Jews . . . there begins the *slave revolt in morality:* that revolt which . . . we no longer see because it—has been victorious.[52]

How does this differ from Vishvamitra? The Jews "brought off that miraculous feat of an inversion of values, thanks to which life on earth has acquired a novel and dangerous attraction for a couple of millennia."[53] I think we must admit that both slaves and *Übermenschen* undergo discipline and torture, which can deepen them, make them more spiritual, and which can allow them to overthrow old values and create a new heaven. One might object that the slaves are reactive, filled with *ressentiment,* and that this is an important difference. But doesn't Vishvamitra react also? Can't he be said to resent the old gods and tradition—it takes him millennia of self-torture in his own hell to build up the power to overthrow this old order.[54] And *ressentiment*, Nietzsche himself admits, is capable of creating new values.[55] It is not easy to find a meaningful difference here.

Both the *Übermensch* and the slave undergo millennia of self-torture. The difference between them is that the Nietzschean *Übermensch* wants to use this suffering to build up the power to create a *new* heaven, whereas Jewish and Christian slaves, who created their heaven a long time ago, do not any longer want a *new* heaven and so undergo their self-torture, accept it, and remain beneath it—perhaps an unsympathetic critic would even say they wallow in it. At any rate, Christianity no longer gains power from its suffering. The priest and the slave, while accepting suffering as necessary, nevertheless, look forward to salvation as the *end* of suffering. In sharp contrast to this, Nietzsche's new heaven is not an escape from the suffering of this world. The *Übermensch* embraces his suffering. He eternalizes it. He turns it into a discipline, so that he can sublimate, so that he can create new meaning and overcome nihilism. That is what the slaves did once, but they are no longer able or willing to do so—and *that* is the difference between the contemporary slave and the *Übermensch*. At the same time, though, we also see the deep *link* between the slave and the *Übermensch*.

III. Christianity, Guilt, and the Ascetic Ideal

To understand the *Genealogy* further, we must say more about the origin of guilt, the development of the ascetic ideal, and Nietzsche's all important notion of punishment. Punishment alone, Nietzsche thinks, will not produce guilt. In fact, punishment tends to harden the criminal and actually hinder the development of guilt.[56] In Nietzsche's view, guilt arises as society develops, becomes peaceful, closes in, encages the individual, and prevents the outward discharge of instincts: "All instincts that do not discharge themselves outwardly *turn inward*—this is what I call the *internalization* of man: thus it was that man first developed what was later called his 'soul.' . . . Hostility, cruelty, joy in persecuting, in attacking, in change, in destruction—all this turned against the possessors of such instincts."[57] And once guilt, or bad conscience, develops, priests are quick to pick it up, interpret it as punishment for sin, nurture it, and push it further as an ascetic ideal:[58]

> The creature imprisoned in the "state" so as to be tamed, who invented the bad conscience in order to hurt himself after the *more natural* vent for this desire to hurt had been blocked—this man of the bad conscience has seized upon the presupposition of religion so as to drive his self-torture to its most gruesome pitch of severity and rigor. Guilt before *God:* this thought becomes an instrument of torture to him.[59]

The state first arises, Nietzsche holds, as beasts of prey conquer a weaker population. These masters "do not know what guilt, responsibility, or considera-tion are, these born organizers. . . . It is not in *them* that the 'bad conscience' developed, that goes without saying—but it would not have developed *without them*."[60] Again, we have a Hegelian master-slave model here. Much as for Hegel, the repression instituted by the masters forces the slaves to internalize, to deepen, and to develop guilt. For Nietzsche, this produces self-discipline and self-overcoming[61]—it builds will to power.[62] Indeed, "'bad conscience'—you will have guessed it—as the womb of all ideal and imaginative phenomena, also brought to light an abundance of strange new beauty and affirmation, and per-haps beauty itself."[63] It is out of this guilt and the ascetic ideal that develops from it that a Vishvamitra, a great man, an *Übermensch,* will gain the creative power to overcome, to sublimate, and to create a new heaven. Torment and mis-treatment, Nietzsche tells us in *Human, All Too Human,* are what produce gen-ius.[64] The intensification of guilt in the Christian ascetic ideal is a form of self-discipline and self-torture that takes an especially internalized and spiritualized form. It especially contributes to imagination and creativity. What "is the mean-ing of the ascetic ideal in the case of the philosopher," Nietzsche asks. "My an-swer is . . . the philosopher sees in it an optimum condition for the highest and boldest spirituality."[65] It is, in Nietzsche's view, the cruelest and most intense form of self-torture. Thus it may be totally crippling. Or it may be the greatest test, the greatest obstacle to be overcome, and thus be capable of generating the greatest power—the power of an *Übermensch.*

It is difficult to decide what Nietzsche means when he says that the masters produce guilt and responsibility in those they conquer but that they themselves do not know what guilt and responsibility are. It may be that since Nietzsche is discussing an extremely early period—the very origin of the state—the masters simply have not yet developed guilt or responsibility. The second essay, after all, is trying to explain how anyone *first* develops these qualities. Perhaps the masters will develop their feelings of guilt at a somewhat later period. We have already seen that the masters do develop responsibility. They, especially, are the truthful ones, as opposed to the *"lying* common man."[66] On the other hand, per-haps it is the case that masters only become responsible, but never develop guilt. Or perhaps they do develop guilt, but not as intensely as priests and slaves. If they never do develop guilt, or to the extent that they do not, then I think we must say that the *Übermensch* and the master simply would have no connection with one another—the *Übermensch* would not develop out of the master at all. This is so because it is Nietzsche's view, I think, that a modern *Übermensch* is not likely to be able to create a new heaven without passing through the intense, tortuous, creative discipline of guilt and the ascetic ideal. "[W]hoever has at some time built a 'new heaven' has found the power to do so only in his *own hell.*"[67] Thus if one tries to keep the master and the slave neatly separate, as the normal interpretation would have it, by claiming that the master does not feel guilt, then the master would not give rise to the *Übermensch.* The master would repress the slave and get the process of internalization started, but all important development would take place on the side of the slave. If one instead decides to admit that the master does develop guilt and does undergo the ascetic ideal, then one must also admit that there is a definite slave-like side to the master, a side that we find to be deeper and more significant the more we continue to probe these issues. Whichever way we look at it, we must admit that the Hegelian slave model figures very centrally in the realization of the *Übermensch*.

There is also a sense in which Nietzsche himself is very much like the slave. Neither is able to change his condition, escape it, or avoid suffering. Perhaps the slave keeps hoping for escape by believing in another, higher, truer world. Nietzsche, for his part, rejects this, but nevertheless, like the slave, he uses his suffering as a self-discipline, a discipline to build up enough power to overthrow the old gods and create a new heaven. The slave does not actually overthrow the master anymore than Nietzsche overcomes his pain and suffering. Slaves merely depict the masters as evil and themselves as good. As Magnus says, since "the slave cannot displace the master in reality, he avenges himself symbolically."[68] However, Magnus says this as if it were objectionable, as if it were not exactly how Nietzsche responded to his own suffering. Indeed, Nietzsche's view seems to be that if you think you can actually change things, you never gain the power to change them symbolically. If you are an Achilles, you never become a Homer.[69] To overthrow the old gods and create a new heaven, we need a new Homer, not a new Achilles. We need the power to change things symbolically. They cannot be changed actually—at least mean- ingless suffering cannot.

The ascetic ideal, we can say, does three things. First, it creates meaning in our world, which otherwise would be a meaningless void. It thus banishes sense- less, meaningless suffering. It interprets suffering as punishment by God for sin.[70] Secondly, the ascetic ideal disciplines those who live under it, builds power in them, which may eventually make it possible for a Vishvamitra to cre- ate a new heaven. This is the Hegelian slave model of discipline, interiorization, spiritualization, and sublimation—which can make possible the master model of imposing new meaning. So far, the ascetic ideal, far from being a denial of life, as it may seem to some, is a powerful affirmation of life.[71]

Thirdly, the ascetic ideal, because it contains and has always contained a powerful will to truth, begins in the modern era to undermine the meaning and the power it has created over the millennia. It begins to rip aside the veil, to close in on the truth, and thus threatens to plunge us into the void—into nihil- ism. The ascetic ideal, Nietzsche thinks, has a rigid and unconditional faith "in a *metaphysical* value, the absolute value of *truth*."[72] Moreover, in Nietzsche's view, science is the latest and noblest form of the ascetic ideal,[73] and certainly modern science has a powerful will to truth. This drive to get at the truth, we have seen, is a problem. It is a problem because reality is terrible. Truth is horri- ble. We live in an empty and meaningless cosmos where we can only expect to suffer. We cannot live without myths and illusions. We have always needed an *Übermensch,* someone powerful enough to impose such myths. And now the will to truth characteristic of the ascetic ideal is pushing aside the veil, leading us to the last thing we want—true reality. We are about to fall into the abyss—plunge into nihilism. We are likely to perish if that occurs. We need a Vishvami-tra, a great man, an *Übermensch,* to create a new heaven. Even the *Übermensch* needs such illusion. No more than anyone else can the *Übermensch* live in the void.

Before we continue here, an important point must be emphasized. If any reader has not yet been convinced that Nietzsche believes in the horror of existence, or if anyone thinks that the horror of existence is something to be found only (or mainly) in early writings like the *Birth of Tragedy,* such readers need pay close attention to the last section of the *Genealogy of Morals.*[74] The *Genealogy of Morals* was published in 1887—that is, at the *end* of Nietzsche's career. It is a very important text. At *Genealogy of Morals,* III, §28, Nietzsche writes:

> Apart from the ascetic ideal, man, the human *animal,* had no meaning so far. . . . "[W]hy man at all?"—was a question without an answer. . . . *This* is precisely what the ascetic ideal means: that something was *lacking,* that man was surrounded by a fearful *void*—he did not know how to justify, to account for, to affirm himself; he *suffered* from the problem of his meaning. He also suffered otherwise . . . but his problem was *not* suffering itself, but that there was no answer to the crying question, *"why* do I suffer?"
>
> Man . . . does *not* repudiate suffering as such; he *desires* it, he even seeks it out, provided he is shown a *meaning* for it. . . . The meaninglessness of suffering, *not* suffering itself, was the curse that lay over mankind so far—*and the ascetic ideal offered man meaning!* It was the only meaning offered so far; any meaning is better than none at all. . . . In it, suffering was interpreted; the tremendous void seemed to have been filled; the door was closed to any kind of suicidal nihilism. This interpretation—there is no doubt of it—brought fresh suffering with it, deeper, more inward, more poisonous, more life-destructive suffering: it placed all suffering under the perspective of *guilt.*
>
> But all this notwithstanding—man was *saved* thereby, he possessed a meaning, he was henceforth no longer like a leaf in the wind, a plaything of nonsense. [75]

One must not misread this text. One certainly should not think that somehow the horror of existence (that is, meaninglessness, suffering, and the void) is merely a construction of, and thus tied exclusively to, limited to, Christianity and the ascetic ideal. The horror of existence exists independently of Christianity and the ascetic ideal. The horror of existence is independently real. Nietzsche believes in it himself. Nietzsche believes in it at the *end* of his career. The ascetic ideal has functioned merely to keep the horror of existence hidden. The ascetic ideal has created meaning for two millennia. It saved us. But now all that is coming to an end. It is failing. And thus the horror of existence will reappear. We are about to be plunged into a meaningless void—into a suicidal nihilism. Something must be done.

If Christianity and the ascetic ideal, for a couple of millennia, have given us meaning in a meaningless cosmos, if they have also disciplined us, built a power in us that may make it possible to create a new heaven, what then is wrong with

Christianity? Why is Nietzsche so critical of it? It cannot be denied that he is highly critical of it.

Schutte suggests that "a religion which glorified unconditional love and suffering . . . left human beings weak and incapable of dealing with the necessarily aggressive aspects of life."[76] But this cannot be the right answer. Nothing glorifies love and suffering more than eternal recurrence and *amor fati*. We must give suffering a meaning. It is not that Christianity gives suffering a meaning by glorifying it that Nietzsche objects to. If anything, Christianity is not positive enough about suffering. It seeks to alleviate it in this world and promises to overcome it in the next. Nietzsche wants to increase it in this world and eternalizes it in all subsequent ones. In this sense, we should not think of eternal recurrence as opposed to the ascetic ideal, as so many commentators do. Eternal recurrence *intensifies* the ascetic ideal—it eternalizes suffering.[77]

What, then, is wrong with Christianity? Well, in many respects, nothing is wrong with it. Nietzsche says, "attack is in my case a proof of good will, sometimes even of gratitude. . . . When I wage war against Christianity I am entitled to this because I have never experienced misfortunes and frustrations from that quarter."[78] After all, Christianity gave suffering a meaning, and did so successfully for a couple of millennia. It kept meaningless suffering at bay and made life possible. As Nehamas puts it, "the ascetic ideal is not to be unequivocally condemned . . . it was for a long time the best (that is, the only) means available for imposing some interpretation upon the fact of 'suffering' and thus for giving human life a purpose and a direction."[79]

Suffering must be given a meaning for life to be possible. We might say that the masters gave suffering a meaning by inflicting it on others as well as themselves. They did so especially in warfare, understood as something to be witnessed by the gods as a sort of festival play and thus an occasion to be remembered by the poets.[80] Those who do not engage in such activity, those who are not warrior-masters, those who are slaves, tend to feel they are wrongfully subjected to the suffering inflicted by the masters. They develop a deep *ressentiment* against the masters and want revenge against them.[81] They eventually develop a God who punishes people for such sins. They too impose suffering to give it meaning. They turn it against the masters out of *ressentiment* and a desire for revenge, and they turn it against themselves as guilt.

It is understandable that one might want to be critical of the slaves for turning against the masters. The masters after all only did what we all must do— they gave suffering a meaning. But at the same time, it would be a mistake to overlook the fact that the slaves are no different in this respect. They too have given suffering a meaning—and successfully so for a couple of millennia. What, then, is Nietzsche's objection to Christianity? He certainly objects to it.

His objection, I suggest, is that Christianity is no longer capable of creativity. On the one hand, Christianity's very powerful and perverse will to truth is leading us into the empty meaningless void, into nihilism, and at the very same time, it is incapable of doing anything about it. It has become decadent. It is incapable of creating a new heaven. This is so because it already has its heaven—it cannot tolerate another. It already has a meaning structure—it cannot believe in another. It already has an explanation for suffering—it cannot accept another. But more than this, it cannot create a new heaven simply because it no longer has the ability to create. Why not? Because it has no power. It has ceased to use its suffering to build up power. It rejects power. It rejects overcoming. Both would threaten its very existence. It does not want the power to overcome the old gods and construct a new heaven—it wants to *keep* its old god and enjoy its old heaven. It has become decadent. It embraces the ascetic ideal. It wallows beneath its suffering. It refuses to turn its suffering into a discipline. It rejects using it as a means to build up power. It shuns a creativity that could topple its old god and create a new heaven.[82]

In all fairness, though, we should add that we could hardly expect master morality to fare any better. No more than Christianity, could we expect it to overthrow its old gods and build a new heaven. It would not be willing to shed its Apollonian shell, its beautiful gods, and accept eternal recurrence of the same.[83] As for creativity, it would likely be inferior to Christianity. It completely lacks the depth of slave morality. It lacks any deep sense of guilt. Masters are the last people we could expect to have the spiritual reserves to help create a new meaning structure. They are even more decadent, more in decline, than Christianity.

IV. A Roman Caesar With Christ's Soul

At this point, we must see that masters and slaves are not two neat and separate classes. The master of the first essay is not someone Nietzsche does anything so simple as just identify with. He plays with the concept of the master— experiments with it. He uses it to dislodge and reveal. He uses it to undermine the morality of the present. He shows us the genealogy of this morality—which embarrassingly leads us back to the opposite of what presently exists. When Nietzsche succeeds in relaxing our grip on the morality of the present, the master is tossed aside, and the master-principle begins to shift, evolve, and become much more subtle:

> *Master morality* and *slave morality*—I add immediately that in all the higher and more mixed cultures there also appear attempts at mediation between these two moralities, and yet more often the interpenetration and mutual misunderstanding of both, and at times they occur directly alongside each other—even in the same human being, within a *single* soul.[84]

Here we have different tendencies, different attitudes, within the same person—not different classes of people. Furthermore, back in the first essay, if we now read even more carefully than before, Nietzsche makes it quite clear that priests—while they are the opposite of the masters and are aligned with the slaves—nevertheless, are themselves aristocrats, nobles, masters.[85] And

Nietzsche speaks of "how easily the priestly mode of valuation can branch off from the knightly-aristocratic and then develop into its opposite; this is particularly likely when the priestly caste and the warrior caste are in jealous opposition."[86] Priests and masters are two parts of the same class. Priests are masters. Even Zarathustra tells us that his blood is related to that of priests "and I want to know that my blood is honored even in theirs.'"[87]

If we admit that the priest is a type of master, then the next step is to notice that for Nietzsche the "Jews . . . were the priestly nation . . . *par excellence*."[88] It follows, doesn't it, that Jews are a type of master. And there is good reason to think that Nietzsche accepts this view. In the Jews, he says, "there dwelt an unequalled popular-moral genius: one only has to compare similarly gifted nations—the Chinese or the Germans, for instance—with the Jews, to sense which is of the first and which of the fifth rank."[89] Clearly the Germans are of the fifth, and the Jews of the first, rank. In *Beyond Good and Evil*, Nietzsche says:

> The Jews, however, are beyond any doubt the strongest, toughest, and purest race now living in Europe; they know how to prevail even under the worst conditions (even better than under favorable conditions). . . . That the Jews, if they wanted it—or if they were forced into it, which seems to be what the anti-Semites want—*could* even now have preponderance, indeed quite literally mastery over Europe, that is certain; that they are *not* working and planning for that is equally certain.[90]

What we must finally accept is that 'master' and 'slave' refer to qualities, characteristics, tendencies that can be found in any society, class, or person. In *Beyond Good and Evil*, while speculating upon the "cultivation of a new caste that will rule Europe," Nietzsche even suggests interbreeding the Jews with the Prussian nobility.[91]

So instead of asking whether Nietzsche endorses or approves of the master or the slave, we should ask which model of history Nietzsche uses, that of the Hegelian slave or that of the master and genealogy? Which will explain the possibility of the great man or the *Übermensch?* Which will explain the possibility of Europe's move to and beyond nihilism? As I have tried to argue, it is definitely not the master model alone that is sufficient to accomplish these things. A complex mix of *both* models is necessary—or as Nietzsche puts it in *Will to Power*, we need a "Roman Caesar with Christ's soul."[92]

V. Virtue

It has been argued that Nietzsche is committed to a virtue ethic.[93] Solomon, for example, claims that Nietzsche is more like Aristotle than Kant. Aristotle's ethics, he holds, is not one of rules and principles—especially not universal ones. It is concerned with excellence and is still involved with the Homeric warrior tradition. The purpose of such an ethic is to maximize people's potential and that will always be unequal for Aristotle as well as Nietzsche. Solomon thinks Nietzsche wants to return to the values of masterly virtue.[94] The *Übermensch* is Aristotle's *megalopsychos*—the great-souled man.[95]

I have already argued that it is a mistake to understand Nietzsche as returning to the values of master morality. But further than that, Solomon's whole approach seems unaware of Nietzsche's belief in the horror of existence. While Nietzsche might have been impressed by Aristotle's *megalopsychos*,[96] Aristotle would be appalled by Nietzsche's *Übermensch*. A life that contains as much suffering as Nietzsche expects a life to contain, could not be considered a good life by Aristotle. To go further, as Nietzsche does, to advocate *loving* such a fate, to refuse to change the slightest detail, Aristotle would find debased—perhaps even demented. At any rate, the life of the *Übermensch* is not a flourishing life in Aristotle's sense. These claims will have to be explained and defended.

While it is quite clear that Nietzsche does believe in virtue, he does not believe in ordinary virtue. He says: "One should defend virtue against the preachers of virtue: they are its worst enemies. For they teach virtue as an ideal *for everyone;* they take from virtue the charm of rareness, inimitableness, exceptionalness and unaverageness—its aristocratic magic."[97] In *Beyond Good and Evil,* he also says: "It is probable that we, too, still have our virtues, although in all fairness they will not be the simpleminded and foursquare virtues for which we hold our grandfathers in honor—and at arms length."[98] Nietzsche thinks that "each one of us should devise *his own* virtue."[99]

He says that he is "actually the very opposite of the type of man who so far has been revered as virtuous."[100] In fact, he thinks that any virtue "becomes a virtue through rising against that blind power of the factual and tyranny of the actual. . . . It always swims against the tide of history."[101] This suggests that a figure like King Vishvamitra, who through millennia of self-torture acquired such a feeling of power and self-confidence that he endeavored to build a new heaven, could be the model for the development of virtue. To overthrow the tyranny of the actual, to overcome the old gods and tradition, one must develop new powers, new self-confidence, new capacities, new virtues. We must:

> confront our inherited and hereditary nature with our knowledge, and through a new, stern discipline combat our inborn heritage and implant in ourselves a new habit, a new instinct, a second nature, so that our first nature withers away. It is an attempt to give oneself, as it were *a posteriori*, a past in which one would like to originate in opposition to that in which one did originate.[102]

The old virtues are at odds with the type of person Nietzsche wants to realize. New and different virtues are required. It is even the case that: "what is good and evil *no one knows yet,* unless it be he who creates. He, however, creates man's goal and gives the earth its meaning and its future. That anything at all is good and evil—that is his creation."[103] Only when a Vishvamitra has created a new heaven, a new meaning structure, will we be able to tell what is good and evil and develop new virtues accordingly.

A virtue ethic is capable of asking what is good for a certain type of person, rather than what is good for everyone or for the majority, and it can take what is good for this person as *good.* Nietzsche thinks that as we move past the ancient world, as we move through Christianity and into the modern world, we move further and further from understanding good in this way. We understand it more and more as the utilitarian does—as what benefits the greatest number. Nietzsche wants to return to the question of what is good for a certain type of person. In this respect Solomon is quite right in claiming that Nietzsche is much the same as Aristotle. But I do not think that Nietzsche and Aristotle have in mind anything like the *same* type of person.

Aristotelian virtue is completely at odds with Nietzsche's vision of the horror of existence and the need to conceal it. If we ask the simplest of questions, if we ask how we should value the traditional virtue of truthfulness, we quickly see that Nietzsche and Aristotle would be deeply opposed. For Nietzsche, we cannot give anything like the traditional answer, the answer Aristotle's would certainly give. While for Nietzsche, as we have seen, it is heroic to accept as much truth as we can bear,[104] nevertheless, we need illusion, we need art, we need lies.[105] We must conceal the truth—we must hide the horror of existence. We do not, for Nietzsche, live in a world where the good and the true will coincide. The truth is that reality is horrible—not good. If we seek what is good for us, if we seek human well-being, if we seek a flourishing life, if we seek happiness, we must shun the true. Traditional morality, on the other hand, assumes that the good and the true coincide. If the good does not in fact coincide with the true, if we must choose between the good and the true, then we cannot have anything like an Aristotelian virtue ethic. If virtues are characteristics, dispositions, or powers that enable us to do what is good for us, and if this must leave out what is true, indeed, even serve to hide what is true,[106] then we cannot have anything like an Aristotelian notion of virtue. For Aristotle, if we develop a characteristic or power that works to hide the true, it would not be a virtue but a vice. For Aristotle, "reasoning must be true and the desire right, if the choice is to be good."[107] If, however, the true is horrible, if it is terrible, then characteristics or powers that enable us to hide the true, characteristics that would normally be called vices, become virtues.[108] And, indeed, Nietzsche says:

> Let us not hide from ourselves this most curious result: I have imparted to virtue a new charm—the charm of something forbidden. . . . Only after we have recognized everything as lies and appearance do we regain the right to this fairest of falsehoods, virtue. . . . Only by exhibiting virtue as a form of immorality do we again justify it . . . it is part of the fundamental immorality of all existence . . . the haughtiest, dearest and rarest form of vice.[109]

Nietzsche is definitely committed to a virtue ethic. He attends to characteristics, dispositions, and powers that he wants developed in individuals (at least some individuals), but the characteristics he values, that he takes to be good, that he takes to be virtues, are not ones that enable us to find the true or to live in accord with it.[110] Rather, Nietzsche seeks the very opposite, powers that hide the true, that make life possible, powers that would normally be called vices.

It is not only the case that virtue is incompatible with the true, but virtues are also incompatible with each other. Nietzsche completely rejects anything like an Aristotelian unity of the virtues:[111] *"By which means does a virtue come to power?*—By exactly the same means as a political party: the slandering, inculpation, undermining of virtues that oppose it and are already in power, by rebaptizing them, by systematic persecution and mockery. Therefore: through sheer 'immorality.'"[112] Indeed, Zarathustra holds that it is difficult to have more than one virtue—they conflict.[113] We do not have anything like an Aristotelian virtue ethic here.

It is true that Nietzsche seeks the sorts of virtues that would empower the great man or the *Übermensch* and allow him to flourish. But this is a radically different kind of flourishing than Aristotle had in mind. As MacIntyre puts it, for Aristotle, virtues enable us to realize our true nature and reach our true end.[114] In realizing our nature, in becoming what we should become, in realizing our true end, we will achieve our good, that is, we will flourish and be happy. This implies and requires a fit between the human essence and the world. It is as if they were designed for each other—certainly they cannot be alien and opposed to each other. For Nietzsche, this is ridiculous. To realize our nature as Aristotle understands nature, to achieve our good as Aristotle understands good, that is, a good that accords with the true, far from allowing us to flourish, far from making us happy, would plunge us into the horror and terror of existence. We live in an alien and hostile cosmos and we need lies to conceal this fact from ourselves.

Moreover, we need the power to create and maintain these illusions. Such powers are virtues. They build a certain kind of character. They build a disposition. They enable one to function in a certain way. To this extent we have a virtue ethic. But it does not realize our essence. If, for Nietzsche, we can even be said to have an essence, it would be some sort of Dionysian chaos, and the task of any virtue would be to conceal it, not realize it.[115] As far as our true end goes, if we can in any way be said to have one, it would be horror and terror, something we do not want to realize, something we want to conceal.

If we can look back over our entire life and say it was a good one, then, for Aristotle, it was a happy life. If in looking back over our entire life, we must instead admit that it was a life of horrible and meaningless suffering, then, for Aristotle, it would be impossible to say it was a happy life.[116] If it is necessary to lie, to live in illusion, in order to conceal this meaningless suffering, then, for Aristotle, it would be impossible to say it was a good life.

What if, however, one was able to look back over such a life and was able to love it? What if one would not be willing to change a single moment of suffering? Would that make one's life a *happy* one? Certainly not for Aristotle. Nietzsche, at least at times, will suggest that it could.[117] But what does he mean by happiness? Certainly not the good life in Aristotle's sense. Happiness is understood as power,[118] or is replaced by power.[119] In the *Genealogy of Morals,* Nietzsche says:

> Every animal—therefore *la bête philosophe,* too—instinctively strives for an optimum of favorable conditions under which it can expend all its strength and achieve its maximal feeling of power. . . . (I am *not* speaking of its path to happiness, but its path to power . . . and in most cases actually its path to unhappiness).[120]

Virtue, for Aristotle, allows us to fit with reality, be at home, and be happy. Virtue, for Nietzsche, allows us to construct a new heaven, conceal an alien cosmos, and experience the satisfaction of power—not happiness.

Something is a virtue for Aristotle if it contributes to living a good life, a happy life. Something is a virtue for Nietzsche if it enables you to love your fate, live with suffering, not want to change a single moment.[121]

If you look back over your life, for Nietzsche, you do not ask the same question Aristotle would have you ask. You do not ask if it was a good life, let alone the best life. If you ask that, you would immediately see that any life could be improved by changing this or adding that. To dwell on such concerns, we have seen, would threaten to re-enslave you to your suffering. Instead, you must have unqualified love for every detail of your life.[122] Why? Not because every detail deserves it, not because your life was the best life in Aristotle's sense, not because it could not be made better in Aristotle's sense, but because if you do not, then the pain and suffering of your life will begin to reassert itself, eat away at you, subjugate you. If you do not love *every* moment of your life, those moments you do not love will reassert their psychological stranglehold. They will begin to dominate you. You will begin to wish you did not have to endure so many of them, you will try to develop strategies for dealing with them, you will fret over them, and pretty soon you will again be enslaved by them. Your attitude toward any moment cannot be a desire to avoid it, change it, reduce it—or it will begin to dominate you. Such love, Aristotle would consider abject and degrading. Aristotle would completely reject the *Übermensch.*

On the other hand, though, if in looking back over your life, for Aristotle, you *were* to find it a good one, a happy one, *even* the best life, there would be nothing about it that would necessarily make you want to affirm it to the point that you would wish to live it again. And if one fine day you were informed by the demon that you *had* to live it again over and over an infinite number of times, even Aristotle, as "this thought gained possession of" him, might "throw [him]self down and gnash [his] teeth and curse the demon who spoke thus."[123]

Chapter Seven

The Truth of Nietzsche's Doctrines

I. Metaphysical Truth

We have seen that truth is conceptually possible for Nietzsche. It has been buried during the course of millennia, but we could dig back to it—we could approach the horror of existence. We have also seen that Christianity as well as modern science have a powerful will to truth that could ultimately get us all the way to that truth and plunge us into the meaningless void of nihilism. We have also seen that this will to truth, while it can accumulate real truth along the way, also serves to distract us from and thus conceal the ultimate truth. Thus there is also something false about such truth.

What about Nietzsche's own doctrines? What about will to power and eternal recurrence? Are they true? Are they metaphysical truths? Are they just *taken to be truths* rather than *real* truths? Are they illusions necessary to mask the truth? We have avoided such questions long enough and must finally face them in this chapter.

Heidegger famously thought that Nietzsche's doctrines are to be understood as metaphysical truths. For Heidegger, eternal recurrence is Nietzsche's fundamental doctrine and it expresses his essential metaphysical position. It can be likened to traditional metaphysical teachings like Plato's notion that "beings have their essence in the 'Ideas'" or the Christian conception that "a personal Spirit, as Creator, has brought forth all beings."[1]

Nietzsche would not seem to agree with such an assessment. In a long passage from *Twilight of the Idols,* entitled "How the 'Real World' at last Became a Myth,"[2] Nietzsche rejects the whole metaphysical notion of a real world opposed to the ordinary world, and thus, it would seem, he rejects the very idea of metaphysics. The passage ends with the following:

> 5. The 'real [*wahre*] world'—an idea no longer of any use . . . —an idea grown useless, superfluous, *consequently* a refuted idea: let us abolish it! . . . Plato blushes for shame; all free spirits run riot. . . .
> 6. We have abolished the real world: what world is left? the apparent world perhaps? . . . But no! *with the real world we have also abolished the apparent world!* . . . end of the longest error; zenith of mankind; INCIPIT ZARATHUSTRA.[3]

Eternal recurrence, we have seen, forces us to accept the world as it is. It rejects any notion of a world as it *ought* to be, a *real* world, a *true* world, a *higher* world, a *better* world. All such notions have the result of making this world, the ordinary world, a *lesser* world, an *inferior* world, something that falls short of a *true* world.[4] In the passage just quoted, Nietzsche says that in abolishing the real world we also abolish the apparent world. That would seem to imply that we abolish any notion of the ordinary world as less than a real world.

Clark suggests that in abolishing the apparent world we would be left with the *empirical* world?[5] What she means, I think, is that we would be left with a world that is not distorted or concealed by its relation, or opposition, to a *true* world. We would be left with the world as it really is. But if that is so, then for Nietzsche we would be plunged into the horror of existence.[6] It *is* the case, for Nietzsche, that we should accept as much of the truth, as much horror and suffering, as much meaninglessness, as possible. But it is also the case that we cannot go all the way.

There is another very plausible way to interpret the claim that in abolishing the real world we also abolish the apparent world. If through millennia of self-torture one gains the power to overthrow the old gods and build a new heaven, if one completely abolishes the old interpretation of the world, both the real world as well as the apparent world, what would one be left with? For the *Übermensch*, one would be left with the opportunity to impose one's *own* interpretation. The way would be cleared for one to create one's *own* meaning. One would be free to construct one's *own* heaven—or as Nietzsche chooses to put it in the passage quoted above, "INCIPIT ZARATHUSTRA," which might be taken to mean: 'here begins the doctrine of eternal recurrence.'

This is to suggest that in overthrowing the old gods, in eliminating the real as well as the apparent world, in constructing a new heaven, that is, in creating new meaning in a meaningless world, the *Übermensch* constructs a new illusion. Is eternal recurrence a new illusion?

The horror of existence is a very powerful concept. It does an impressive job of eliminating a true world. A higher, true, or real world—that is, a world up outside the cave where the true, the good, and the beautiful are held to be one—is made impossible, is undermined and flatly rejected, if we decide that existence in fact is horrific. But at the same time, the horror of existence implies the necessity of some sort of veil. We cannot look into the horror of existence without perishing. Eternal recurrence takes us closer to the horror of existence than ever before. It accepts every moment of suffering and pain—indeed, it eternalizes it. But it cannot go all the way.

Where, then, is the illusion? Is the illusion in the claim that the world will return? Is this an illusion for Nietzsche? It *is* what allows us to impose meaning on a meaningless world. The determinism it entails *is* what allows us to construct the world as innocent.[7] This determinism *is* what forces us to love every moment of our life as the only way to escape the stranglehold our suffering would otherwise have over us.[8]

If we decide that eternal recurrence *is* an illusion, then it certainly cannot be a metaphysical truth. Heidegger admits as much himself, though he thinks that such an interpretation demeans Nietzsche's thought.[9] Nietzsche himself, however, says that "it is in itself a matter of absolute indifference whether a thing be true, but a matter of the highest importance *to what extent* it is believed to be true."[10] Even Clark admits that Nietzsche does not put forth his doctrines of will to power and eternal recurrence as metaphysical truths, but merely as interpretations.[11]

If eternal recurrence is an illusion, at least it is a minimal illusion. It rejects any notion that meaning can be derived from a higher world, a true world, a real world. It affirms this world. *This* world returns eternally. And it accepts the horror of existence. It accepts a world of meaningless suffering and pain. It comes very close to the truth. But doesn't it need a small illusion? To affirm this world, doesn't it need to *exaggerate* it? It must have it repeat—repeat *eternally*. Only thus do we construct meaning in a meaningless void. Only thus are we forced to experience existence as innocent.[12] Only thus are we forced to love every moment of our life so as to escape the stranglehold our suffering would otherwise have over us—only eternal recurrence of the horror of existence forces us to accept our life fully if we are not to be crushed by it.[13]

II. The Truth of the Horror of Existence

Well, then, are Nietzsche's doctrines true or not? One very possible response is to say that, no, they definitely are not true—and they damned well better not be. It is their function to conceal, if only in a minimal way, the horror of existence and only thus do they foster life. It is quite possible, then, that for Nietzsche the doctrines of eternal recurrence and will to power are not true. For them to function successfully in handling the horror of existence, it is sufficient that they merely be *taken to be true.*

What about Nietzsche's doctrine of the horror of existence? Must it be true? It certainly seems that Nietzsche thought it was true. And that was certainly his personal experience in the world. But could it be just that Nietzsche *believed* it true, *took it to be* true, that is, that it was an illusion, not a *real* truth?[14] I have presented the horror of existence as the foundation of Nietzsche's vision—the basic truth from which all else follows. Is it possible to turn around at this point and deny that it is true? Wouldn't that undermine the whole argument of this book?

If we were to deny that it is true, the denial would go something like this. Nietzsche lived a life of horrible suffering. That made him want to ask *why* he suffered. He could not accept the traditional answer—that his suffering was punishment. He refused to believe his suffering was due to some sin of which he was to be considered guilty. He decided that there was no reason for it at all. He decided that this was just the way things are. He found that he was unable to eliminate or even significantly reduce his suffering. He decided that it was just his fate. And from there he began more and more to generalize on the basis of his particular experience. He decided that suffering was the human condition. He decided that existence in general, not just his personal existence, was horrible and terrifying. Then he began to make a real breakthrough. He decided that he would not change a thing—after all, he could not anyway. He decided that he would will nothing differently. He decided to accept his fate. And he was astonished to find that this began to break the psychological stranglehold his suffering had had over him. It made him innocent. He began to impose his own meaning on his situation. This began to give him a feeling of power. Moreover, he discovered that the more pain and suffering he could endure, the greater his feeling of power. He continued to reflect on these experiences and general philosophical doctrines eventually emerged—will to power, eternal recurrence, and the *Übermensch*. What ends up being most important here is not whether the horror of existence is actually a general truth about the cosmos. What is most important is how one handles one's personal suffering. What is most important is achieving the ability to impose one's own meaning upon it. What is most important is achieving the ability to create a new heaven out of one's own hell. In successfully accomplishing this one moves closer and closer toward becoming a great man or an *Übermensch*. All of this required starting from the horror of existence, but if one moves closer toward becoming a great man or an *Übermensch*, does it matter whether or not the horror of existence will hold up as a general truth about the world?

But this is to suggest that after Nietzsche develops his thought, builds up his power, imposes his new meaning, gets closer and closer to becoming a great man or an *Übermensch,* we can turn around and admit that it was all a lie (the horror of existence, will to power, and eternal recurrence—all of it), a lie to make an *Übermensch* possible? Is that a tenable interpretation? Well, Zarathustra says: "You say it is the good cause that hallows even war? I say unto you: it is the good war that hallows any cause."[15] So also, in *Will to Power,* Nietzsche says: "The Revolution made Napoleon possible: that is its justification."[16] So, we might say that the horror of existence, will to power, and eternal recurrence can make an *Übermensch* possible. That is their justification. After all, the *Übermensch "shall be* the meaning of the earth!"[17]

Can eternal recurrence, will to power, and the horror of existence all be lies? Can their only justification be that they can make an *Übermensch* possible? It is almost as if Nietzsche had climbed into a hot-air balloon, tossed overboard the last rope anchoring him to the ground, and as he slowly floats off toward the high mountains, never to return, we can see behind that walrus mustache a mocking grin—though, to be honest, we cannot be entirely certain it isn't a worried grimace.

III. The Value of Illusions

So, then, is the horror of existence true or not? Well, it can certainly serve Nietzsche as *his truth*. It gives him power and allows him to move toward becoming a great man or an *Übermensch*. Fine, but *is* it true? Well, it is certainly something he could *believe* to be true—and as we have seen Nietzsche thinks it a matter of indifference whether something is true, "but a matter of the highest importance *to what extent* it is believed to be true."[18] Fine, fine, but is it *actually* true? Well, even if it turns out not to be true, even if it is actually false, still, it can work to make an *Übermensch* possible.

All right, but we must push even further than this in our probing of Nietzsche's commitments. Nietzsche, we concede, can *believe* his doctrines, and thus work to make an *Übermensch* possible, even if his doctrines *turn out* to be false. But what if—going further—it is the case that Nietzsche actually *knows* his doctrines *are* false? Could he still *believe* them? Could they still enable an *Übermensch?* What if he knows that his doctrines are *lies?* Can he believe *lies?* Could lies make an *Übermensch* possible? I do not think it impossible to answer these questions in the affirmative. Let me try to explain.

In *Will to Power,* Nietzsche holds that the hypothesis that gives rise to the greatest feeling of power is the one that is accepted and believed true.[19] At the same time, however, he makes it quite clear that no matter how powerful a belief might be, this does not at all establish its actual truth. For Nietzsche we are capable of seeing that our most deeply held beliefs are not true. He even says that the measure of our strength is the degree to which we can admit the necessity of lies.[20]

Nietzsche seeks to undermine traditional thought by showing us that it is interpretation, illusion, a lie. But Nietzsche's task is not merely a negative one. He also has positive aims. He seeks something higher and better, and he thinks he has found it in the *Übermensch* and eternal recurrence. The question is whether these positive aims can be established if they too are illusions and lies? If they are, how can Nietzsche hold that his illusions are privileged—higher, better, more valuable? How can Nietzsche avoid the conclusion that one illusion is no better than another, that his illusions are no better than traditional illusions?

Nietzsche claims that we have never been able to accept great ideas as simply our own. To give our ideas objectivity we have traditionally attributed their origin to God—and thus devalued ourselves.[21] Nietzsche himself, we must notice, is doing something quite similar, though he definitely wants to avoid the self-devaluation. He says that "to live alone 'without God and morality' I had to invent a counterpart for myself."[22] He also says: "What sets *us* apart is not that we recognize no God . . . but that we find that which has been reverenced as God not 'godlike'."[23] After all, "there can be an infinite variety of ways of being . . . god."[24] In order to establish the higher value of the ideas of the *Übermensch,* Nietzsche substitutes the *Übermensch* for God: "since the old God is abolished, I am prepared *to rule the world*—"[25] Also Nietzsche tells Burckhardt that he "would much rather be a Basle professor than God; but I have not ventured to carry my private egotism so far as to omit creating the world."[26] What is the point of replacing God with the *Übermensch?*

Martin Luther wrote:

> God is He for Whose will no cause or ground may be laid down as its rule and standard; for nothing is on a level with it or above it, but it is itself the rule for all things. If any rule or standard, or cause or ground, existed for it, it could no longer be the will of God. What God wills is not right because He ought, or was bound, so to will; on the contrary, what takes place must be right, because He so wills it. Causes and grounds are laid down for the will of the creature, but not for the will of the Creator—unless you set another Creator over him![27]

Also, in *The Ego and His Own,* Max Stirner wrote:

> Has [God], as is demanded of us, made an alien cause, the cause of truth or love, his own? You are shocked by this misunderstanding, and you instruct us that God's cause is indeed the cause of truth and love, but that this cause cannot be called alien to him, because God is himself truth and love; you are shocked by the assumption that God could be like us poor worms in furthering an alien cause as his own. "Should God take up the cause of truth if [he] were not himself truth?" He cares only for *his* cause . . . —Now it is clear, God cares only for what is his, busies himself only with himself, thinks only of himself, and has only himself before his eyes; woe to all that is not well-pleasing to him! He serves no higher [person], and satisfies only himself. His cause is—a purely egoistic cause.[28]

For the Christian tradition, God was the source of all truth, value, and meaning. This God did not depend upon a higher principle from which to derive this truth, value, or meaning. God was the source himself, and for some voluntarists, God was even able to establish these truths and values in *any* way he wished. Thus, we cannot say that one interpretation is no better than any other. God's truths are nothing, we might say, but his interpretations, and they are the highest interpretations because they are God's—because of God's power.

So too the *Übermensch* needs no higher alien truth. He simply posits his own. He himself is the sole source of the highest meaning and value. He is subordinate to nothing. And just as the Christian God created all reality, so too the *Übermensch* overthrows the old gods and creates a new heaven. Just as the God of Genesis found after creation that all was good, so the *Übermensch* would have it no other way. It is true that the *Übermensch* cannot change anything, but then neither could the Christian God change himself if he was to remain perfect. Moreover, like the Christian God the *Übermensch* is eternally the same and has no desire to change. If it is the case that the *Übermensch* lives in illusion, lives a lie, well, so too, for Nietzsche, did Christianity.

Nietzsche makes it very clear that we are able to see that our beliefs are not true. It is quite possible, he says, that "a belief, however necessary it may be for the preservation of a species, has nothing to do with truth."[29] And he says that "it is the measure of strength to what extent we can admit to ourselves, without perishing, . . . the necessity of lies."[30] But how is this possible? How is it possible to believe an ungrounded interpretation that we actually see is not true? Nietzsche says:

> It might seem as though I had evaded the question of "certainty." The opposite is true; but by inquiring after the criterion of certainty I tested the scales upon which men have weighed in general hitherto—and that the question of certainty itself is a dependent question, a question of the second rank.[31]

Certainty is secondary, dependent upon something more fundamental—on will to power. We do not accept or believe things because they are true or because we find them certain. We hold they are true, we find them certain, because we accept or believe. Is this *really* so odd? Augustine's *credo ut intelligam* (I believe in order to know) is an example of this position, and the Christian God did not hold things true because he found them true according to an independent standard. His power established their truth. So also for Nietzsche, the great human being should be the standard of measure.[32] Acceptance or belief is determined by will to power, not by truth or certainty. For Nietzsche the ground of belief comes not from some higher and alien standard. The great man becomes the standard himself. The *Übermensch* replaces God and finds sufficient greatness, power, and self-confidence to establish his own truths.

According to the doctrine of will to power, the hypothesis that gives us the greatest feeling of power is the one that we believe, accept, or take to be true. Thus, the *Übermensch* believes his illusion, prefers it, values it as higher for the same reason that anyone else does, for the only reason for doing so—it gives a feeling of power.[33]

But all of this, you say, is mere interpretation? The doctrine of will to power is an interpretation—not a truth but a mere belief—and to rank interpretations, to hold that the highest interpretation is the one that will give us the greatest feeling of power, is itself just a second interpretation. Nietzsche is holding that it is will to power that establishes and ranks our beliefs and at the same time that it is a mere belief to hold that will to power establishes and ranks beliefs.

For Nietzsche, it is clear to us that our deepest beliefs are not true, that we can see that they are not true, that we can see that they are only interpretations. "[W]ell, so much the better."[34] It involves a lower level of existence, a lower level of power, to depend upon, to subordinate ourselves to, something independent of us as the ground of truth, certainty, or belief. The highest level of existence involves being the source of one's own truth, certainty, or belief—without alien reasons or justifications. To accept that there is nothing but interpretation, that even this claim is an interpretation, that to hold that my interpretation is better than others is simply another interpretation—such is the *highest* form of existence.[35] Any other would be to depend upon and subjugate oneself to something alien and higher.

Finally, then, what are we to say about the truth of Nietzsche's doctrines? We can say, I think, that after he fully develops his thought, builds up his power, creates his new heaven, comes closer and closer to becoming a great man or an *Übermensch*, it *could* turn out that all his doctrines were untrue—will to power, eternal recurrence, the horror of existence, all of them could be false. After all, Nietzsche himself says, I sought "to replace the improbable with the more probable, possibly one error with another."[36] Nevertheless, these beliefs could work to make an *Übermensch* or a great man possible, and that is their justification. To hold that they are mere interpretations imposed by a great man would only be to make that man greater—more godlike.

On the other hand, Nietzsche must actually *believe* in eternal recurrence— or at least he runs a very serious risk if he ceases to believe in it.[37] Certainly, he must fully accept his fate, he must turn all "it was" into a "thus I willed it," he must love *every* moment of his life. If he does not, if he begins to think that eternal recurrence is not true, if he begins to feel that anything can be changed, if he begins to think that even one moment of suffering can be avoided, then he runs the risk that his suffering will slowly begin to reassert its stranglehold and that he would soon cease to be anything approaching an *Übermensch*.

On the other hand, I do not see any reason why he could not admit to himself that will to power and the horror of existence as general theories were lies. In fact, in *Beyond Good and Evil* he comes pretty close to admitting this with respect to will to power when he says of it, "Supposing that this also is only interpretation—and you will be eager enough to make this objection?—well, so much the better."[38]

However, I just do not think we can find any support for thinking that Nietzsche takes the horror of existence to be a lie. Nietzsche's own life was certainly a life of pain, suffering, and horror. We could decide that his attempt to generalize this condition, to claim that *existence* in general was horrible, was to construct a lie, a lie necessary to generate an *Übermensch*. That is possible. But, finally, I can find no reason for thinking that this is what Nietzsche actually did. He just says or implies too many times that the horror of existence is the truth. And he never says anything to make us think that it should be seen as a lie.[39]

IV. Contradiction Between Doctrines

Before concluding our discussion of how we are to take Nietzsche's doctrines, we must consider one more issue. There are scholars who think that Nietzsche's doctrines contradict one another. Stambaugh argues that will to power strives for *increase* whereas eternal recurrence is recurrence of the *same*.[40] Heller argues that while the *Übermensch* is expected to *create* something new and original, the doctrine of eternal recurrence holds that the *same* will return eternally.[41] Lampert argues that eternal recurrence renders obsolete, and replaces, the *Übermensch*.[42] Conway argues that the notion of an *Übermensch* or a redeemer betrays a nihilistic belief in the deficiency of the human condition incompatible with eternal recurrence and *amor fati*.[43]

If we leave aside the question of whether Nietzsche's doctrines are true, or are to be taken to be true, if we focus solely on the question of their consistency, and if we take Nietzsche's commitment to the horror of existence seriously, I must say that I do not see any contradiction or incompatibility between these doctrines. Will to power, we have seen, seeks the highest expression of power. We have also seen that to achieve power one must confront and overcome obstacles, and the higher the obstacle overcome, the greater the power achieved.[44] Once we recognize the horror of existence, we would necessarily see that if eternal recurrence of the horror of existence is not the very highest obstacle, it would at least be one of the very highest. Thus will to power in its drive for the highest power would drive us to the idea of eternal recurrence, at least in the sense that, once the idea of the eternal recurrence of the horror of existence had occurred to us, will to power would push us toward belief in it. Will to power pushes us to believe in what gives us the greatest feeling of power.[45] Thus, eternal recurrence is an obstacle, one of the highest obstacles, but that is not at all to contradict will to power, rather, just the opposite, it elicits greater will to power. If will to power drives us toward the idea of eternal recurrence, we could even say that the idea of eternal recurrence could be seen as a manifestation or expression of will to power.

The *Übermensch* is simply the person in whom this highest realization of power is achieved, the person in whom will to power expresses itself as the idea of eternal recurrence, the person in whom eternal recurrence produces the highest feeling of power, and thus the person most able to accept eternal recurrence, love his fate, and creatively impose this vision on the world, thereby veiling the horror of existence and making life possible.[46]

Still, it might seem as if the emphasis on necessity and determinism implied in eternal recurrence would be at odds with the emphasis on creativity and self-overcoming implied in will to power. The person who aspires to be an *Übermensch* must be concerned with facing greater and greater obstacles so as to overcome them and thus build up greater and greater power. But if all is determined, if every slightest detail of one's life is fated, if one's life can only repeat one's past lives, if that is all already decided, wouldn't that be at odds with any hope of building up power, wouldn't that be at odds with any hope of change, wouldn't that be at odds with the attitude needed for becoming an *Übermensch*? Not at all. The sort of determinism implied in eternal recurrence, we saw in Chapter 5, unlike ordinary determinism, in no way enables prediction concerning the future of one's current life.[47] If you believe in eternal recurrence, you believe that everything you have done in the past has been determined and you believe that everything you will ever do in the future will be determined, but eternal recurrence tells you nothing whatsoever about what it is you are determined to do in the future of your existing life. The fact that you believe that each of your recurring lives must be exactly the same gives you no information at all about what in particular is going to happen at any future point in your present life. Eternal recurrence is simply irrelevant to such matters. In your current life, eternal recurrence has its effect with respect to the past and the present—it can tell you nothing one way or the other about whether or not you will be able to build up the power to become an *Übermensch* in the future. It is just that if you do build up this power, you must accept that it occurred in exactly the same way in each and every cycle. Furthermore, if you do build up the power to become an *Übermensch*, eternal recurrence tells you that it was always fated to happen. It had to happen. Far from contradicting your *Übermenschlichkeit*, eternal recurrence confirms it, secures it, and makes it absolute—you have succeeded in becoming an *Übermensch* in an infinite number of past lives and the very same will happen again in an infinite number of future lives.

Still, one might think that belief in eternal recurrence would have to stifle all creativity because no act that you will ever perform will be new, spontaneous, original, creative. Every act that you will ever perform, every slightest detail of your life, will be a repetition of all your past lives. Eternal recurrence would seem to crush any creativity, indeed, it would seem to crush life. Is this the consequence Nietzsche wanted from his doctrine of eternal recurrence? Well, yes, in one sense, it is. For most people, eternal recurrence would have exactly this effect. For most people it would be eternal recurrence of the horror of existence, with no possible escape, with no possibility of anything new, with no possibility of any change.

But not for the *Übermensch*. The very opposite would be the case for him. Indeed, eternal recurrence is the *Übermensch's* own creation. The *Übermensch* invents it. Moreover, it is a creation that empowers the *Übermensch*. Even if one rejects this interpretation, even if one insists that eternal recurrence is not to be viewed as something *invented* by the *Übermensch*, that it is not merely an illusion the *Übermensch* dreams up, even if one insists that eternal recurrence is something *discovered* by the *Übermensch*, or at least that it is experienced as a discovery by the *Übermensch*, that would change nothing here. Any great discovery involves creativity on the part of its discoverer. Any great discovery is certainly experienced as involving the creativity of the discoverer. If one wins a Nobel Prize in Physics for the discovery of a new particle, is anyone going to deny that the process of discovery involved a great deal of creativity?

At any rate, as the *Übermensch* invents or discovers eternal recurrence (however one wishes to interpret it), the *Übermensch* begins to experience the creative and transformative effect of this great discovery or invention. Let us try to imagine Nietzsche's situation once again. Imagine him reflecting on his life, on the meaningless suffering that it has involved, the nausea, the vomiting, the migraines, and on the fact that he has been unable to change any of this. No medication has worked. No change in climate has worked. No change in diet has worked. He has been dominated by his illness—subjugated to it. But then he imagines the idea of eternal recurrence—or he discovers it. And this idea begins to grow on him. It begins to take him over. After each migraine, after each bout of nausea and vomiting, he asks himself whether he would be willing to live that episode over again without the slightest change—live it over again an infinite number of times. He asks himself whether he is able to accept such an extreme form of determinism. Each time he is able to answer yes, each time he is able to accept that determinism, each time he is able to love that fate, he begins to break the stranglehold his suffering has had over him. Something begins to change in him. A new power is created in him. He becomes stronger. Determinism and creativity are not at odds in the *Übermensch*. Rather, they are fused—each feeds and increases the other. The more determinism the *Übermensch* finds, the more determinism he can accept, the more he is able to love his fate, then the more he breaks the stranglehold of that fate and the more power he creates in himself. And reciprocally, the more he breaks the stranglehold of his fate, the more power he creates in himself, then the more he is able to love his fate and to embrace the creative idea of eternal recurrence.

Moreover, as the *Übermensch* feels this power being created in himself, as he increasingly breaks the stranglehold his suffering has had over him, he begins to see that what produces this empowerment is his own creativity, his own invention of eternal recurrence, or his discovery of it. His belief in eternal recurrence and his commitment to this creative notion are precisely what give him power. As long as he is able to view his illness as fate, as long as he is able to see every detail of his suffering as eternally recurring, as long as he is able to impose this creative interpretation on his life, or discover it in his life, as long as he is able to embrace it, he gains power and ever more solidly confirms his *Übermenschlichkeit.*

Moreover, if the *Übermensch* can break the stranglehold his suffering has had over him, if he can triumph over it, if he can embrace eternal recurrence, if he can love his fate, then, as we saw earlier, he can even experience a godlike joy—a joy like the joy of triumph in battle.[48] The *Übermensch* can welcome his suffering, take joy in getting through it, take joy in the increased power it brings him, take joy in triumphing over it. Indeed, through this self-torture he creates his new heaven.

Just as the Apollonian gave us enough distance, enough of a veil, that we could feel the Dionysian suffering of the tragic hero as powerful, creative, and joyous, without being annihilated by it,[49] so too eternal recurrence gives us a perspective such that we can triumph over the horror of our life, be empowered by it, and experience it creatively and joyously.

The doctrines of eternal recurrence, will to power, and the *Übermensch* are not at odds. They are not contradictory. Moreover, it is not merely the case that they can be reconciled. More than that, they are actually integrated. They reinforce each other. Each feeds the others. And each needs the others.

Before closing this chapter, there is one other matter that should be discussed. Throughout this book I have been quoting freely from Nietzsche's *Nachlass*—including the parts of it collected by his sister and published as *Will to Power*. Use of this material is controversial. At one end of the spectrum, Heidegger thought it contained Nietzsche's true philosophy.[50] At the other end, there are those who tend toward the position that the *Nachlass* should not be used at all—except perhaps where it agrees with texts actually published by Nietzsche.[51]

I do not see how such generalized conclusions can be sustained. I certainly do not think we can establish in a priori fashion that some of Nietzsche's texts have a first class status and others only a second class status. It may be the case that Nietzsche decided not to publish certain fragments because he thought they were wrong, inferior, or lacking in some way. But it is also possible that he did not do so for very different reasons. He could have thought some of them were among his best thoughts, but he had not yet found the place for them, or was saving them for something special, or was not yet satisfied with the way they were phrased.[52]

But suppose we could somehow prove that in fact it was Nietzsche's opinion that all of his unpublished fragments were seriously lacking, inferior, and second class. I have always found *Will to Power* to be one of Nietzsche's most interesting and valuable texts. Suppose we could prove that Nietzsche thought it was not. Is the author the last word on such matters? Certainly we would have to take the author's opinion very seriously. But surely scholars are not obliged to agree with the author concerning the significance, value, or import of each bit of text.

I have a colleague who once told me, only half jokingly, that he wished he could actually talk to Plato so that he could find out once and for all what Plato actually meant in certain difficult passages. But clearly if Plato could somehow appear and give one this information, all one would have would be a new bit of text to place alongside the texts one was worried about in the first place. One would still have to interpret all of these texts oneself—the original ones and now Plato's new additions. And it is not at all obvious that Plato's new additions would make the overall task of interpretation easier. It might even make it more complicated and difficult. After all, if there are already cases where his original texts seem inconsistent, contradictory, or obscure, his new commentary might just introduce further inconsistencies, contradictions, or obscurities.[53]

Clark argues that what Nietzsche says in the *Nachlass* may be interesting for biographical speculation about what Nietzsche believed but is completely irrelevant to philosophical questions concerning the doctrines found in his published books.[54] Would Plato's comments, were he to appear to my colleague, be merely biographical? We are assuming that he *actually* appeared to my colleague. I think that just as my colleague was wrong in thinking that Plato could give him the final and definitive answer, that is, more than another piece of text, so Clark is wrong in thinking that the *Nachlass* constitutes mere biography, that is, less than another piece of text.

Chapter Eight

Should We Accept Nietzsche?

I. Covering Up for Nietzsche

I have tried to understand Nietzsche and to explain his insight into the horror of existence—and I do think he had real insight here. I have also tried to show the consequences of this for the rest of his thought. It is now time to ask whether we should agree with Nietzsche, accept his views, and make them our own? My answer will be, finally, that we should not accept his views. Nietzsche is a fascinating thinker, and this leads readers to want to agree with him in far more places than they should. Nietzsche holds some atrocious views that should be soundly rejected.

Recently, some commentators have been willing to be more critical of Nietzsche's thought. Schutte, for example, writes:

> To many of us who appreciate Nietzsche's other insights on creativity and art, his statements on slavery are not appealing. Therefore, they tend not to be discussed. . . . I take it . . . we have a responsibility not to cover up for him, especially when issues of justice and injustice are at stake. His positive contributions to knowledge should be distinguished from the justification of cruelty which he offers in the name of the superior culture and the superior man.[1]

As Holub puts it:

> When Nietzsche's advocacy of nobility is interpreted simply as a call for more freedom and creativity, for an end to repression and levelling of individual differences, his philosophy quite rightly meets with general approval. But the darker side of Nietzsche's views should not be ignored: at times he affirms a return to an aristocratic social order in which the happiness of the vast majority would be sacrificed for an elite caste.[2]

Warren, however, thinks that while Nietzsche's political vision involves objectionable and insupportable distortions, nevertheless, these are extraneous to the rest of Nietzsche's thought and thus the valuable postmodern possibilities of his philosophy can be disconnected from them.[3] I am not persuaded of this. I think these objectionable views cannot easily be separated from Nietzsche's core philosophical commitments and thus cannot easily be abandoned.[4]

Nietzsche is deeply opposed to the liberation of women and of workers.[5] The concept of 'liberation,' in its ordinary meaning, suggests that if we get people to see things as they actually are, see them in all their ugliness and brutality, if we drag all discrimination and abuse out into the open, we will be better able to work toward the elimination of oppression and the liberation of those oppressed. Nietzsche would think this nonsense. In his view, the suffering of women and workers has not in any very significant sense been due to an oppressor. Reality itself is the problem. We live in a terrible void. Existence is horrible. And we certainly cannot drag it all out into the open—otherwise all would be likely to perish. We cannot end suffering. Moreover, it would be counterproductive to try to do so—because that would end up showing us all the more quickly how hopeless things are. Instead, we must give suffering a meaning. To give suffering a meaning, we have seen in earlier chapters,[6] we inflict it ourselves—for a reason. This is the context in which we must view oppression.

Most of the things that liberals, socialists, and feminists say about oppression, most of their complaints, are perfectly valid. But they also completely miss the point. They see only the surface of things and entirely miss what is really going on underneath. Workers and women, it is true, are oppressed. But oppression is not the fundamental source of their suffering and misery. In fact, it may even make their suffering more tolerable—it gives it meaning. To eliminate this oppression would not eliminate suffering and misery. It might even make it worse. It might lead us to see the meaninglessness of suffering in general—and thus plunge us into a nihilistic void.

I do not think Nietzsche's views on women and workers can quickly and easily be dismissed as if they were nothing but groundless prejudices extraneous to his basic philosophical commitments. They follow directly from his core philosophical doctrines, and to reject them, it seems to me, we would have to reject those doctrines. Indeed, I think we must choose between liberalism, socialism, or feminism, on the one hand, and Nietzsche's basic doctrines, on the other. I do not think it is possible to hold to both.

Nietzsche has a lot of objections to liberalism, socialism, feminism, and Christianity, but one of his main objections is to their notion that we can change things, improve them, reduce suffering: "It is a disgrace for all socialist systematizers that they suppose there could be circumstances—social combinations—in which vice, disease, prostitution, distress would no longer grow.— But that means condemning life."[7] "The whole moral struggle against vice, luxury, crime, even disease, appears a naiveté and superfluous: there is no 'improvement'."[8] Nietzsche also says:

> Herd-animal morality . . . is striving with all its power for a universal green-pasture happiness on earth, namely for security, absence of danger, comfort, the easy life, and ultimately, "if all goes well," hopes to do away with any kind of shepherd or bellwhether. The two doctrines it preaches most often are: "equal

rights" and "sympathy with all that suffers"—and it takes suffering itself to be something that must absolutely be abolished. . . . Whoever has thought profoundly about where and how the plant man has hitherto grown most vigorously must conclude that this has happened under *reverse* conditions: that the dangerousness of his situation must grow to tremendous proportions, that his power of invention and dissembling must struggle up beneath protracted oppression and compulsion, that his will to live must be enhanced to an unconditional will to power and to overpower, and that danger, severity, violence . . . inequality of rights . . . in short the opposite of all the herd thinks desirable, are necessary for the elevation of the type man.[9]

In Nietzsche's view: "When the anarchist, as the mouthpiece of *declining* strata of society," thus, he no doubt means, as the mouthpiece of liberals, socialists, feminists, and Christians, "demands with righteous indignation 'his rights,' 'justice,' 'equal rights,' he is only acting under the influence of his want of culture, which prevents his understanding *why* he is really suffering—in *what respect* he is impoverished, in life."[10] To explain why he is really suffering we would have to discuss the horror of existence.[11] This is something our anarchist cannot face:

A cause-creating drive is powerful within him; someone must be to blame for his feeling vile. . . . His 'righteous indignation' itself already does him good; every poor devil finds pleasure in scolding—it gives him a little of the intoxication of power. Even complaining and wailing can give life a charm for the sake of which one endures it: there is a small dose of *revenge* in every complaint, one reproaches those who are different for one's feeling vile, sometimes even with one's being vile, as if they had perpetrated an injustice or possessed an *impermissible* privilege. 'If I am *canaille,* you ought to be so too': on the basis of this logic one makes revolutions.—Complaining is never of any use: it comes from weakness. Whether one attributes one's feeling vile to others or to *oneself*—the Socialist does the former, the Christian for example the latter—makes no essential difference. What is common to both, and *unworthy* in both, is that someone has to be to *blame* for the fact that one suffers.[12]

Such people hold the state, or the upper classes, or the capitalists, or the aristocracy, or the clergy, or patriarchy, or some such group responsible for their suffering—and they want *them* to remove their suffering. Nietzsche's objection is not that such groups are not involved in causing suffering, his objection is that to focus on such groups as the cause and to expect them to cease being the cause, is to obscure the real issue—that existence itself is horrible and suffering unavoidable. Furthermore, liberal, socialist, and feminist movements, with their emphasis on reducing suffering, improving social conditions, making progress, once these are accepted by culture, make it extremely difficult to even suggest what in Nietzsche's opinion is really necessary—that we need *more* suffering, not less. Such notions are made to appear insane. If this sort of cultural environment does not directly hinder the development of a great man, it definitely does not help. It makes it virtually impossible to encourage suffering as a discipline necessary to build up power in the hope of producing an *Übermensch.* Nietzsche says, "The socialists crave to produce a good life for as many people as possible. If the lasting site of this good life, the perfect state, really were attained, that good life would ruin the soil from which great intellect and any powerful individual grow."[13]

He says: "The lower species ('herd,' 'mass,' 'society') . . . blows up its needs into cosmic and metaphysical values. In this way the whole of existence is vulgarized: in so far as the mass is dominant it bullies the exceptions, so they lose their faith in themselves."[14] He also says that the "revolution, confusion, and distress of peoples is, in my view, inferior to the distress of great [*grossen*] individuals during their development."[15]

Nietzsche also says: "Liberal institutions . . . undermine the will to power, they are the levelling of mountain and valley exalted to a moral principle, they make small, cowardly and smug—it is the herd animal which triumphs with them every time."[16] He says, "the slavish morality of meekness, chastity, selflessness, absolute obedience, has triumphed—ruling natures were thus condemned . . . to torments of conscience—creative natures felt like rebels against God, uncertain and inhibited by eternal values."[17] Also, "the higher men measured themselves according to the standard of virtue of slaves—found they were 'proud,' etc., found all their higher qualities reprehensible."[18]

Nietzsche is especially hostile to Christianity as perhaps the major obstacle to the development of strength:

> What is it we combat in Christianity? That it wants to break the strong, that it wants to discourage their courage, exploit their bad hours and their occasional weariness, convert their proud assurance into unease and distress of conscience, that it knows how to poison and sicken the noble instincts until their strength, their will to power turns backward, against itself—until the strong perish through orgies of self-contempt and self-abuse: that gruesome way of perishing of which Pascal provides the most famous example.[19]

Women are an obstruction of the same sort. They need "a religion of weakness that glorifies being weak, loving, and being humble as divine: or better, she makes the strong weak—she rules when she succeeds in overcoming the strong. Woman has always conspired with the types of decadence, the priests, against the 'powerful,' the 'strong,' the men—."[20]

II. Pity and Compassion

It is also the case that the suffering of others can pose a threat to the strong, as is implied in the following passage: "not to perish of internal distress and uncertainty when one inflicts great suffering and hears the cry of this suffering—that is great, that belongs to greatness."[21] Pity, we have seen in an earlier chapter,[22] implies looking down upon, and therefore demeaning, even showing a certain contempt for, the sufferer. But it can also be harmful to the one who pities:

> Pity stands in antithesis to the tonic emotions which enhance the energy of the feeling of life: it has a depressive effect. One loses force when one pities. The loss of force which life has already sustained through suffering is increased and multiplied even further by pity. Suffering itself becomes contagious through pity; sometimes it can bring about a collective loss of life and life-energy. . . . Aristotle, as is well known, saw in pity a morbid and dangerous condition which one did well to get at from time to time with a purgative: he understood tragedy as a purgative.[23]

On the other hand pity can work as a self-defense:

> suffering incurred by another constitutes a signpost to some danger to us; and it can have a painful effect upon us simply as a token of human vulnerability and fragility in general. We repel this kind of pain and offence and requite it through an act of pity; it may contain a subtle self-defence or even a piece of revenge. That at bottom we are thinking very strongly of ourselves can be divined from the decision we arrive at in every case in which we *can* avoid the sight of the person suffering, perishing or complaining: we decide *not* to do so if we can present ourselves as the more powerful and as a helper . . . if we want to feel how fortunate we are in contrast.[24]

Identifying with the suffering of another can weaken us, thus pity, insofar as it emphasizes our superiority to the sufferer, can preserve us. This means that pity would be less a threat to the strong than real compassion. The difference between pity and compassion, I suggest, is that pity looks down from a secure higher position and feels sorry for the poor soul suffering beneath one. Pity is better than contempt, certainly, but it is not that noble a feeling. In feeling compassion, on the other hand, one empathizes with the sufferer—one is transported to the sufferer's own level. One sees that such suffering could occur to anyone, and one identifies with the sufferer. Compassion, for Nietzsche, would seem to pose a greater threat to the strong than would pity.

Once again let us try to imagine Nietzsche's life—a life of migraines, nausea, and vomiting. It is a life of pain and suffering that has gone on for years. He has been unable to do anything about it. It is out of his control. But he decides that he would not change the slightest detail. He turns all "it was" into a "thus I willed it." He loves his fate. He transforms his suffering into a discipline. He begins to gain strength from this and it grows over the years. Let us then imagine him viewing the suffering of others, great suffering—poverty, misery, oppression. Imagine that Nietzsche is a decent human being and that he begins to feel sorry for these sufferers. Imagine that he empathizes with them and that he even begins to work to ease their suffering. Imagine that at moments he is even tempted to become a liberal—or, even better, a socialist. Suppose he begins to devote his life to such work, or at least that he develops an attitude which supports such work.

How would this affect Nietzsche's attitude toward his own suffering? Could he continue to accept it, will it, refuse to change it, love his fate? Could he continue to treat his suffering as a discipline from which to derive strength? Wouldn't it be schizophrenic for him to have one attitude toward the suffering of others and the opposite attitude toward his own suffering? If Nietzsche were to continue to care about easing the suffering of others, wouldn't that erode the determination to increase his own suffering, wouldn't it undermine the process of gaining strength through the discipline of his own suffering? And if existence really is horrible, wouldn't it subvert the attitude one needs to develop toward suffering in general?

We might stop a moment, however, and ask whether it is really so obvious that compassion weakens the one who feels compassion? The suffering of others seems naturally to evoke some sort of response in us. If we can avoid the self-defensive superiority of pity, if we can experience compassion for the sufferer, if we can empathize with the sufferer, then we might begin to feel that the same suffering could also befall us. Compassion shows a willingness to identify with the sufferer and to share their suffering—at least psychologically. If this is so, then we must say that compassion allows one to take on some of the suffering of the other—which thus increases one's own suffering. And if one is a Nietzschean, if one believes that greater strength comes from facing greater suffering, then it would seem that the *more* compassion we can feel, the *stronger* we can become.[25] Compassion is not incompatible with strength. In the last book of the *Iliad,* Achilles, the greatest of warriors, after killing Hektor, dragging his body around the city twelve times and leaving it for the dogs, finally begins to feel compassion for Hektor's father, Priam. Thinking of his own father, who will never see him again, Achilles is able to identify with Priam and to feel compassion for him.[26] This does not weaken Achilles. It only enhances his greatness.

Insofar as liberalism, socialism, feminism, and Christianity promote compassion, then, there is no reason to believe that they must promote weakness. There are passages in which one wonders whether Nietzsche might actually agree with such a view. He says in the *Genealogy of Morals:* "This self-overcoming of justice: one knows the beautiful name it has given itself—*mercy;* it goes without saying that mercy remains the privilege of the most powerful man, or better, his—beyond the law."[27] Nevertheless, this is not Nietzsche's general position. In far and away the most cases he argues that the obstacles created by liberalism, socialism, feminism, and Christianity drag down the strong.

Furthermore, one wonders whether the person who could write the following passage is really capable of serious compassion:

> If someone who is rich takes a possession away from someone who is poor (for example, a prince takes the beloved from some plebian), an error arises in the poor person; he thinks that the rich person must be completely vile to take from him the little that he has. But the rich person does not feel the value of a *single* possession nearly so deeply because he is accustomed to having many of them:

so he cannot put himself in the place of the poor person and does not do nearly so much of an injustice as the latter believes. Both have a false conception of the other. The injustice of the powerful, which infuriates people the most in history, is not nearly so great as it seems. The inherited sense of being a higher being with higher claims already makes a person fairly cold and leaves his conscience in peace: all of us, in fact, when the difference between us and another being is quite large, no longer feel any sense of injustice, and so we kill a gnat, for instance, without any remorse. So it is no sign of wickedness in Xerxes (whom even all the Greeks depict as outstandingly noble), when he takes a son from his father and has him cut to pieces, because the father had expressed an anxious, ominous mistrust of the whole campaign: the individual is in this case done away with like a disagreeable insect; he ranks too low to be permitted to cause a world ruler any further annoying sensations.[28]

Like the passage quoted above concerning pity as self-defense, Nietzsche here, it seems to me, hides behind a sense of superiority in order to avoid feeling compassion. And doing so does not increase his greatness—in fact, it makes him rather contemptible.

Still, if compassion leads the liberal, socialist, feminist, or Christian to want to set about eliminating suffering, if they loudly complain about it and campaign to reduce it, if they convince society that this is the proper attitude to take to suffering, how will this make the sufferer feel? How will it make the sufferer whose suffering is incurable feel? What will it do to the sufferer who is about to face his suffering, accept it, love it, work to become an *Übermensch?* What if existence really is horrible and suffering really cannot be significantly reduced?

To produce an *Übermensch,* Nietzsche thinks, we must increase suffering and oppression, not reduce it: "Slavery is . . . the indispensable means of spiritual discipline and cultivation."[29] "Almost everything we call 'higher culture' is based on the spiritualization of *cruelty.*"[30] "The discipline of suffering, of *great* suffering . . . has created all enhancements of man so far."[31] He says that he would like to have suffering "higher and worse than ever."[32]

Unfortunately (from Nietzsche's perspective), contemporary society holds the very opposite values—values which Zarathustra, in talking about the *last man,* ridicules:

"Alas, the time is coming when man will no longer give birth to a star. Alas, the time of the most despicable man is coming, he that is no longer able to despise himself. Behold, I show you the *last man.* . . .

"The earth has become small, and on it hops the last man, who makes everything small. . . .

"'We have invented happiness,' say the last men. . . . One still loves one's neighbor. . . .

"One still works, for work is a form of entertainment. But one is careful lest the entertainment be too harrowing. One no longer becomes poor or rich: both require too much exertion. Who still wants to rule? Who obey? Both require too much exertion.

"No shepherd and one herd! Everybody wants the same, everybody is the same. . . .

And here ended Zarathustra's first speech . . . for at this point he was interrupted by the clamor and delight of the crowd. "Give us this last man, O Zarathustra," they shouted. "Turn us into these last men! Then we shall make you a gift of the overman!"[33]

If one can see through the ridicule, much of which I have left out, the values of the last man are the values of Christians, liberals, and especially socialists.[34] And I must say that I agree with the view of the crowd expressed in the last paragraph of the quotation. I too would work to realize the last man and let Zarathustra keep the *Übermensch.*

III. Best Argument for Nietzsche

The best argument that could be made in defense of Nietzsche's position would run something like this. Existence is horrible. To look into it too deeply would likely mean our annihilation. For our culture to face up to the meaninglessness of suffering would over time destroy it. What must be done to prevent this? We must construct meaning where there is none. We need illusion, art, lies. We must mask the void. But things are not so simple. We have a powerful enemy in our midst. Liberalism, socialism, feminism, Christianity, science, all have a very powerful will to truth. If this will to truth is allowed to pursue its course, it will eventually drive us into nihilism. This makes the task of creating meaning much more difficult. It will not work for each of us to create our own meanings— small meanings. Such meanings are inadequate to conceal the horror and terror of existence, let alone stand up to a powerful will to truth. We need a creative artist with the ability of a Homer, a Jesus, a Buddha, a Mohammed. We need a Vishvamitra who through millennia of self-torture acquires the power and self-confidence to build a new heaven. To produce such an *Übermensch,* we must increase suffering, oppression, cruelty, and slavery. We must fight those who would seek to reduce this discipline. We must eternalize suffering—make it infinite. The point of such oppression is not so much to give a master class domination over the masses as it is to empower an *Übermensch* capable of saving the masses. Indeed, the *Übermensch* has a duty to them.[35] The *Übermensch* is needed by *all* of us. This is Nietzsche's best argument. We will all perish, our entire culture will perish, unless we produce an artist great enough to create new meaning. We must all sacrifice to that end. Only the *Übermensch* can save us from the abyss. If this is so, if we need the *Übermensch* for our survival, then we must abandon any notion of equality as well as any concept of justice based upon equality: "That which is fair to one *cannot* by any means be fair to another. The demand of one morality for all means an encroachment upon precisely a superior type of man."[36] Here Nietzsche agrees with Aristotle, who argued:

If, however, there be some one person . . . whose excellence is so pre-eminent that the excellence . . . of all the rest admit of no comparison with his . . . he . . . can be no longer regarded as part of a state; for justice will not be done to the superior, if he is reckoned only as the equal of those who are so far inferior to him in excellence. . . . Such a man may truly be deemed a God among men.[37]

But is this really a good argument? In saving our culture from the abyss, how many does the *Übermensch* really benefit? Nietzsche says: "The problem of *culture* is seldom grasped correctly. The goal of a culture is not the greatest possible *happiness* of a people, nor is it the unhindered development of *all* their talents; instead . . . the production of great works is the aim of culture."[38] What Nietzsche means by culture involves very few people:

The time will come when one . . . will regard not the masses but individuals, who form a kind of bridge across the turbulent stream of becoming. These individuals . . . live as that republic of genius of which Schopenhauer once spoke; one giant calls to another across the desert intervals of time and, undisturbed by the excited chattering dwarfs who creep about beneath them, the exalted spirit-dialogue goes on. . . . The goal of humanity cannot lie in its end but only in its highest exemplars.[39]

Nietzsche also says: "The goal of humankind cannot possibly be found in its end stage, but only in the highest specimens, who, dispersed throughout millennia, conjointly represent all the supreme powers that are buried in humanity."[40] "The highest men live beyond the rulers . . . and in the rulers they have their instruments. . . . He who *determines* values and directs the will of millennia by giving direction to the highest natures is the *highest* man."[41] "A people is a detour of nature to get to six or seven great men."[42] Indeed, "a single individual can under certain circumstances justify the existence of whole millennia."[43]

Nietzsche has said that we cannot stand the meaningless suffering that makes up the horror of existence. We either construct meaning or we are likely to perish. Past *Übermenschen* constructed meaning structures able to give large numbers of people meaning over long periods of time. They made life possible. Homer did so. Jesus certainly did so. So did Buddha and Mohammed. But eternal recurrence seems different. The *Übermensch* finds it meaningful. But not most people. Most people would be crushed by it. Most people, it would seem, are to be sacrificed for an *Übermensch* capable of carrying on a dialogue with a few other giants "across the desert intervals of time . . . undisturbed by the excited chattering dwarfs who creep about beneath them." Eternal recurrence is the "triumphant idea of which all other modes of thought will ultimately perish. It is the great cultivating idea: the races that cannot bear it stand condemned; those who find it the greatest benefit are chosen to rule."[44] Eternal recurrence ranks people. Those with the greatest power end up at the top. The weakest are likely to perish.

We can also say that eternal recurrence insulates the *Übermensch* from the herd. It makes it more difficult for the values of the herd to weaken the *Übermensch*. If the *Übermensch* believes that all will return eternally, that he will return eternally, that even the slightest change is impossible, then it becomes much more difficult for him to find his "higher qualities reprehensible"[45]—as if they could be changed. It becomes more difficult for him to experience "unease and distress of conscience," let alone "orgies of self-contempt and self-abuse"[46]—as if everything about him were not fated.

Eternal recurrence makes suffering eternal, suffering which is near meaningless except that for the *Übermensch* its meaninglessness creates the innocence of existence. But for most people, eternal recurrence destroys meaning—meaning established by Christianity, science, socialism, liberalism, feminism. How serious could we be about reducing suffering, improving things, making progress, if in the next cycle we would lose everything we had accomplished and have to start all over again from scratch like Sisyphus. For most people eternal recurrence would increase suffering. It would discourage attempts to reduce suffering, it would strip suffering of meaning—it would rub our noses in the meaninglessness of existence. Eternal recurrence offers little that would be of value to ordinary people. The "'underprivileged,'" Nietzsche says, "will experience the belief in the eternal recurrence as a curse."[47] Those who cannot handle meaninglessness, those who seek a god, or science, or socialism, or feminism, or some cause to serve will be hurt by eternal recurrence. They would be likely to perish—and rightly so, in Nietzsche's opinion:

> The essential characteristic of a good and healthy aristocracy . . . is that it experiences itself *not* as a function (whether of the monarchy or the commonwealth) but as their *meaning* and highest justification—that it therefore accepts with a good conscience the sacrifice of untold human beings who, *for its sake,* must be reduced and lowered to incomplete human beings, to slaves, to instruments. Their fundamental faith simply has to be that society must *not* exist for society's sake but only as the foundation and scaffolding on which a choice type of being is able to raise itself to its higher task and to a higher state of *being.*[48]

Nietzsche simply believes in: "mankind in the mass sacrificed to the prosperity of a single *stronger* species of man."[49] He tells us: "I am actually the very opposite of the type of man who so far has been revered as virtuous. Between ourselves, it seems to me that precisely this is part of my pride. . . . The last thing *I* should promise would be to 'improve' mankind."[50]

We should notice that Nietzsche's perspectivism is perfectly compatible with his elitism. Some of Nietzsche's critics suggest that he contradicts himself in holding that his views are merely his views, his perspectives, while at the same time wanting his readers to accept those views. But it is not at all clear that Nietzsche in fact cares whether his readers accept his views. It seems that he would be content to set up a dialogue with six or seven giants scattered across the desert intervals of time. He tells us that he writes "for a species of man that does not yet exist."[51] He says, "The time for me hasn't come yet: some are born posthumously. . . . It would contradict my character entirely if I expected ears and hands for my truths today: that today one doesn't hear me and doesn't accept my ideas is not only understandable, it even seems right to me."[52] Nietzsche also says: "There can be no doubt that the artist creates his work for other human beings. Nevertheless he knows that no one will ever understand and love his work the way he does."[53] Nietzsche does write for other people, he does hope that others will understand him, but realistically he expects only a very few to do so for a long time to come.

IV. Benefiting Culture

Nietzsche views culture in a peculiar way. He views it, we might say, on the model of the military or on the model of an athletic team. All of culture is a training. It should be made to undergo the severest discipline. Suffering should be increased. Most will be crushed by this—and may well drop out or even die off. Some will do a bit better, but at best be no more than mediocre. But what will finally emerge, Nietzsche hopes, will be a grand specimen, someone who achieves great feats, breaks all records, defeats all enemies. Some few of the rest will be able to take pride in having undergone the same discipline as this great figure. They may even feel that in some way, at least in spirit, they contributed to his development. They will see this great man as *theirs*—the product of their team or their corps. They will identify with this *Übermensch* and his greatness will prove all their effort meaningful and valuable. Think of the spirit that could seize them in the heat of battle or in some great game—as their *Übermensch* triumphs. This would also increase their feeling of power. Nietzsche thinks, "the masses are willing to submit to slavery of any kind, if only the higher-ups constantly legitimize themselves as higher, as *born* to command."[54] He also says: "One may be quite justified in continuing to fear the blond beast at the core of all noble races and in being on one's guard against it: but who would not a hundred times sooner fear where one can also admire than *not* fear but be permanently condemned to the repellent sight of the ill-constituted, dwarfed, atrophied, and poisoned?"[55]

What Nietzsche has in mind, of course, is much more complex than this simple model can convey. But sometimes a simplified model can bring into focus what a more complex treatment obscures. At any rate, this model, I think, shows us the only way that those who are not *Übermenschen* can find meaning in the new heaven created by the *Übermensch*. Eternal recurrence empowers the *Übermensch* while crushing almost everyone else. Eternal recurrence strips all meaning from the world for most people. The only meaning possible for them comes through the awe that admiring the *Übermensch* can inspire in them.

Thus, the *Übermensch* speaks to very few. Eternal recurrence is accepted and *amor fati* is possible only for the *Übermensch* and perhaps a few others. Beyond that, a small number will be able to identify with the *Übermensch*, admire him, see him as their own. Eternal recurrence will crush most of the rest.

Besides this, over time Nietzsche hopes for a natural selection. Hopefully, the weak will grow less numerous, die off,[56] and the strong will propagate themselves and increase. Nietzsche says: "The problem I raise here is not what ought to succeed mankind in the sequence of species . . . but what type of human being one ought to *breed*, ought to *will*, as more valuable, more worthy of life, more certain of the future."[57] Nietzsche wants to breed a stronger human being; he wants "mankind in the mass sacrificed to the prosperity of a single *stronger* species of man."[58] Eventually, then, in some distant future there will be human beings able to understand Nietzsche's thought: "Some day institutions will be needed in which men live and teach as I conceive of living and teaching; it might even happen that a few chairs will then be set aside for the interpretation of *Zarathustra*."[59]

V. Against Nietzsche

Accepting eternal recurrence, we have seen, breaks the stranglehold that one's suffering imposes on one. But it also implies that as I turn all "it was" into a "thus I willed it," I will eternal recurrence on others. I will that they relive their suffering eternally. If they could accept eternal recurrence and love their fate, they might break the stranglehold their suffering has over them, but my willing eternal recurrence will not have that effect for them. Eternal recurrence, of course, is not dependent upon my willing it. It is not due to my choice. It is not that history will only recur if the *Übermensch* wills it and will not if he does not. It will return anyway—or at least one risks allowing one's suffering to reassert its stranglehold if one ceases to believe this.[60] Nevertheless, we have a definite parallel here to what Nietzsche says about Thomas Aquinas in the *Genealogy of Morals*. Nietzsche quotes the *Summa Theologiae*, where Thomas says that part of the reward of those who get to heaven will be to enjoy for eternity the spectacle of the damned suffering in hell.[61] Nietzsche certainly does not believe in the Christian hell, but the fact that Christians imagine a hell, imagine certain people in it, and imagine enjoying the spectacle for eternity in the afterlife, seems the furthest thing possible from loving one's enemies and suggests that there is a good deal of *ressentiment* and revenge operating at the core of Christianity.

But wouldn't we have to say much the same about Nietzsche himself? Eternal recurrence does not condemn the *Übermensch* to hell—he *loves* his fate. But eternal recurrence certainly condemns all who are not *Übermenschen* to hell. It certainly does so if there is anything to the horror of existence. It certainly does so if eternal recurrence would be met by all but the *Übermensch* with the greatest anguish. The *Übermensch*, then, like Thomas Aquinas, as part of his reward, gets to enjoy the suffering of those incapable of loving their fate, and gets to enjoy it in each and every cycle repeated eternally—indeed, he himself turns all this "it was" into a "thus I *willed* it." He *loves* this fate. If enjoying the eternal suffering of others suggests that *ressentiment* and revenge operate at the core of

Christianity, mustn't we conclude much the same about Nietzsche who must *love* the hell-like suffering of others?

We must decide whether to accept the horror of existence and its eternal re- currence if it condemns most people to hell. We must decide whether to accept the increase in suffering necessary to produce an *Übermensch* if it means reject- ing liberalism, socialism, feminism, and Christianity's attempt to reduce suffer- ing. We must decide whether women, workers, and most of humanity should be sacrificed for an *Übermensch.*

Nietzsche's position on these issues makes some sense if existence really is horrible and if suffering really cannot be reduced significantly. If he is wrong about these matters, if liberals, socialists, and feminists are right, if suffering can be reduced, then Nietzsche might begin to appear as a rather ugly little charac- ter, as someone who over-reacted to his own suffering, as someone who blew up his "needs into cosmic and metaphysical values," such that "the whole of exis- tence [was] vulgarized."[62] He might begin to appear as someone who would drag the whole of humanity down so that he might face his own suffering. One might be tempted to treat such a person with pity—if he had not taught us the ugliness of such an attitude.

I do not think we can *prove* that Nietzsche is wrong. I do not think we can *prove* that suffering can be significantly reduced. We are certainly nowhere near doing so worldwide. But do we have to give suffering the ontological weight that Nietzsche gives it? Must it be taken as the primary reality? Must it be seen as the essence of the human condition? Does it force us to believe in the horror of existence? I must confess—perhaps I should have done so earlier—that I have never felt the horror of existence. I think it acceptable to reject Nietzsche re- sponse to suffering and to push liberalism, socialism, feminism, and Christianity as alternative responses to suffering (personally, I favor socialism and feminism, but this is not the place to develop that argument). The point here is that it is legitimate to treat suffering *as if* it can be reduced even if we cannot *prove* that it can be.

We can even learn from Nietzsche in this regard. We can admit to ourselves that Nietzsche is right, that we have imposed our own meaning on suffering. We can admit to ourselves that we have just decided to view suffering as something that with effort can be significantly reduced. That is how we find meaning in our world. It is our view that if we have not yet reduced suffering significantly, that is because we have not exerted enough effort and thus must do more. We can even say that we ourselves are responsible for suffering—at least for not having yet reduced it. Let us admit that Nietzsche is right, that this is simply our con- struction, our myth, our illusion. Why is it worse than Nietzsche's?

After all, our construction has certain desirable consequences. Given the meaning we impose upon suffering, we do not have the slightest need for an .*Übermensch*—he would not help us in the least to remove suffering. Further- more, we would have no need for a doctrine of eternal recurrence—indeed, we should reject it as an abomination. We should view every moment of suffering as something new, original, and terrible. We do not want it repeated—we want it eliminated. We also reject the innocence of existence. *We accept the responsibility* for suffering *ourselves,* at least in the sense that if we had worked a little harder we might have been able to reduce it. Moreover, our meaning derives from improving *this* world. Thus we do not need a heaven, let alone a Vishvamitra to construct a *new* one.

But what if Nietzsche is right? What if we cannot reduce the overall suffering that exists in the world? Even if we cannot, even if Nietzsche is right, what we can do is reduce this particular suffering, the suffering of this person who needs a meal, of this person who needs housing, of this person who needs a job, of this person who needs medical care, of this person who has been abused, or brutalized, or oppressed. Even if we cannot significantly reduce the total suffering in the world, we can alleviate the particular suffering of the particular person that stands before us.

Moreover, there is no good reason to think that this will weaken us. We can face with compassion the totality of suffering that we have not yet alleviated— even the suffering we may be forced to doubt we will ever be able to alleviate. If we can face it with compassion, not pity, we can identify with that suffering. We can empathize. That will cause us to suffer ourselves, but that can strengthen us, not weaken us. And compassion will drive us to work harder to reduce suffering.

We do not need any *Übermenschen* or masters. We slaves can work on the world as we always have. Instead of making it a pleasant place for the master, we can begin to make it a pleasanter place for all of us members of the herd. Indeed, in getting rid of the masters, we may well have gotten rid of a not insignificant part of the suffering.[63]

Nietzsche would still insist that we patronize and demean those whose suffering we seek to reduce. Perhaps that is true with respect to the *Übermensch* and a few like him. But it should be obvious by now that in my opinion such persons should not be the privileged object of our philosophical concern—let alone, the *meaning* of the earth. Indeed, such an attitude should by now appear obscene. As for the rest of humanity, we should work to reduce suffering in the sense that we work to stop inflicting it ourselves, that we root out the myriad hidden ways in which we do so, and that we work to make available to all the means to reduce the rest of their suffering if they want to. There is nothing demeaning here—or nothing sufficiently demeaning to convince us to abandon such a project. At any rate, we have no business inflicting suffering, tolerating it, or encouraging it in order to give any sort of meaning (Christian, Homeric, or Nietzschean) to existence. We can get plenty of meaning by working to *reduce* suffering. If we decide to become socialists, we can advocate each working with others collectively to reduce our common suffering, which would go even further in avoiding anything possibly demeaning for the sufferer. What is wrong with having *your* suffering alleviated if you have been working for a long time with others to reduce *all* suffering?

Nietzsche would abhor the equality implied in this view. Given the enormous actual differences between human beings, Nietzsche thinks the myth of human equality rests upon the lie of essential equality before God, and must be abandoned once we see that God is dead.[64] Even if we share Nietzsche's lack of religious belief, we need not accept such a conclusion if our view of religion is Feurbachian or Marxist, if we hold that religion is capable of expressing the highest truths, just that it mistakenly locates them in another world. Thus, we might say that when human beings first started to think they were equal, or felt they should be treated equally, they were (as Nietzsche himself shows us) unable to accept this as just their own judgment—they attributed it to God.[65] Why did God see all people as equal? Because God is compassionate and because God loves all equally. In other words, we projected our *own* compassion onto God. If that is so, then there is no reason that this compassion could not or should not continue if we have decided that God is dead. Indeed, that might even work to *increase* our compassion, at least in the sense that we might feel an increased responsibility for acting compassionately—that being the only source of compassion in the world.

The serious risk for liberals, socialists, feminists, and Christians is that we fail to reduce suffering significantly. After all, there is still a *very* great deal of it in the world given the amount of time we have been seeking to reduce it. I am not suggesting in this chapter that Nietzsche had no insight. It is not ridiculous to think as he did that we might never reduce suffering significantly. It is not impossible that Nietzsche is right. And the problem for us is that if we start to think that we cannot significantly reduce suffering, if we start to think that we will never make significant headway in reducing the *very* great amount of suffering that continues to exist in the world, it can grievously demoralize us. It could even throw us into despair—even lead to nihilism. For this reason, *compassion* is especially important. Compassion can protect us from despair. Even if we cannot reduce suffering, compassion can bond us with the sufferer. It can strengthen us, without it doing so at the expense of the sufferer. We must see that compassion is even compatible with a tragic vision of life. Oedipus and Lear, when they are crushed, not only evoke our compassion but feel it themselves for others. And they do not despair. Indeed, they are even strengthened a bit. If this is so, then we can continue on working to reduce suffering.

Notes to Chapter One

1. I have used various translations of Nietzsche and, for the German, *Nietzsche Werke: Kritische Gesamtausgabe* (hereafter *NWKG*), ed. G. Colli and M. Montinari (Berlin: de Gruyter, 1967–). I will cite the page of the translation but also the section so that any other editions, English or German, may be used. *The Birth of Tragedy* (hereafter *BT*), in *The Birth of Tragedy and The Case of Wagner*, tr. W. Kaufmann (New York: Vintage, 1967), §3, p. 42.

2. *BT,* §3, p. 42. See also Sophocles, *Oedipus at Colonus,* tr. R. Fitzgerald, in *Sophocles I* (Chicago: University of Chicago Press, 1954), 134. For other texts which indicate Nietzsche's belief in the horror of existence, see *Philosophy in the Tragic Age of the Greeks,* tr. M. Cowan (South Bend, IN: Gateway, 1962), §5, p. 55. Nietzsche also speaks of the "original Titanic divine order of terror" (*BT,* §3, p. 42) and of the "terrors of nature" (*BT,* §9, p. 67). See also *On the Uses and Disadvantages of History for Life* (hereafter *U&DHL*), in *Untimely Meditations* (hereafter *UM*), tr. R.J. Hollingdale (Cambridge: Cambridge University Press, 1997), §1, p. 66. Also see *Daybreak* (hereafter *D*), tr. R.J. Hollingdale (Cambridge: Cambridge University Press, 1997), §241, p. 141. He also speaks of the mere thought of pain as a "reproach against the whole of existence"; *The Gay Science* (hereafter *GS*), tr. W. Kaufmann (New York: Vintage, 1974), §48, p. 113. See also *The Will to Power* (hereafter *WP*), tr. W. Kaufmann and R.J. Hollingdale (New York: Vintage, 1968), §4, p. 10; for the German of this text, see *Nietzsche's Werke* (hereafter *NW*) (Leipzig: Kröner, 1901-23), vols. XV and XVI. Nietzsche speaks of Christianity as creating "sublime words and gestures to throw over a horrible reality . . . " (*WP,* §685, p. 364). He also speaks of the world as "false, cruel, contradictory, seductive, without meaning" and of "the terrifying and questionable character of existence" (*WP,* §853, p. 451). See also *WP,* §4, p. 10. In one of his last texts, Nietzsche says: "In every age the wisest have passed the identical judgement on life: *it is worthless.*" See *Twilight of the Idols* (hereafter *TI*), in *Twilight of the Idols and The Anti-Christ,* tr. R.J. Hollingdale (Harmondsworth: Penguin, 1977), "The Problem of Socrates," §1, p. 29.

3. In these matters, Nietzsche was influenced by Schopenhauer, who tells us of "The unspeakable pain, the wretchedness and misery of mankind, the triumph of wickedness, the scornful mastery of chance, and the irretrievable fall of the just and the innocent. . . . Here is to be found a significant hint as to the nature of the world and of existence. . . . 'For man's greatest offence/Is that he has been born,' as Calderón . . . frankly expresses it" (A. Schopenhauer, *The World as Will and Representation* [hereafter *WW&R*], tr. E.F.J. Payne [New York: Dover, 1966], I, §51, pp. 253-54; also see II, p. 605). Furthermore, "If, finally, we were to bring to the sight of everyone the terrible sufferings and afflictions to which his life is constantly exposed, he would be seized with horror. If we were to conduct the most hardened and callous optimist through hospitals, infirmaries, operating theatres, through prisons, torture-chambers, and slave-hovels, over battlefields and to places of execution; if we were to open to him all the dark abodes of misery, where it shuns the gaze of cold curiosity . . . he too would certainly see in the end what kind of a world is this *meilleur des mondes possibles.* For whence did Dante get the material for his hell, if not from this actual world of ours?" (*WW&R,* I, §59, p. 325; see also §54, p. 283. See also I. Soll, "Pessimism and the Tragic View of Life: Reconsiderations

of Nietzsche's *Birth of Tragedy,"* in *Reading Nietzsche,* ed. R.C. Solomon and K.M. Higgins [New York: Oxford University Press, 1988], esp. 109, 114).

4. *On the Genealogy of Morals* (hereafter *GM*), in *On the Genealogy of Morals* and *Ecce Homo,* tr. W. Kaufmann (New York: Vintage, 1969), III, §28, p. 162.

5. *GM,* III, §28, p. 162. See also *WP,* §55, p. 35.

6. *Beyond Good and Evil* (hereafter *BGE*), tr. W. Kaufmann (New York: Vintage, 1966), §39, p. 49. Also see *WP,* §822, p. 435.

7. See L. Salomé, *Nietzsche,* tr. S. Mandel (Redding Ridge, CT: Black Swan Books, 1988), 10.

8. Nietzsche to Brandes on 10 April 1888, in *Selected Letters of Friedrich Nietzsche,* tr. C. Middleton (Chicago: University of Chicago Press, 1969), 294.

9. *Nietzsche Contra Wagner,* in *The Complete Works of Friedrich Nietzsche* [hereafter *CWFN* (Levy)], ed. O. Levy (New York: Russell & Russell, 1964), VIII, "Epilogue," 79. For a very similar passage, see *GS,* "Preface," §3, p. 36.

10. *BGE,* §6, p. 13.

11. This paradigm was also found in Novalis and Goethe, and even, I have argued elsewhere, in Hegel and Marx; see my *Schiller, Hegel, and Marx: State, Society, and the Aesthetic Ideal of Ancient Greece* (Montreal: McGill-Queen's University Press, 1982). For an extended discussion of Nietzsche's relation to these and other figures in 19th century aesthetics, see G.E. McCarthy, *Dialectics and Decadence: Echoes of Antiquity in Marx and Nietzsche* (Lanham, MD: Rowman & Littlefield, 1994), esp. Ch. 4.

12. F. Schiller, *On the Aesthetic Education of Man,* tr. E.M. Wilkinson and L.A. Willoughby (Oxford: Clarendon Press, 1967), Letter 6, p. 31.

13. F. Schiller, *On Naive and Sentimental Poetry,* in *Friedrich Schiller: Essays,* ed. W. Hinderer and D.O. Dahlstrom (New York: Continuum, 1998), 180-81.

14. *Naive and Sentimental Poetry,* 193-95.

15. *BT,* §1, p. 33.

16. *BT,* §3, p. 43. See also *TI,* "What I Owe to the Ancients," §4, p. 109.

17. *BT,* §§1-4, pp. 33-47.

18. *BT,* §§1-4, pp. 33-47. The Dionysian is also associated with the ugly; *BT,* §24, p. 140.

19. *BT,* §1, p. 37.

20. *BT,* §1, p. 37.

21. *BT,* §2, p. 40.

22. *BT,* §3, pp. 42-43. Also *GS,* §107, p. 163. Schiller's position is quite close to Nietzsche's on this issue. Schiller writes: "Once he begins to assert his independence in the face of nature as phenomenon, then he also asserts his dignity *vis-à-vis* nature as force, and with noble freedom rises in revolt against his ancient gods. Now they cast off those ghastly masks which were the anguish of his childhood and surprise him with his own image by revealing themselves as projections of his own mind. The monstrous divinity of the Oriental, which rules the world with the blind strength of a beast of prey, shrinks in the imagination of the Greeks into the friendly contours of a human being. The empire of the Titans falls . . . " (*Aesthetic Education,* Letter 25, p. 185). Indeed, one could say that Nietzsche's view of Greece is already here in Schiller; it just never gets developed any further by Schiller.

23. This is anticipated in Hegel, for whom classical art is not to be regarded as the beginning of art, but as a result; see G.W.F. Hegel, *Aesthetics,* tr. T.M. Knox (Oxford: Clarendon Press, 1975), I, 441. For an anticipation of Nietzsche's Dionysian, see *Aesthetics,* I, 365. For an anticipation of the distinction between the Apollonian and the Dionysian, see *Aesthetics,* I, 436-37.

24. *BT*, §1, p. 37.
25. *GS*, §1, p. 75.
26. *BT*, §10, pp. 73-74.
27. *BT*, §10, p. 73.
28. Aristotle, *Nicomachean Ethics* (hereafter *NE*), in *The Complete Works of Aristotle*, ed. J. Barnes, Bollingen Series LXXI (Princeton, NJ: Princeton University Press, 1984), II, 1097^b-1098^a.
29. *BT*, §25, p. 143.
30. *BT*, §8, pp. 65-66.
31. *BT*, §§16-17, 21, pp. 104-5, 128.
32. *BT*, §10, pp. 73-74.
33. *BT*, §17, pp. 104-5.
34. *BT*, §21, p. 125.
35. *BT*, §21, pp. 127-28.
36. *BT*, §9, pp. 71-72.
37. *TI*, "What I Owe to the Ancients," §5, p. 110. *Ecce Homo* (hereafter *EH*), in *On the Genealogy of Morals* and *Ecce Homo*, "The Birth of Tragedy," §3, p. 273.
38. Aristotle, *Poetics*, in *Complete Works of Aristotle*, II, 1449^b; also 1453^a.
39. *Poetics*, 1452^b.
40. *BT*, §9, pp. 67-68.
41. *BT*, §15, p. 93.
42. *BT*, §15, p. 94.
43. *BT*, §20, p. 123.
44. *BT*, §19, p. 119.
45. *BT*, §24, p. 142. *On the Future of Our Educational Institutions*, in *CWFN* (Levy), III, 68.
46. *BT*, §15, pp. 98-99, n. 11. W. Kaufmann, *Nietzsche: Philosopher, Psychologist, Antichrist*, 4th ed. (Princeton, NJ: Princeton University Press, 1974), 393-94. For a defense of Nietzsche's addition of these later sections, see M.S. Silk and J.P. Stern, *Nietzsche on Tragedy* (Cambridge: Cambridge University Press, 1981), 59-60. See also N. Martin, *Nietzsche and Schiller: Untimely Aesthetics* (Oxford: Clarendon Press, 1996), 87ff.
47. Nietzsche still holds the same view on both the Greek ideal and on Wagner in *Richard Wagner in Bayreuth*, in *UM*, §4, p. 209. Also *U&DHL*, §7, p. 97.
48. *EH*, "The Birth of Tragedy," §4, p. 274. See also *WP*, §419, p. 225.
49. For a similar view of nature, see J.W. von Goethe, *The Sorrows of Young Werther*, tr. E. Mayer and L. Bogan (New York: Vintage, 1973), "August 18," 64-66. Also Schopenhauer, *WW&R*, II, pp. 350-51, 473.
50. *U&DHL*, §3, p. 76.
51. *WP*, §1052, p. 543.
52. *WP*, §1050, p. 539. See also *TI*, "What I Owe to the Ancients," §5, p. 110. *EH*, "The Birth of Tragedy," §§2-3, pp. 272-73.
53. M. Clark, *Nietzsche on Truth and Philosophy* (Cambridge: Cambridge University Press, 1990), 200.
54. The following show little or no awareness that the horror of existence is central to Nietzsche's thought. B. Magnus, *Nietzsche's Existential Imperative* (Bloomington: Indiana University Press, 1978). W. Kaufmann, *Nietzsche: Philosopher, Psychologist, Antichrist*. O. Schutte, *Beyond Nihilism: Nietzsche without Masks* (Chicago: University of Chicago Press, 1984). J. Richardson, *Nietzsche's System* (New York: Oxford University Press, 1996). M. Heidegger, *Nietzsche*, tr. D.F. Krell, et. al. (San Francisco: Harper &

Row, 1979-82), 4 vols. J. Derrida, *Spurs: Nietzsche's Styles*, tr. B. Harlow (Chicago: University of Chicago Press, 1979). There are scholars who note the presence in Nietzsche's thought of the concept of the horror of existence, but for whom it does not in any significant way inform their interpretation. A.C. Danto, *Nietzsche as Philosopher* (New York: Macmillan, 1967). R. Schacht, *Nietzsche* (London: Routledge & Kegan Paul, 1983), esp. 376, 478. A. Nehamas, *Nietzsche: Life as Literature* (Cambridge, MA: Harvard University Press, 1985). Some scholars do appreciate the central importance of the concept of the horror of existence. J. Sallis, *Crossings: Nietzsche and the Space of Tragedy* (Chicago: University of Chicago Press, 1991). K. Ansell-Pearson, *An Introduction to Nietzsche as Political Thinker: The Perfect Nihilist* (Cambridge: Cambridge University Press, 1994). D.R. Ahern, *Nietzsche as Cultural Physician* (University Park: Pennsylvania State University Press, 1995). The book that pays the most attention to the importance of suffering in Nietzsche's thought and which agrees with my views in many respects, while approaching Nietzsche quite differently, is that of B. Reginster, *The Affirmation of Life: Nietzsche on Overcoming Nihilism* (Cambridge, MA: Harvard University Press, 2006). Nevertheless, as I hope to show, even these scholars have not fully appreciated how deeply Nietzsche's thought has been affected by the horror of existence.

55. *WP*, §12A, p. 12.

56. My three models, that of the perfectible, the designed, and the horrific cosmos, should be compared to the three models that Nietzsche sets out in *BT*, §§18ff., pp. 109ff., that of the Socratic, the artistic, and the tragic. See also *WP*, §333, pp. 181-82.

57. See, e.g., *WP*, §§40, 90, 684, pp. 25, 55, 363.

58. *BGE*, §225, pp. 153-54; also §44, pp. 54-55. *WP*, §957, p. 502. *GM*, II, §7, pp. 67-68.

59. Danto, *Nietzsche as Philosopher*, 226.

60. *BT*, §7, p. 60.

61. *BT*, §15, p. 95.

62. *BT*, §7, p. 60. Also see *TI*, "Morality as Anti-Nature," §6, p. 46.

63. "On Truth and Lies in a Nonmoral Sense" (hereafter *T&L*), in *Philosophy and Truth: Selections from Nietzsche's Notebooks of the Early 1870's*, tr. D. Breazeale (Amherst, NY: Humanity Books, 1999), §1, p. 79. Nietzsche probably got this view from Frederick Lange, who thought it followed from the mechanical theory of heat; see *The History of Materialism*, 3rd edn., tr. E.C. Thomas (New York: Humanities Press, 1950), Second Book Continued, 11. Also see Schopenhauer, *WW&R*, II, p. 583.

64. For Schopenhauer, "constant suffering is essential to all life . . . " (*WW&R*, I, §54, p. 283).

65. See especially Section V of Chapter 5 below. See also *BT*, §17, pp. 104-5. *WP*, §1050, p. 539.

Notes to Chapter Two

1. *BGE*, §39, p. 49. Also see *WP*, §822, p. 435.
2. *TI*, "'Reason' in Philosophy," §4, p. 37. Also see Plato, *Republic*, in *The Collected Dialogues of Plato*, ed. E. Hamilton and H. Cairns, Bollingen Series LXXI (New York: Pantheon, 1961), 505a-505b, 508d-509b, 515c-516b.
3. *TI*, "The Problem of Socrates," §4, p. 31. See also *BT*, §14, p. 91; also §12, p. 84.
4. *NE*, 1177ª.
5. Sophocles, *Oedipus the King*, tr. D. Greene, in *Sophocles I*, 64, 69. Also *Oedipus at Colonus*, 134.
6. *Eudemian Ethics*, in *Complete Works of Aristotle*, II, 1216ª.
7. *NE*, 1168ª.
8. *Republic*, 517b-517c.
9. *Republic*, 519d-519e. See also P. Berkowitz, *Nietzsche: The Ethics of an Immoralist* (Cambridge, MA: Harvard University Press, 1995), 55.
10. *Oedipus the King*, 52, 57.
11. On the influence of Lange on Nietzsche, see G.J. Stack, *Lange and Nietzsche* (Berlin: de Gruyter, 1983).
12. *History of Materialism*, First Book Continued, 121.
13. *History of Materialism*, Second Book Continued, 284-85.
14. *WP*, §822, p. 435.
15. *Human, All Too Human, I* (hereafter *HAH, I*), tr. G. Handwerk, in *The Complete Works of Friedrich Nietzsche* (hereafter *CWFN*), ed. B. Magnus (Stanford, CA: Stanford University Press, 1995), III, §517, p. 269; also §36, p. 44.
16. E.g., *TI*, "How the 'Real World' at last Became a Myth," pp. 40-41.
17. *GM*, III, §24, p. 153.
18. Kaufmann, *Nietzsche: Philosopher, Psychologist, Antichrist*, 357-60. J.T. Wilcox, *Truth and Value in Nietzsche* (Ann Arbor: University of Michigan Press, 1974), esp. 155-70. M. Clark, *Nietzsche on Truth and Philosophy*.
19. Danto, *Nietzsche as Philosopher*. Also A. Danto, "Nietzsche's Perspectivism," in *Nietzsche: A Collection of Critical Essays*, ed. R.C. Solomon (Garden City, NY: Anchor, 1973), 35. M.S. Green, *Nietzsche and the Transcendental Tradition* (Urbana: University of Illinois Press, 2002). See also S.D. Hales and R. Welshon, *Nietzsche's Perspectivism* (Urbana: University of Illinois Press, 2000), 21-36.
20. Nehamas, *Nietzsche: Life as Literature*, 2. There are some, for whom such contradictions do not pose a problem. For Derrida, we cannot do without the concepts of metaphysics in attacking metaphysics; J. Derrida, *Writing and Difference*, tr. A. Bass (Chicago: University of Chicago Press, 1978), 280. Also, Heidegger writes: "Herr Nietzsche says that truth is an illusion. And if Nietzsche wants to be 'consistent' . . . his statement about truth is an illusion, too, and so we need not bother with him any longer. . . . However . . . [this] forgets one thing, to wit, that if Nietzsche's statement is true, then not only must Nietzsche's own statement as true become an illusion, but just as necessarily so must the consequent statement that is brought forward as a refutation of Nietzsche be an 'illusion.'" See M. Heidegger, *Nietzsche: Volume III: The Will to Power as Knowledge and as Metaphysics*, in *Nietzsche: Volumes III and IV*, tr. J. Stambaugh,

D.F. Krell, F.A. Capuzzi (San Francisco: HarperCollins, 1991), 26. Heidegger goes on to attack such attempts to catch relativism in self-contradiction.

21. Schutte, 11.

22. Twenty five years ago, I myself held a different position than I do now. I then defended the view that Nietzsche did not believe in truth; see "Nietzsche, Skepticism, and Eternal Recurrence," *Canadian Journal of Philosophy*, 13 (1983): 365-87.

23. Here, I prefer Golffing's translation; see *The Birth of Tragedy* [hereafter *BT* (Golffing)], in *The Birth of Tragedy and The Genealogy of Morals*, tr. F. Golffing (Garden City, NY: Doubleday, 1956), §7, pp. 51-52. In comparing Apollonian and Dionysian art, Nietzsche also says, "The muses of the arts of 'illusion' paled before an art that, in its intoxication, spoke the truth. The wisdom of Silenus cried 'Woe! woe!' to the serene Olympians" (*BT*, §4, p. 46; see also *BT*, §17, p. 107). See also *HAH, I*, §225, p. 155.

24. *GM*, III, §27, pp. 160-61.

25. *GM, I*, §1, p. 25.

26. *BT*, §3, p. 42 (my italics). See also *BT*, §3, p. 43; also §4, p. 45.

27. Here again I prefer Golffing's translation, *BT* (Golffing), §9, pp. 59-60 (my italics). See also *D*, §507, p. 206. Also *BGE*, §4, pp. 11-12; also §34, p. 46.

28. *WP*, §853, p. 451. Also *TI*, "'Reason' in Philosophy," §5, pp. 37-38.

29. *WP*, §480, pp. 266-67. See also *WP*, §513, p. 277.

30. *GS*, §111, p. 171. See also *GS*, §307, pp. 245-46. Also *HAH, I*, §§517, 519, pp. 269-70.

31. *GS*, §110, p. 169. See also *GS*, §354, p. 299. Also *T&L*, §1, pp. 79-81.

32. *WP*, §503, p. 274.

33. *BGE*, §24, p. 35. For an extended discussion of these matters, see Green, 58-94.

34. *BGE*, §192, p. 105. See also *TI*, "The Four Great Errors," §5, p. 51.

35. *WP*, §493, p. 272. See also *WP*, §535, p. 290.

36. *T&L*, §1, p. 84. See also *BGE*, §296, p. 236.

37. "The Philosopher: Reflections on the Struggle Between Art and Knowledge," in *Philosophy and Truth*, §47, p. 16.

38. *BGE*, §231, p. 162; also §43, p. 53. Also, e.g., *Thus Spoke Zarathustra* (hereafter *Z*), tr. W. Kaufmann (New York: Viking, 1966), IV, "On Science," p. 302. *HAH, I*, §261, p. 177.

39. Derrida argues for a congruence of Nietzsche's "*apparently feminist* propositions" and "the overwhelming *corpus* of Nietzsche's venomous anti-feminism . . . "; see Derrida, *Spurs*, 57. Despite the objectionableness of Nietzsche's views on women, there is something interesting going on here. Nietzsche gathers together a lot of traditional stereotypes—stereotypes of women and stereotypes of truth. Nietzsche considers the traditional stereotypes of truth to be false. Truth is *not* desirable, it is not to be sought, it is not good or beautiful, it is not better than illusion. While *we* would also consider the traditional stereotypes of women to be false, that unfortunately does not seem to be Nietzsche's view. Women according to these stereotypes concern themselves with beauty, appearance, illusion, lie—and not with real truth. Thus, the things men stereotypically say about women are objectionable and false—though Nietzsche would not agree. The things philosophers traditionally say about truth are also objectionable and false—for Nietzsche. But what is stereotypically said about women turns out to be true about truth—for Nietzsche. We are certainly getting a revaluation of truth here. Truth, rather than being opposed to woman, as tradition would have it, is being aligned with woman. What would seem to follow from this is that a revaluation of the traditional view of women would also be called for. Nietzsche, however, nowhere carries that out.

This raises an interesting question. In great thinkers, we often find a mixture of two things: (1) prejudice, racism, sexism, that is, the *inability* to break through certain stereotypes of their age and culture, and (2) insight, originality, depth of thought, that is, the *ability* to break through other stereotypes of their age and culture. Which of these should weigh more heavily in assessing that thinker? It does not seem to me that we want to say that (2) is simply more important than, and that it excuses, (1). But neither should we say that the presence of (1) makes meaningless or unimportant the accomplishments of (2).

40. *BGE*, "Preface," p. 2.

41. *BGE*, §232, pp. 162-63.

42. *Nietzsche Contra Wagner*, "Epilogue," §2, pp. 81-82. See also *GS*, §64, p. 125. Also *GS*, "Preface," §4, p. 38. Also *TI*, "Maxims and Arrows," §16, p. 24.

43. See also *BGE*, §220, p. 149.

44. There is one thing that Nietzsche says on these matters that appears contradictory. In *Beyond Good and Evil*, he says, "Ultimately Truth is a woman: we must not violate her" (here I prefer Cowan's translation; see *Beyond Good and Evil* [hereafter *BGE* (Cowan)], tr. M. Cowan [Chicago: Henry Regnery, 1955], §220, p. 145). On the other hand, in *Thus Spoke Zarathustra*, Nietzsche seems to hold to the opposite: "Brave, unconcerned, mocking, violent—thus wisdom wants us: she is a woman and always loves only a warrior" (*Z*, I, "On Reading and Writing," p. 41. This passage is also quoted at the beginning of the third essay of the *Genealogy of Morals;* see *GM*, III, p. 97). The passage from *Zarathustra* echoes, and the passage from *Beyond Good and Evil* contrasts with, Machiavelli's famous: "fortune is a woman and whoever wishes to win her must importune and beat her. . . . Like a woman, too, she is well disposed to young men, for they are less circumspect and more violent and more bold to command her" (N. Machiavelli, *The Prince*, tr. T.G. Bergin [New York: Appleton-Century-Crofts, 1947], Ch. XXV, p. 75). But the contradiction between the two passages is only apparent. We must see that Nietzsche, as I have been claiming, understands truth in two senses. The passage from *Zarathustra* advocates violence, which is to say, aggressive effort, if we are to gain wisdom, that is, get at the actual truth, which because it is horrible has been buried through millennia of masking. Whereas the passage from *Beyond Good and Evil* rejects violence and suggests we should be content with truth as appearance, as illusion, what we *take to be* truth, which is necessary to mask the horror of real truth and make life possible.

45. G. Lukács, *The Destruction of Reason*, tr. P. Palmer (London: Merlin, 1980), 389. Also see Nehamas, *Nietzsche: Life as Literature*, 52-53.

46. *WP*, §497, p. 273. See also *BGE*, §4, pp. 11-12.

47. *BGE*, §22, pp. 30-31.

48. D. Smith, "Introduction" to *On the Genealogy of Morals* [hereafter *GM* (Smith)], tr. D. Smith (Oxford: Oxford University Press, 1996), xxii.

49. *BGE*, §§4, 34, pp. 11-12, 46. Also see Green, 150-65.

50. *GM* (Smith), xxv.

51. *GM*, III, §24, p. 150.

52. *WP*, §§13, 602, pp. 14, 326.

53. *GM*, III, §§24, 25, 27, pp. 150-54, 159-61.

54. *BGE*, §24, p. 35.

55. If we were to decide that Nietzsche's claim that 'will to knowledge is not the opposite, but a *refinement*, of will to ignorance' is to be taken as true, wouldn't that mean that this statement itself would be part of will to ignorance, and so don't we have self-contradiction here? Not on my view. Will to knowledge or will to truth must serve to conceal the horror of existence (that is, keep us *ignorant* of this horror). To do that, we might very well argue, it must give us *real* knowledge, *real* truth. If it did not, it would

not serve to mask the horror. It must find truth, get us focused on it, absorb our interest in it, give us the hope of meaningfulness, if it is going to hide the horror of existence (keep us ignorant of it).

56. *Human, All Too Human* (hereafter *HAH, II*), tr. R.J. Hollingdale (Cambridge: Cambridge University Press, 1986), II, §113, pp. 238-39. In a similar vein, Nietzsche also writes: "'That other saying of Lessing's . . . that, if God held all truth in his right hand and in his left the never-sleeping quest for truth with the condition of continually erring in this quest, and then offered him a choice between them, he would humbly fall upon God's left hand and beg for the contents of it. . . . This saying has always made so powerful an impression upon me because behind its subjective significance I have heard resounding an objective one of immense range. For does it not contain the best reply to Schopenhauer's crude conception of an ill-advised God who knows nothing better to do than to enter into so wretched a world as this is? May it not be that the Creator himself shares Lessing's opinion and prefers continual striving to peaceful possession?' A God, that is to say, who reserves to himself *continual error* and at the same time a striving for truth . . . " (*David Strauss, the Confessor and the Writer,* in *UM,* §7, p. 32).

57. *GM,* III, §25, p. 153.

58. *GM,* III, §27, p. 161.

59. For Nietzsche, abstract concepts cannot grasp reality; see *HAH, I,* §11, pp. 21-22. Also *WP,* §§512-16, pp. 277-80.

60. *BT* (Golffing), §8, p. 53.

61. *BGE,* §39, p. 49. See also *EH,* "Preface," §3, p. 218. Also *WP,* §1041, p. 536.

62. *The Anti-Christ (hereafter AC),* in *Twilight of the Idols and The Anti-Christ,* tr. R.J. Hollingdale (Harmondsworth: Penguin, 1977, §50, p. 167.

63. "The Philosopher: Reflections on the Struggle Between Art and Knowledge," §73, p. 28.

Notes to Chapter Three

1. *GM*, III, §28, p. 162. See also *TI*, "Maxims and Arrows," §12, p. 23. Also see, *Schopenhauer as Educator*, in *UM*, §5, p. 157.
2. *GM*, II, §7, pp. 68-69. See also *D*, §78, p. 48. Also *The Wanderer and His Shadow*, in *HAH, II*, §14, p. 307.
3. *GM*, II, §§6-7, p. 67; see also p. 68. See also *D*, §18, p. 17; also §77, p. 46. Also *GS*, §48, p. 113; also §325, p. 255.
4. A.C. Danto, *Nietzsche as Philosopher*, 176-77. See also Ahern, 32. Also B. Magnus and K.M. Higgins, "Introduction," *The Cambridge Companion to Nietzsche*, ed. B. Magnus and K.M. Higgins (Cambridge: Cambridge University Press, 1996), 49. Also see my "Nietzschean Genealogy and Hegelian History in the *Genealogy of Morals*," *Canadian Journal of Philosophy*, 26 (1996): 142-43. For an explanation of why the infliction of suffering is so enjoyable that is based upon the influence of Schopenhauer, see Reginster, 139-47.
5. *GM*, II, §§16-17, pp. 84-87.
6. *GM*, III, §20, p. 140.
7. *Z*, II, "On Redemption," p. 140.
8. *GM*, III, §20, p. 141.
9. *GM*, III, §20, p. 141.
10. *GM*, III, §20, p. 141.
11. *GM*, III, §28, p. 162.
12. *BGE*, §225, pp. 153-54; see also §229, p. 158; also §270, p. 220. Also see *GS*, "Preface," §3, p. 36. Also *Nietzsche Contra Wagner*, "Epilogue," 79-80. Also *TI*, "Expeditions of an Untimely Man," §24, p. 82.
13. *WP*, §765, pp. 401-2. Also *TI*, "The Four Great Errors," §7, p. 53. Also *D*, §13, p. 13. See also *Z*, II, "On Redemption," p. 140.
14. See note 13 above.
15. *GS*, §125, p. 181; also see §345, p. 279.
16. See, e.g., *D*, §95, p. 54.
17. *GM*, III, §§27-28, pp. 160-62. *TI*, "Expeditions of an Untimely Man," §5, pp. 69-70. *WP*, §253, p. 147.
18. See L. Feuerbach, *The Essence of Christianity*, tr. G. Eliot (New York: Harper & Row, 1957).
19. *GS*, §109, p. 168.
20. *WP*, §569, p. 307.
21. *WP*, §§518-20, p. 281; also §489, p. 270; also §12A, pp. 12-13.
22. *WP*, §521, p. 282; see also §715, p. 380. *HAH, I*, §11, pp. 21-22; also §19, p. 30. *T&L*, §1, p. 83.
23. "The Greek State," *CWFN* (Levy), II, 8.
24. *Philosophy in the Tragic Age of the Greeks*, §5, p. 54.
25. *TI*, "'Reason' in Philosophy," §1, p. 35. *WP*, §407, p. 220; also §§517-20, pp. 280-81; also §569, pp. 306-7; also §576, p. 309.

26. *GM*, I, §13, p. 45. *TI*, "'Reason' in Philosophy," §6, p. 39; also "How the 'Real World' at last Became a Myth," pp. 40-41. *WP*, §12A, pp. 12-13; also §17, pp. 15-16; also §461, pp. 253-54; also §485, pp. 268-69.
27. *GS*, §111, pp. 171-72. *WP*, §§512-16, pp. 277-80. Also *BGE*, §4, pp. 11-12. For a lengthier discussion of Nietzsche's views on logic, see Hales and Welshon, 37-56.
28. *T&L*, §1, pp. 81-84. *HAH, I,* §11, pp. 21-22. *BGE,* §20, pp. 27-28. *TI,* "'Reason' in Philosophy," §5, pp. 37-38. *WP*, §484, p. 268; also §631, p. 336.
29. *GS*, §57, p. 121. *BGE*, §192, pp. 104-5. *TI*, "'Reason' in Philosophy," §5, pp. 37-38; also "The Four Great Errors," §4, pp. 50-51. *WP*, §481, p. 267; also §500, p. 273; also §505, pp. 274-75; also §507, pp. 275-76; also §512, p. 277; also §§515-17, pp. 278-81; also §521, pp. 282-83; also §556, pp. 301-2; also §604, p. 327; also §616, p. 330.
30. Chaos means that: (1) truth is impossible. We must simplify, reduce, distort, i.e., lie, before we can get what we *take to be* truth, logic, order, coherence. But chaos also means that: (2) existence *is* horrible and terrifying—and that is the *actual* truth. It is, however, a truth we must avoid by constructing the sort of truth discussed under (1).
31. *BGE*, §224, p. 151.
32. *BGE*, §12, p. 20; also §§16-19, pp. 23-27. *TI*, "The Four Great Errors," §3, pp. 48-50. *WP*, §§476-90, pp. 263-70; also §523, pp. 283-84. *Unpublished Writings from the Period of Unfashionable Observations*, tr. R.T. Gray, in *CWFN*, XI, 106.
33. *TI*, "'Reason' in Philosophy," §5, pp. 37-38; also "The Four Great Errors," §3, pp. 48-50. *WP*, §485, pp. 268-69; also §560, pp. 302-3; also §569, p. 307; also §635, p. 338.
34. I. Kant, *Critique of Pure Reason* (hereafter *CPR*), A97 (brackets in the original); I have used the N. Kemp Smith translation (New York: St. Martin's Press, 1965) and, for the German, *Kant's gesammelte Schriften* (hereafter *KGS*), ed. Königlich Preussischen Akademie der Wissenschaften (Berlin: Georg Reimer, 1910-55), but I cite the standard A and B edition pagination so that any editions may be used. For a very good historical discussion of what Kant means by a deduction, see D. Henrich, "Kant's Notion of a Deduction and the Methodological Background of the First *Critique*," in *Kant's Transcendental Deductions,* ed. E. Förster (Stanford, CA: Sanford University Press, 1989), 29-46. The material on Kant which follows first appeared in my *Hegel and the Other* (Albany: State University of New York Press, 2005).
35. *CPR,* A98-A100, A102, A120-A121.
36. *CPR,* A100-A101, A121.
37. *CPR,* A102.
38. *CPR,* A103.
39. *CPR,* A121.
40. *CPR,* A103, A106; also B233-A201.
41. *CPR,* A106-A107.
42. *A Treatise of Human Nature,* ed. L.A. Selby-Bigge (Oxford: Clarendon Press, 1967), Book I, Part IV, Section VI, pp. 251-63.
43. *CPR,* A106-A107.
44. *CPR,* A112, A122, B132-B133.
45. *CPR,* B131.
46. *CPR,* A112.
47. *CPR,* A105, A108, A111-A112, A125, B138-B139, B143.
48. *CPR,* A122. For a more extended discussion of Kant's influence on Nietzsche, see Green, esp. 36-57.
49. *CPR,* A98-A101, A120, A122, B134, B154, A156. See also my "Kant and the Possibility of Uncategorized Experience," *Idealistic Studies,* 19 (1989): 163, also 158-63.

Allison also makes this point; see H.E. Allison, *Kant's Transcendental Idealism: An Interpretation and Defense* (New Haven: Yale University Press, 1983), 141-42.

50. *WP*, §552c, p. 298.

51. *WP*, §483, pp. 267-68; also §487, p. 269; also §485, pp. 268-69. *CWFN*, XI, 148. Also see, J. Stambaugh, *Nietzsche's Thought of Eternal Return* (Baltimore: Johns Hopkins University Press, 1972), 74-75.

52. *WP*, §518, p. 281.

53. *WP*, §635, p. 338; also §483, pp. 267-68. Also see *BGE*, §54, p. 67.

54. *WP*, §552b, p. 297.

55. *BGE*, §11, p. 19.

56. See *CWFN*, XI, 148.

57. *U&DHL*, §1, p. 62.

58. *Treatise of Human Nature*, Book I, Part IV, Section VI, pp. 251-63.

59. See, e.g., *CPR*, A108, B133-B134.

60. *GM*, II, §§1-3, pp. 57-61.

61. *WP*, §532, p. 289; also §520, p. 281.

62. *GM*, II, §1, p. 58.

63. *WP*, §521, p. 282. "The Greek State," 8.

64. *WP*, §512, p. 277.

65. *WP*, §568, p. 306. *T&L*, §1, p. 83.

66. *WP*, §521, p. 282.

67. *BGE*, §192, p. 105. See also *TI*, "The Four Great Errors," §§4-5, pp. 50-51.

68. *U&DHL*, §1, pp. 60-61.

69. See also *WP*, §477, p. 264.

70. *CPR*, A97, A94, A116.

71. For a good discussion of these matters, see D. Owen, *Nietzsche, Politics and Modernity: A Critique of Liberal Reason* (London: Sage Publications, 1995), 21-32, esp. 27.

72. *BGE*, §17, p. 24. Also *WP*, §483, pp. 267-68.

73. *WP*, §485, pp. 268-69. See also *BGE*, §12, p. 20.

74. *WP*, §552, p. 297. See also *GM*, I, §13, p. 45.

75. *TI*, "The Four Great Errors," §3, p. 49.

76. *WP*, §490, p. 270.

77. *WP*, §481, p. 267

78. *WP*, §488, p. 270.

79. *WP*, §492, p. 271. We must also recognize, Nietzsche says, "the dependence of these regents upon the ruled" and also "an order of rank and division of labor." Moreover, the "relative ignorance in which the regent is kept concerning individual activities and even disturbances within the communality is among the conditions under which rule can be exercised. In short, we also gain a valuation of *not-knowing*, . . . of simplification and falsification . . ." (*WP*, §492, p. 271). See also *BGE*, §12, p. 20; also §19, pp. 26-27. Nietzsche here anticipates a Freudian conception of the self. For a lengthier discussion of the bundle theory of the self, see Hales and Welshon, 157-82.

80. *WP*, §480, p. 266.

81. See, e.g., *CPR*, A351ff.

82. Nietzsche's discussion of chaos and the composite self compliments and reinforces his theory of Dionysian reality. If the self is overwhelmed, if it dissolves, as we saw earlier that it does in a Dionysian experience (see Section II of Chapter 1), we can now see that it would dissolve into chaos, which, we have also seen in the present chapter, is another way of understanding the horror of existence.

So also, if will to truth drives us toward the truth, real truth, as we have earlier seen that it does (see Section IV of Chapter 2), this would mean, we now see, that we would eventually be driven to recognize that neither subject nor object are fixed and solid realities—we would be driven toward the realization that at bottom they are chaos. Subject and object, then, would begin to dissolve. Will to truth would drive us toward the *knowledge that* reality is a horrible chaos. Were we to go beyond such *knowledge that,* were we to move toward a Dionysian experience, then rational, scientific, philosophical knowledge as well as coherent experience would dissolve into a Dionysian chaos from which we might not return.

83. Magnus, *Nietzsche's Existential Imperative,* 22.

84. *WP,* §636, p. 340.

85. *WP,* §675, p. 356.

86. *WP,* §§481, 636, pp. 267, 339-40.

87. *BGE,* §21, p. 29. *GM,* I, §13, pp. 44-45. *TI,* "The Four Great Errors," §§1-4, pp. 47-51. *WP,* §531, pp. 288-89; also §§550-51, pp. 294-97; also §624, p. 334; also §631, p. 336.

88. *TI,* "Morality as Anti-Nature," §6, p. 46; also "The Four Great Errors," §8, p. 54. *WP,* §331, pp. 180-81; also §373, p. 200; also §556, pp. 301-2; also §§634-35, pp. 337-39; also §1032, p. 532. For a discussion, from the perspective of modern science, of many of these issues (though Nietzsche is never mentioned), see B. Russell, "On the Notion of Cause, with Applications to the Free-Will Problem," in *Readings in the Philosophy of Science,* ed. H. Feigl and M. Brodbeck (New York: Appleton-Century-Crofts, 1953), 387-407.

89. There is considerable disagreement as to whether will to power applies beyond the realm of human psychology to the natural world in general. Texts that suggest it does are the following. *BGE,* §36, pp. 47-48; also §259, p. 203. *Z,* II, "On Self-Overcoming," p. 114. Also *Z,* III, "On the Vision and the Riddle," §2, pp. 157-59. *GM,* II, §12, pp. 77-78. *WP,* §619, pp. 332-33; also §675, p. 356; also §704, pp. 374-75. Kaufmann thinks that the projection of will to power beyond the human sphere to the cosmos is an afterthought on Nietzsche's part unsubstantiated by the evidence and at variance with Nietzsche's own critical principles; see Kaufmann, *Nietzsche: Philosopher, Psychologist, Antichrist,* 420. Clark thinks Nietzsche's concern is the human world, not the cosmos; see Clark, 209-10. Magnus thinks there is little evidence for extending will to power to cosmology; see B. Magnus, "The Use and Abuse of *The Will to Power,"* in *Reading Nietzsche,* 226-27. On the other hand, see M. Haar, "Heidegger and the Nietzschean 'Physiology of Art,'" in *Exceedingly Nietzsche: Aspects of Contemporary Nietzsche-Interpretation,* ed. D.F. Krell and D. Wood (London: Routledge, 1988), 26.

90. *BGE,* §13, p. 21. *GM,* III, §7, pp. 107-8. *WP,* §46, pp. 28-29; also §633, p. 337; also §636, pp. 339-40.

91. *D,* §109, p. 65. See also *BGE,* §6, p. 13.

92. *GS,* §354, p. 299. See also *BGE,* §3, p. 11; also §32, p. 44. Also *WP,* §478, p. 265; also §523, p. 283.

93. *BGE,* §51, p. 65; also §61, pp. 72-73; also §§188-89, pp. 100-102; also §225, pp. 153-55; also §227, p. 155. *GM,* II, §§16-17, pp. 84-87; also III, §1, p. 97; also §7, pp. 107-8; also §16, pp. 128-29; also §§27-28, pp. 159-62. *TI,* "Morality as Anti-Nature," §3, pp. 43-44. Ahern is very good on this matter; see *Nietzsche as Cultural Physician.*

94. See, e.g., *BGE,* §259, p. 203. Clark and Schutte go too far, in my opinion, in suggesting that domination has little or nothing to do with will to power. See Clark, 211. Schutte, 78.

95. See, e.g., *WP,* §619, p. 333; also §776, p. 407.

96. *BGE*, §259, p. 203; see also §9, pp. 15-16. Also *WP*, §617, p. 330.

97. *GM*, II, §12, p. 77.

98. *WP*, §534, p. 290; see also §455, p. 249.

99. *WP*, §533, p. 290.

100. *WP*, §480, pp. 266-67.

101. *WP*, §497, p. 273. See also *BGE,* §4, pp. 11-12.

102. *BGE*, §4, pp. 11-12.

103. See also M. Haar, *Nietzsche and Metaphysics,* tr. M. Gendre (Albany: State University of New York Press, 1996), 121-22.

104. *GM*, II, §12, p. 77.

105. *WP*, §481, p. 267.

106. Here I prefer Golffing's translation, see the *Genealogy of Morals*, in *The Birth of Tragedy and The Genealogy of Morals,* III, §12, p. 255.

107. *BGE*, §287, p. 228.

108. *WP*, §556, pp. 301-2.

109. *WP*, §600, p. 326. In the *Genealogy of Morals,* Nietzsche says something just a bit different: "There is *only* a perspective seeing, *only* a perspective 'knowing'; and the *more* affects we allow to speak about one thing, the *more* eyes, different eyes, we can use to observe one thing, the more complete will our 'concept' of this thing, our 'objectivity,' be" (*GM*, III, §12, p. 119). This passage says the more perspectives the better. It does not say, I do not think, the more perspectives we have the more *truth* we get. Moreover, in this passage Nietzsche could well be talking about what we *take to be true,* illusions necessary to hide the real truth—the horror of existence. Thus, the more perspectives, the more 'objectivity' we would have—an 'objectivity' which of course would be a lie. And, indeed, the more 'objectivity' we have, the more convergence of perspectives we have, the better we will be able to hide the horror of existence—the truth.

110. *GS*, §374, p. 336.

111. *BGE*, §22, pp. 30-31.

112. R.C. Solomon, *Living With Nietzsche: What the Great "Immoralist" Has to Teach Us* (Oxford: Oxford University Press, 2003), 38.

113. See Section IV of Chapter 2.

114. See Section II of Chapter 1.

115. *BGE*, §38, p. 49.

116. Ahern, 4.

117. Nehamas, *Nietzsche: Life as Literature,* 72.

118. *WP*, §563, p. 304.

Notes to Chapter Four

1. Here I prefer Smith's translation, see *GM* (Smith), III, §27, pp. 134-35.
2. *GM*, III, §28, p. 162.
3. *WP*, §1, p. 7.
4. *WP*, §§2-3, p. 9.
5. *WP*, §7, pp. 10-11.
6. *WP*, §12A, p. 12; see also §12B, pp. 13-14.
7. *GM*, II, §24, p. 96. This passage suggests that Nietzsche himself is not the *Über-mensch*. Or at least it suggests that Nietzsche is not *yet* the *Übermensch*. It does leave open the possibility that Nietzsche might some day become the *Übermensch* (also see note 35 of Chapter 7).
8. *BGE*, §211, p. 136.
9. *Schopenhauer as Educator*, §8, pp. 188-89. See also "The Philosopher: Reflections on the Struggle Between Art and Knowledge," §44, pp. 14-15.
10. *BGE*, §203, p. 117.
11. I intentionally do not use the term 'great person.' Given what Nietzsche has to say about women, I do not think it should be suggested that he could believe in a 'great woman.' For the same reason I will not use gender neutral language when referring to the *Übermensch*.
12. *U&DHL*, §9, p. 111; see also §2, p. 68.
13. *BGE*, §126, p. 87.
14. The term first appears in *GS*, §143, p. 191.
15. It does appear at *GM*, I, §16, p. 54. Also *TI*, "Expeditions of an Untimely Man," §37, p. 89. Also *AC*, §4, p. 116. Also *EH*, "Why I Write Such Good Books," §1, p. 261; also "Thus Spoke Zarathustra," §6, p. 305; also "Why I Am a Destiny," §5, p. 331.
16. *GM*, III, §10, p. 115. See also *D*, §113, pp. 113-14. The *death of God* is not something that happens merely once. Any *Übermensch* overthrows the old gods and creates a new heaven.
17. *Z*, "Prologue," §3, p. 13.
18. B. Magnus, "Jesus, Christianity, and Superhumanity," in *Studies in Nietzsche and the Judaeo-Christian Tradition*, ed. J.C. O'Flaherty, T.F. Sellner, and R.M. Helm (Chapel Hill: University of North Carolina Press, 1985), 312-13.
19. *WP*, §999, p. 519; see also §§997, 998, pp. 518-19.
20. *GS*, §341, pp. 273-74. See also *Z*, III, "On the Vision and the Riddle," §2, pp. 157-59; also "The Convalescent," §§1-2, pp. 215-21. *WP*, §§1057-67, pp. 544-50. *NW*, XII, §§90-132, pp. 51-69. *NWKG*, V 2, pp. 421, 432-33. In the early writings, Nietzsche several times formulated or came close to formulating the doctrine of eternal recurrence, but did not embrace it. See *U&DHL*, §1, p. 65; also §2, p. 70. *Schopenhauer as Educator*, §1, p. 127. See also *D*, §124, p. 77. For a discussion of earlier approximations to the doctrine of eternal recurrence in the history of philosophy, see Magnus, *Nietzsche's Existential Imperative*, 47-68. For a good discussion of Nietzsche's proofs for eternal recurrence, see Kaufmann, *Nietzsche: Philosopher, Psychologist, Antichrist*, pp. 326 ff.
21. *EH*, "Why I Am So Clever," §10, p. 258. See also *GS*, §276, p. 223.

22. *Z*, II, "On Redemption," p. 139. See also *Z*, III, "On Old and New Tablets," §3, p. 198.

23. *Z*, IV, "The Drunken Song," §1, p. 318.

24. *TI*, "The Four Great Errors," §8, p. 54.

25. See Section VII of Chapter 3.

26. *HAH, I*, §106, p. 82. *WP*, §1064, p. 547; also §1066, p. 549.

27. *Z*, III, "The Convalescent," §2, p. 220.

28. Magnus, *Nietzsche's Existential Imperative*, 67-68, 103-10. Also, Magnus, "Asceticism and Eternal Recurrence: A Bridge Too Far," *Southern Journal of Philosophy*, 37, Supplement (1999): 100.

29. Stambaugh, *Nietzsche's Thought of Eternal Return*, 31.

30. I. Soll, "Reflections on Recurrence: A Re-Examination of Nietzsche's Doctrine, *die Ewige Wiederkehr des Gleichen,*" in *Nietzsche: A Collection of Critical Essays*, 335, 339-40. See also Solomon, *Living With Nietzsche*, 202.

31. Also, if one believes in anything like a Christian afterlife, eternal recurrence would hardly be a matter of indifference. If eternal recurrence were true, the Christian would be deprived of an afterlife that made any sense—at the very least it would have to be interrupted eternally, each time one had to relive one's earthly life.

32. *Z*, III, "On the Vision and the Riddle," §2, pp. 158-59; also IV, "The Ugliest Man," p. 263. For a very interesting development of this view, see P.S. Loeb, "Time, Power, and Superhumanity," *Journal of Nietzsche Studies*, 21 (2001): 27-47.

33. G. Braddock seems to assume this in "Personal Identity, Determinism, and the Eternal Recurrence," *Eidos*, 14 (1997): 35.

34. *Z*, III, "On the Vision and the Riddle," §2, pp. 157-58. *WP*, §1066, p. 548. For a very interesting amplification of this whole point, see P.S. Loeb, "Identity and Eternal Recurrence," in *A Companion to Nietzsche*, ed. K. Ansell Pearson (Blackwell), 171-88.

35. Soll, "Reflections on Recurrence," 340.

36. *WP*, §55. p. 36.

37. *WP*, §1057, pp. 544-55; also §1062, pp. 546-47; also §1064, p. 547; also §§1066-67, pp. 548-50. *NW*, XII, §§90-114, pp. 51-63. *NWKG*, V 2, pp. 421, 432-33.

38. Salomé, 131.

39. Danto, *Nietzsche as Philosopher*, 203-13. Magnus, *Nietzsche's Existential Imperative*, 74-117. M.C. Sterling, "Recent Discussions of Eternal Recurrence: Some Critical Comments," in *Nietzsche-Studien* (Berlin: de Gruyter, 1977), VI, 261-68. For another defense, see J.H. Combee, "Nietzsche as Cosmologist," *Interpretation*, 4 (1974): 38-47.

40. *BGE*, §14, pp. 21-22; also §24, p. 35. *GS*, §344, pp. 280-83; also §373, pp. 334-36. *GM*, III, §§23-25, pp. 145-56. *WP*, §516, pp. 279-80; also §521, pp. 282-83; also §555, p. 301; also §606, p. 327.

41. *WP*, §853, pp. 451-52.

42. D. Wood, "Nietzsche's Transvaluation of Time," in *Exceedingly Nietzsche*, 38-39. Stack argues that Nietzsche subscribes to Lange's view of science as hypothetical or fictive, such that scientific views would be quite compatible with the claim that all is interpretation; see Stack, esp. 240, 248.

43. *WP*, §1066, pp. 548-49. Stack argues that Nietzsche's concept of force comes from Boscovich and Lange; see Stack, 224-61.

44. *WP*, §1066, pp. 548-49. A. Zuboff, "Nietzsche and Eternal Recurrence," in *Nietzsche: A Collection of Critical Essays*, 350-52. J. Krueger, "Nietzschean Recurrence as a Cosmological Hypothesis," *Journal of the History of Philosophy*, 16 (1978): 442-43.

45. Sterling, 279-81.

46. See also Section II of Chapter 5 which will reinforce this latter point.

47. *NWKG*, V 2, pp. 421-22.

48. Soll, "Reflections on Recurrence," 322-25. Magnus, *Nietzsche's Existential Imperative*, 116-17. Nehamas, *Nietzsche: Life as Literature*, 142ff., 146ff. Clark, 246ff. L.J. Hatab, *Nietzsche and Eternal Recurrence: The Redemption of Time and Becoming* (Washington, DC: University Press of America, 1978), 93-94.

49. Salomé, 133.

50. *Z*, IV, "The Drunken Song," §10, p. 323.

51. *WP*, §1032, p. 532.

52. B. Magnus, "Jesus, Christianity, and Superhumanity," 317-18.

53. *EH*, "Why I Am So Clever," §10, p. 258 (the last emphasis is in the text, the rest are mine).

54. *EH*, "The Birth of Tragedy," §2, p. 272.

55. See *BGE*, §39, p. 49. See also *EH*, "Preface," §3, p. 218. Also *WP*, §1041, p. 536.

56. It "impose[s] upon becoming the character of being . . ." (*WP*, §617, p. 330).

57. See also M. Haar, *Nietzsche and Metaphysics*, 121-22.

58. Shapiro thinks eternal recurrence entails a radical dissolution of selfhood. I think that is only one side of the story. See G. Shapiro, *Nietzschean Narratives* (Bloomington: Indiana University Press, 1989), 86. As Wood points out, "identity is not a fixed point we need to presuppose for differences to be possible; matters are rather the other way around. The possibility that a thing can appear again and again at different times is what *gives it* an identity; it is not dependent on it having a prior atemporal identity"; see D. Wood, "Nietzsche's Transvaluation of Time," 54-55.

Notes to Chapter Five

1. *WP*, §55, p. 35.

2. Even Reginster, who pays more attention to suffering than do other commentators, does not emphasize this point in his chapter on Eternal Recurrence; see Reginster, 201-27. Brodsky, however, comes close; see G.M. Brodsky, "Nietzsche's Notion of *Amor Fati*," *Continental Philosophy Review*, 31 (1998): 35-57. Also see McCarthy, 198-99. In many ways, my views overlap with those of McCarthy.

3. Salomé, 130. It is quite clear that Nietzsche wavered on eternal recurrence; see Salomé, 133 (this passage is quoted in Section II of Chapter 4). At times Nietzsche even said: "I do not wish for life again" (*NWKG*, VII I, p. 139).

4. See Kaufmann's Preface and Notes to *Z*, pp. xiii-xiv, 4-5.

5. *BGE*, §157, p. 91. Nietzsche to Overbeck on 11 February 1883, also on 24 March 1883, in *Selected Letters of Friedrich Nietzsche*, 206, 210.

6. In the *Nachlass*, Nietzsche writes: "Just ask yourself, . . . David Hume demands of us, . . . or all of your acquaintances whether they would like to relive the last ten or twenty years of their lives. No! But the next twenty will be better, they will say . . . " (*CWFN*, XI, 288).

7. If one has experienced a grand moment, a peak experience, I can well imagine wanting to relive moments *like* that moment. I can even imagine someone wanting to eternally relive a series of *different* moments each *like* that grand moment. What I cannot imagine is someone desiring to relive the very *same* moment over and over again an infinite number of times. The prospect of such eternal repetition, if the idea grew upon you and gained possession of you, would sap *any* moment of its appeal. Even if you would not remember earlier repetitions of this moment, even if you would not realize it was a repetition, even if you experienced the moment afresh in each cycle, nevertheless, right now, in your present life, if the idea of repeating this grand moment grew upon you and gained possession of you, it would sap that moment of its freshness, sap it of its grandness, it would lessen and demean it.

8. See, e.g., Hatab, 114. This also seems to be Schopenhauer's view; *WW&R*, I, §54, pp. 283ff.

9. F. Schiller, "Concerning the Sublime," in *Friedrich Schiller: Essays*, 70-72. Nietzsche makes a similar point himself: "In a certain state it is indecent to go on living. To vegetate on in cowardly dependence on physicians and medicaments after the meaning of life, the *right* to life, has been lost ought to entail the profound contempt of society. . . . Death of one's own free choice, death at the proper time, with a clear head and with joyfulness . . . in contrast to the pitiable and horrible comedy Christianity has made of the hour of death. . . . '[N]atural' death is death for the most contemptible reasons, an unfree death, a death at the *wrong* time, a coward's death. From love of *life* one ought to desire to die differently from this: freely, consciously, not accidentally, not suddenly overtaken. . . . We have no power to prevent ourselves being born: but we can rectify this error—for it is sometimes an error. When one *does away with* oneself one does the most estimable thing possible; one thereby almost deserves to live . . . " (*TI*, "Expeditions of an Untimely Man," §36, pp. 88-89). Nietzsche's sister tells us that even as a schoolboy at Pforta Nietzsche once, without flinching, burned his own hand; see Frau

Förster-Nietzsche, *The Young Nietzsche,* tr. A.M. Ludovici (London: William Heinemann, 1912), 81.

    10. *Z,* IV, "The Drunken Song," §1, p. 318.

    11. *WP,* §382, p. 206. See also *BGE,* §225, p. 153. *GM,* III, §9, p. 114.

    12. *TI,* "Maxims and Arrows," §8. p. 23.

    13. *WP,* §910, p. 481.

    14. See, e.g., *GM,* II, §11, p. 76. Also *WP,* §1030, p. 532.

    15. *WP,* §1041, p. 536. See also *BGE,* §39, p. 49. *AC,* §50, p. 167.

    16. Nietzsche says: "Never have I felt happier with myself than in the sickest and most painful periods of my life . . . " (*EH,* "Human, All-To-Human," §4, p. 288).

    17. *GM,* III, §10, p. 115.

    18. B. Magnus, "Jesus, Christianity, and Superhumanity," 317-18.

    19. *Z,* IV, "The Drunken Song," §10, p. 323. *WP,* §1032, p. 532.

    20. *EH,* "Why I Am So Clever," §10, p. 258 (the last italics are in the text, the rest are mine).

    21. *EH,* "The Birth of Tragedy," §2, p. 272 (my italics).

    22. One great moment may be enough to get you interested in, and excited by, eternal recurrence, but then, as Nietzsche says, the thought has to "[gain] possession of you." I suggest that for it to gain possession of you you must come to love every moment of your life or eternal recurrence will crush you; see *GS,* §341, pp. 273-74. However, see *Z,* IV, "The Drunken Song," §10, p. 323. Also see note 7 above.

    23. *EH,* "Why I Am So Wise," §6, p. 231. Clark objects to Sartre's claim "that Nietzsche needed the dogma . . . of eternal recurrence to try to cope with his unacceptable present, that it justified his pretense that he was the 'legislator of a pre-established order' and thus that he actually willed the misery of his own life." (Clark, 259n. Also J-P. Sartre, *Saint Genet: Actor and Martyr,* tr. B. Frechtman [NY: Braziller, 1963], 346ff.) Sartre's reading here is very close to my own and I think he is quite correct. Clark, however, dismisses Sartre on the grounds that for Nietzsche eternal recurrence is true, thus that Nietzsche was forced to undergo it, and that he was not the creator of it (Clark, 259n). I think that is completely beside the point. *Amor fati* requires Nietzsche to turn all "it was" into a *"thus I willed it."* It does not matter whether eternal recurrence is true or false, whether Nietzsche was forced to undergo it or not, or whether he created it or discovered it. He *himself* must will it, love it—and if he does so it is capable of transforming the misery of his life.

    24. As I said above in note 7 of this chapter, I can imagine someone wanting to eternally relive a series of *different* moments each *like* a great moment, but I cannot imagine someone desiring to relive the very *same* moment over and over again an infinite number of times.

    25. Nietzsche writes in the *Nachlass:* "Human beings of greater profundity have always felt compassion with animals precisely because they suffer from life and yet do not possess the strength to turn the sting of suffering against themselves and understand their existence metaphysically; and the sight of senseless suffering arouses profound indignation" (*CWFN,* XI, 373).

    26. *GM,* III, §10, p. 115.

    27. *AC,* §23, p. 132.

    28. *D,* §13, p. 13.

    29. *WP,* §55, p. 35.

    30. See, e.g., *BGE,* §39, p. 49; also §225, pp. 153-54. *WP,* §585A, p. 318.

    31. *TI,* "The Four Great Errors," §8, p. 54. *HAH, I,* §99, pp. 75-76.

    32. *GM,* III, §28, p. 162.

33. *BGE*, §56, p. 68.

34. See *EH*, "The Birth of Tragedy," §3, p. 273. Also *GS*, §12, p. 85; also §45, p. 110. Also see Section V of Chapter 5.

35. *BT*, §21, pp. 127-28.

36. Eternal recurrence itself does not entail that it is impossible in the present cycle to do something about reducing suffering, but eternal recurrence does entail that in the next cycle, as for Sisyphus, all would be undone and we would start over again from scratch.

37. *GM*, III, §20, p. 141. As Reginster puts it, we must see not merely the necessity of suffering, but its desirability; Reginster 230-31, 234.

38. *GM*, III, §10, p. 115.

39. *GS*, §338, p. 269. *D*, §135, p. 86.

40. See, e.g., *Z*, IV, "The Ugliest Man," pp. 264-65.

41. Nietzsche might well have had such treatment in mind when (in the revised text of *Ecce Homo*, deleted by his mother and sister) he says: "Wherever I search for my profoundest opposite, to wit, incalculable vulgarity of instinct, I always find my mother and sister—if I thought I were actually related to such canaille it would be a veritable blasphemy against my divinity. The treatment I have always received from my mother and sister—up to the present moment—fills me with unutterable horror: here a highly perfected, infernal machine is at work, one that operates with unfailing accuracy at the very moment when I am most vulnerable and most likely to bleed—during my supreme moments . . . for in these one lacks all the energy that would be needed to defend oneself against venomous vipers. . . . But I confess that the most profound objection to the eternal return, that is, to my properly *abyssal* thought, is always mother and sister." Quoted from D.F. Krell, "Consultations with the Paternal Shadow: Gashé, Derrida and Klossowski on *Ecce Homo*," in *Exceedingly Nietzsche*, 83-84; for the German see *NWKG*, VI 3, p. 266.

42. *WP*, §910, p. 481.

43. S. Kierkegaard, *Fear and Trembling*, in *Fear and Trembling and The Sickness unto Death*, tr. W. Lowrie (Garden City, NY: Doubleday, 1954), 26-64, esp. 46.

44. *Fear and Trembling*, 64-77.

45. Many commentators reject the notion that Nietzsche holds eternal recurrence as a cosmological doctrine, that is, that he takes it to be true cosmologically (see, e.g., Nehamas, *Nietzsche: Life as Literature*, 142, 146ff.). Instead, what is important is the effect it has on those who accept it or the life-affirming attitude that follows from it (Soll, "Reflections on Recurrence," 322-26. Magnus, *Nietzsche's Existential Imperative*, 111-54. Clark, 246ff.). I agree that Nietzsche does not hold to eternal recurrence as a cosmological truth and I agree that its importance is in the effect it has on those who can embrace it, but I think that its effect is expected to be more than the generation of an attitude. I think it is expected to produce a real power in those who accept it—see Section I of Chapter 4.

46. B. Magnus, "The Deification of the Commonplace: *Twilight of the Idols*," in *Reading Nietzsche*, ed. R.C. Solomon and K.M. Higgins (New York: Oxford University Press, 1988), 171ff. Clark, 279. Owen, 111.

47. Clark, 279.

48. *GM*, I, §10, p. 39.

49. *GS*, §325, p. 255.

50. *WP*, §910, p. 481.

51. *WP*, §382, p. 206.

52. *BGE*, §251, pp. 187-88. Also *HAH*, I, §475, p. 258. Also *D*, §205, pp. 124-25.

53. Magnus, "Asceticism and Eternal Recurrence," 107.

54. This point was made by an anonymous referee.

55. See also note 3 above. See also Magnus, who argues in "Asceticism and Eternal Recurrence" that after the holocaust accepting eternal recurrence is both impossible *and* a necessity (see esp. 108).

56. *GS*, §337, p. 268.

57. E.g., *EH*, "The Birth of Tragedy," §3, p. 273. *WP*, §1030, p. 532.

58. This is like the joy of childbirth, a joy that also does not eliminate the pain. You feel the pain and you experience joy. See *TI*, "What I Owe to the Ancients," §4, p. 110.

59. *BGE*, §44, p. 54.

60. This question is raised and rejected by Kaufmann, Löwith, Magnus, Hatab, and Braddock. See Kaufmann, 322-25. K. Löwith, *Nietzsche's Philosophy of the Eternal Recurrence of the Same*, tr. J.H. Lomax (Berkeley: University of California Press, 1997), 88. Magnus, *Nietzsche's Existential Imperative*, 57, 73, 111-13, 139-40. Hatab, 111. G. Braddock, 45-46. Jaspers argues that eternal recurrence is like an ethical imperative; see K. Jaspers, *Nietzsche: An Introduction to the Understanding of His Philosophical Activity*, tr. C.F. Wallraff and F.J. Schmitz (Tucson: University of Arizona Press, 1966), 359ff. Ansell-Pearson argues that eternal recurrence represents a version of the categorical imperative; see K. Ansell-Pearson, *Nietzsche Contra Rousseau: A Study of Nietzsche's Moral and Political Thought* (Cambridge: Cambridge University Press, 1991), 183, 194-99. Also see G. Deleuze, *Nietzsche and Philosophy*, tr. H. Tomlinson (New York: Columbia University Press, 1983), 68ff.

61. *NWKG*, V 2, p. 403; quoted in Magnus, *The Existential Imperative*, 73.

62. *TI*, "Morality as Anti-Nature," §6, p. 46.

63. B. Magnus, Foreword to K. Löwith, *Nietzsche's Philosophy of the Eternal Recurrence of the Same*, xv. Also see Löwith, 88. Also Magnus, *The Existential Imperative*, 73, 111-13. Also B. Magnus, "Eternal Recurrence," in *Nietzsche-Studien*, VIII (1979), 363ff.

64. See Ansell-Pearson, *Nietzsche Contra Rousseau*, 97. Also see Jaspers, 359ff. Also Deleuze, 48.

65. E.g., *Z*, "The Convalescent," §2, p. 221.

66. *GS*, §341, p. 274.

67. On the other hand, this attitude would still have to be found in all our other lives. There can be no difference between cycles without contradicting the notion of eternal recurrence of the *same*.

68. *Z*, III, "On Old and New Tablets," §9, p. 201.

69. Even for Kant himself, there is an analogy between the categorical imperative and the laws of nature: "The universality of law according to which effects are produced constitutes what is properly called nature in the most general sense. . . . [By analogy], then, the universal imperative of duty can be expressed as follows: Act as though the maxim of your action were by your will to become a universal law of nature." Furthermore: "A realm of ends is thus possible only by analogy with a realm of nature. The former, however, is possible only by maxims, i.e., self-imposed rules, while the latter is possible by laws of efficient causes of things externally necessitated." See *Foundations of the Metaphysics of Morals*, tr. L.W. Beck (Indianapolis: Bobbs-Merrill, 1959), 39, 57 (brackets in the text); for the German, see *KGS*, IV, 421, 438. So also we could say that for Nietzsche too there would be an analogy between a deterministic and externally necessitated realm of nature and the self imposed "thus I willed it" of loving one's fate. Certainly, Nietzsche could endorse completely and without reservation the Kantian imperative to: 'Act as though the maxim of your action were by your will to become a universal law of nature'—indeed, he could even add: 'it will anyway.'

70. See F.A. Olafsen, "Nietzsche, Kant, and Existentialism," in *Nietzsche: A Collection of Critical Essays*, 200.

71. *Foundations*, 16-18 and *KGS*, IV, 400-401. Even if one were to try to argue that the Kantian moral law could engender *amor fati*, a Kantian would certainly have to hold that the love involved could not be a pathological love, but must be rational love. One would have to love one's life out of duty, not because one were inclined to love it. But it would not be enough, for Nietzsche, to say that I am willing to live my life again, not because I am inclined to, but because it is my duty, because it can be universalized, because it follows from the categorical imperative. That is not loving one's life. That will not turn a thus "it was" into a real "thus I willed it." That will not break the stranglehold that your suffering has over you. You must love it completely—pathologically.

72. Virgil, *Aeneid*, Book VI.

73. Kant's categorical imperative would imply that at least some acts in one's life would have to be changed if one were to will to live one's life over again *and* be moral in doing so. It would not be possible, in Kant's view, that every act in one's past life was moral; see, e.g., *Foundations*, 23-24 and *KGS*, IV, 406-8. Also *Critique of Practical Reason*, tr. L.W. Beck (Indianapolis: Bobbs-Merrill, 1956), 33, 133 and *KGS*, V, 32-33, 128. Kant's categorical imperative, in this sense also, would not be compatible with eternal recurrence of the same.

74. Kant, *Foundations*, 53-54, 56 and *KGS*, IV, 434-36, 438.

75. *WP*, §765, pp. 401-2. Also *TI*, "The Four Great Errors," §7, p. 53. Also *D*, §13, p. i3.

76. *TI*, "The Four Great Errors," §8, p. 54.

77. Nietzsche writes, "to recreate all 'it was' into a 'thus I willed it'—that alone should I call redemption" (*Z*, II, "On Redemption," p. 139).

78. *D*, §13, p. 13.

79. *WP*, §585A, p. 316.

80. *WP*, §12A, p. 13.

81. *TI*, "How the 'Real World' at last Became a Myth," pp. 40-41.

82. *EH*, "Why I Am a Destiny," §8, p. 334.

83. *WP*, §136, p. 87.

84. *WP*, §583B, p. 314.

85. *WP*, p. 85.

86. Nietzsche thinks that atheism will bring a decrease in guilt and give rise to "a kind of *second innocence*" (*GM*, II, §20, pp. 90-91). Freud certainly would not agree. One might even imagine that his *Civilization and Its Discontents* was written against such a position; see S. Freud, *Civilization and Its Discontents*, tr. J. Strachey (New York: Norton, 1961).

87. See Haar, *Nietzsche and Metaphysics*, 29.

88. Richardson, 159.

89. *WP*, §708, p. 377.

90. Y. Yovel, "Nietzsche and Spinoza: *amor fati* and *amor dei*," in *Nietzsche as Affirmative Thinker*, ed. Y. Yovel (Dordrecht: Martinus Nijhoff, 1986), 198.

91. Magnus, *Nietzsche's Existential Imperative*, 62.

92. See K. Higgins, "Reading Zarathustra," in *Reading Nietzsche*, 145. Also D. Wood, "Nietzsche's Transvaluation of Time," in *Exceedingly Nietzsche*, 40.

Notes to Chapter Six

1. E.g., see Magnus, *Nietzsche's Existential Imperative*, 32. Schacht is an exception here; he does not think that the *Übermensch* simply grows out of master morality; Schacht, 466.

2. Nehamas, *Nietzsche: Life as Literature*, 206. Deleuze, 10. Danto, *Nietzsche as Philosopher*, 158-60, 166. Lukács, 351. Also see Schutte, 108. R. Solomon, "Nietzsche *ad hominem:* Perspectivism, personality, and *ressentiment*," in *Cambridge Companion to Nietzsche*, 204, but also see 214. On the other hand, Kaufmann does not think that Nietzsche necessarily identifies with the master; Kaufmann, *Nietzsche: Philosopher, Psychologist, Antichrist*, 297.

3. Deleuze, 10, 156, 195. Also M. Foucault, "Nietzsche, Genealogy, History," in *Language, Counter-Memory, Practice*, ed. D.F. Bouchard (Ithaca, NY: Cornell University Press, 1977), 151-54. M. Greene, "Hegel's 'Unhappy Consciousness' and Nietzsche's 'Slave Morality,'" in *Hegel and the Philosophy of Religion*, ed. D.E. Christensen (The Hague: Martinus Nijhoff, 1970), 125-41. S. Houlgate, *Hegel, Nietzsche and the Criticism of Metaphysics* (Cambridge: Cambridge University Press, 1986), 19-20. However, Schacht thinks that Nietzsche holds a revised view of Hegelian development; Schacht, 395. For a good review of the literature on the relationship of Hegel to Nietzsche, though for the most part dealing with issues other than those that I will treat, see D. Breazeale, "The Hegel-Nietzsche Problem," in *Nietzsche-Studien*, IV (1975), 146-58.

4. This was not even Nietzsche's own view of the origin of morality in earlier writings. See *HAH, I*, §39, pp. 47-48; also §94, pp. 71-72. *BGE*, §32, pp. 43-44. See also Salomé, 110, also 63.

5. *GM*, I, §2, pp. 25-26; also §5, p. 29; also §10, p. 36.

6. *GM*, I, §2, p. 26.

7. *GM*, I, §4, pp. 27-28.

8. *GM*, I, §10, pp. 36-37.

9. E.g., *GM*, I, §16, pp. 53-54.

10. *Phenomenology of Spirit*, tr. A.V. Miller (Oxford: Clarendon Press, 1977), 114-16. I think it inappropriate, when referring to the master and the slave, to try to replace Hegel's language with gender neutral language. While the master-slave dialectic can have implications for both genders, nevertheless, the master and the slave, it seems to me, are basically masculine in the way they have been conceived by Hegel.

11. *Phenomenology*, 116-17.

12. *Phenomenology*, 118-19.

13. *Philosophy of History*, ed. J. Sibree (New York: Dover, 1956), 407.

14. *Philosophy of Right*, tr. T.M. Knox (Oxford: Clarendon Press, 1952), 125.

15. *Phenomenology*, 138. Also Greene, 137.

16. *GM*, I, §2, p. 26.

17. *GM*, II, §12, p. 77.

18. *GM*, II, §13, p. 80.

19. *GM*, II, §13, pp. 80-81.

20. Deleuze, 3-4.

21. G. Shapiro, "Translating, Repeating, Naming: Foucault, Derrida, and the *Genealogy of Morals,"* in *Nietzsche as Postmodernist,* ed. C. Koelb (Albany: State University of New York Press, 1990), 39.

22. *GS,* §335, p. 264.

23. *U&DHL,* §8, pp. 104-5. See also *BGE,* §207, p. 128.

24. Here I prefer Collins' translation; see *The Use and Abuse of History,* tr. A. Collins (Indianapolis: Bobbs-Merrill, 1957), §VI, p. 40.

25. *Use and Abuse of History,* §VI, p. 40.

26. *GM,* I, §6, p. 33. Also *WP,* §864, p. 460.

27. *GM,* I, §7, p. 33.

28. *GM,* I, §10, p. 37.

29. *GM,* I, §10, p. 38. See also *TI,* "Expeditions of an Untimely Man," §14, p. 76.

30. *GM,* I, §9, p. 36.

31. *GM,* II, §1, pp. 57-58. See Section V of Chapter 3.

32. *U&DHL,* §1, p. 62; see also pp. 60-64.

33. *GM,* II, §3, p. 61.

34. Deleuze, 114-15. A.C. Danto, "Some Remarks on *The Genealogy of Morals,"* in *Reading Nietzsche,* 17, 26. M. Warren, *Nietzsche and Political Thought* (Cambridge, MA: MIT Press, 1988), 23.

35. *GM,* II, §2, pp. 58-60.

36. *GM,* I, §5, p. 29. Also *BGE,* §260, p. 205.

37. *GM,* I, §11, p. 40.

38. *GM,* II, §16, pp. 84-85.

39. *GM,* II, §11, p. 76.

40. *BGE,* §225, p. 154. Also *WP,* §382, p. 206.

41. *GM,* II, §10, p. 73.

42. *GM,* III, §4, p. 101.

43. *GM,* III, §10, p. 115. *GS,* §338, p. 269. Also *WP,* §1030, p. 532. See Section I of Chapter 4.

44. *CWFN,* XI, 294.

45. Danto thinks that in discussing slave morality, Nietzsche had in mind the Aristotelian notion of natural slaves (Danto, *Nietzsche as Philosopher,* 156). I think Nietzsche had in mind the Hegelian notion of the slave who subverts the master.

46. *BGE,* §188, p. 101.

47. Richardson (138) thinks the *Übermensch* is a synthesis of master and slave.

48. *GM,* I, §2, p. 26.

49. Though Nietzsche would insist on a more radical break than Hegel has between the Homeric-Greek and the Judeo-Christian eras—between master morality and slave morality.

50. Foucault, "Nietzsche, Genealogy, History," 154.

51. Even Homer had to overthrow the empire of the Titans to build the Apollonian-Olympian realm of the masters (*BT,* §3, p. 43).

52. *GM,* I, §7, p. 34. Christianity, too, promised a revaluation of all values; see *BGE,* §46, p. 60. *WP,* §4, pp. 9-10.

53. *BGE,* §195, p. 108.

54. Deleuze seems to suggest that a reactive force can only become active as a kind of baseness, meanness, stupidity; see Deleuze, 66. This hardly fits Vishvamitra. And Nietzsche admits that *ressentiment* is not impossible for the noble man; *GM,* I, §10, p. 39.

55. *GM,* I, §10, p. 36. Also see Solomon, *Living With Nietzsche,* 103.

56. *GM,* II, §14, pp. 81-82.

57. *GM,* II, §16, pp. 84-85.
58. *GM,* III, §20, p. 140.
59. *GM,* II, §22, p. 92.
60. *GM,* II, §17, p. 87. See also *BGE,* §§257-58, pp. 201-2.
61. *GM,* III, §16, p. 128.
62. *GM,* II, §18, p. 87.
63. *GM,* II, §18, pp. 87-88.
64. *HAH, I,* §233; also §231, p. 159.
65. *GM,* III, §7, pp. 107-8.
66. *GM,* I, §5, p. 29.
67. *GM,* III, §10, p. 115.
68. "Jesus, Christianity, and Superhumanity," 306.
69. *GM,* III, §4, p. 101.
70. *GM,* III, §28, p. 162.
71. *GM,* III, §11, p. 117; also §13, p. 120. See also *BGE,* §51, p. 65. The standard notion, found all too frequently among Nietzsche scholars, of dividing moralities into those that promote life, are natural, instinctual, healthy, on the one hand, and those that are hostile to life, anti-natural, anti-instinctual, on the other, is over-simplified. It overlooks the horror of existence and the fact that to affirm life requires concealing the horror of existence. Once we realize this, we cannot help but see that Christianity, supposedly the quintessence of hostility to life, to the natural, and to the instinctual, did a perfectly adequate job for more than a millennium of concealing the horror of existence and thus making life possible. So also to see master morality as simply and straightforwardly natural, instinctual, earthly, and healthy is to see only surface appearance. Master morality is deceptive. It presents itself, it expresses itself, it sums itself up, in the figure of an Achilles. But we know that it takes a Homer to create an Achilles (*GM,* III, §4, p. 101)—poor, blind Homer. To think that master morality, the Homeric heroes, are simply natural is to fail to see that they are *sublimations* necessary to conceal the natural—the horror of existence. Homer as well as Christianity, master morality as well as slave morality, both of them, have to conceal the horror of existence and create meaning in a meaningless void. And *both* of them succeeded in doing so.
72. *GM,* III, §24, p. 151.
73. *GM,* III, §23, p. 147; also §27, p. 160.
74. GM, III, §28, p. 162.
75. *GM,* III, §28, p. 162.
76. Schutte, 147.
77. It eternalizes *suffering.* It does not eternalize guilt—it eliminates guilt.
78. *EH,* "Why I Am So Wise," §7, pp. 232-33. In a discarded draft for a section of *Ecce Homo,* Nietzsche even says, "I want nothing differently, not backward either. . . . Even Christianity becomes necessary: only the highest form, the most dangerous, the one that was most seductive in its No to life, provokes its highest affirmation—me." See *EH,* "Appendix," §4(d), p. 343.
79. A. Nehamas, "Will to Knowledge, Will to Ignorance and Will to Power in *Beyond Good and Evil,"* in *Nietzsche as Affirmative Thinker,* 101.
80. *GM,* II, §7, p. 69.
81. Owen argues that *ressentiment* expresses the view that one is wrongfully subject to suffering; see Owen, 63.
82. Nietzsche might seem to hold contradictory views. On the one hand he holds that Christianity and the ascetic ideal involve repression, set up obstacles to be overcome, thus build up power, and therefore enhance life (e.g., *BGE,* §51, p. 65; also §§188-89, pp.

100-102. *GM*, III, §1, p. 97; also §7, pp. 107-8; also §§27-28, pp. 159-62). On the other hand, he holds that Christianity and the ascetic ideal cause decadence, decline, a weakening, a turning away from life (e.g., *TI*, "Expeditions of an Untimely Man," §34, pp. 86-87. *WP*, §864, p. 460). Is this just a contradiction? I suggest that *both* are true, that Christianity and the ascetic ideal *began* by producing power and enhancing life and *end up* powerless, decadent, and weak.

83. Clark, on the other hand, thinks the masters are Nietzsche's paradigm of those who could embrace eternal recurrence; Clark, 283.

84. *BGE*, §260, p. 204. Also see *GM*, I, §16, pp. 52-53.

85. *GM*, I, §6, pp. 31-32.

86. *GM*, I, §7, p. 33; see also §6, p. 31. This, it seems to me, sets up a dialectic that is quite Hegelian—a possibility vigorously rejected by Deleuze, 8-10.

87. *Z*, II, "On Priests," p. 91.

88. *GM*, I, §16, p. 53; also §7, p. 33.

89. *GM*, I, §16, p. 53.

90. *BGE*, §251, pp. 187-88. Also *HAH, I*, §475, p. 258. Also *D*, §205, pp. 124-25. I think Kaufmann is correct in arguing that Nietzsche is not anti-Semitic (Kaufmann, *Nietzsche: Philosopher, Psychologist, Antichrist*, Chapter 10). At least, Nietzsche is not anti-Semitic in the ordinary sense—he does not hate Jews, think them inferior, and so forth. But Nietzsche is often guilty of what might be called positive racism. He is all too willing to generalize about races or nations, to assign them a character, a unified identity, perhaps even an essence. In doing so, he often points to what he takes to be the strengths of a people. But to ignore variation between individuals, to rank a people against other peoples, to lump them together and to generalize in this way, only differs from ordinary racism in that it approves of this people rather than disapproves and demeans.

91. *BGE*, §251, pp. 188-89.

92. *WP*, §983, p. 513.

93. R.C. Solomon, "A More Severe Morality: Nietzsche's Affirmative Ethics," in *Nietzsche as Affirmative Thinker*, 69-89. Also T.H. Brobjer, *Nietzsche's Ethics of Character: A Study of Nietzsche's Ethics and its Place in the History of Moral Thinking* (Uppsala: Uppsala University, 1995). Also L.H. Hunt, *Nietzsche and the Origin of Virtue* (London: Routledge, 1991). Also M. Slote, "Nietzsche and Virtue Ethics," in *International Studies in Philosophy*, 30 (1998): 23-27.

94. Solomon, "A More Severe Morality," 74-76, 85; also *Living With Nietzsche*, 93, 122.

95. Solomon, "A More Severe Morality," 83; also *Living With Nietzsche*, 130. Also see Brobjer, 241-62. Magnus argues against this view, see B. Magnus, "Aristotle and Nietzsche: *Megalopsychia* and *Uebermensch*," in *The Greeks and the Good Life*, ed. D.J. Depew (Indianapolis: Hackett, 1980), 260-95.

96. See, e.g., *AC*, §50, p. 167.

97. *WP*, §317, p. 175. Also *The Wanderer and His Shadow*, in *HAH, II*, §34, pp. 318-19.

98. *BGE*, §214, p. 145.

99. *AC*, §11, p. 122. See also *HAH, I*, §94, pp. 71-72. Also *GS*, §120, pp. 176-77; also §335, p. 265. Also *WP*, §326, p. 178. There are passages, however, in which Nietzsche rejects virtue; see *HAH, I*, §56, p. 58.

100. *EH*, "Preface," §2, p. 217.

101. *U&DHL*, §8, p. 106.

102. *U&DHL*, §3, p. 76.

103. *Z*, III, "On Old and New Tablets," §2, p. 196.

104. See Section IV of Chapter 2. Also *AC*, §50, p. 167. "The Philosopher: Reflections on the Struggle Between Art and Knowledge," §73, p. 28.

105. Owen, for example, thinks that truthfulness and integrity are virtues for Nietzsche; Owen, 143, 118.

106. Thus creativity becomes one of the highest virtues.

107. *NE*, 1139ᵃ.

108. In this respect, contrary to Slote, I think Nietzsche holds to (rather than rejects) an agent-independent theory of virtue—that is, one in which the agent sees and enacts what is morally called for in various situations. And so, in this respect (again contrary to Slote), Nietzsche is *like* Aristotle; see Slote, 24-25.

109. *WP*, §328, p. 179. See also *WP*, §308, p. 172; also §272, p. 155. Also see, *TI*, "The 'Improvers' of Mankind," §5, p. 59. *HAH, I*, §40, p. 49. *The Wanderer and His Shadow, HAH, II*, §190, pp. 357-58. *GS*, §347, p. 287. *WP*, §306, p. 171.

110. So also Nietzsche does not endorse the "ancient notion of a life according to nature," as Schatzki suggests he does; see T.R. Schatzki, "Ancient and Naturalistic Themes in Nietzsche's Ethics," in *Nietzsche-Studien*, XXIII (1994), 156ff.

111. *NE*, Book VI, Chapter 13. Also see Solomon, *Living With Nietzsche*, 155.

112. *WP*, §311, p. 172.

113. See *Z*, I, "On Enjoying and Suffering the Passions," p. 37.

114. A. MacIntyre, *After Virtue: A Study in Moral Theory*, 2nd ed. (Notre Dame, IN: University of Notre Dame Press, 1984), 52.

115. *U&DHL*, §3, p. 76.

116. Aristotle does say that no virtuous man can become miserable, but he admits that one who meets with wretchedness like that of Priam, "no one calls happy" (*NE*, 1100ᵃ-1101ᵃ).

117. *EH*, "Human, All-Too-Human," §4, p. 288. One might do better looking to Cicero rather than Aristotle as the model for a Nietzschean virtue ethic. Cicero argues that one can be happy even while undergoing torture; see Cicero, *Tusculan Disputations*, tr. J.E. King, Loeb Classical Library (Cambridge, MA: Harvard University Press, 1950), Book V. Nevertheless, even Cicero is committed to a designed cosmos, not a horrific one; see, e.g., *Tusculan Disputations*, 497-99.

118. *AC*, §2, p. 115.

119. See *WP*, §688, p. 366.

120. *GM*, III, §7, p. 107. Nietzsche contrasts eudaemonistic philosophers to the pre-Socratics, who lack "the detestable pretension to happiness" (see "The Struggle Between Science and Wisdom," in *Philosophy and Truth*, §193, p. 133).

121. Nietzsche says: "Every basic character trait that is encountered at the bottom of every event . . . would have to lead every individual who experienced it as his own basic character trait to welcome every moment of universal existence with a sense of triumph. The crucial point would be that one experienced this basic character trait in oneself as good, valuable—with pleasure" (*WP*, §55, p. 36).

122. *EH*, "Why I Am So Clever," §10, p. 258.

123. *GS*, §341, pp. 273-74. For a discussion of other differences between Aristotle and Nietzsche, see F. Cameron, *Nietzsche and the 'Problem' of Morality* (New York: Peter Lang, 2002), 152-57.

Notes to Chapter Seven

1. Heidegger, *Nietzsche*, II, 5-6. For a good summary of Heidegger's position, see Hatab, 114-15. Richardson also thinks that Nietzsche's thought is metaphysical; see Richardson, *Nietzsche's System.*

2. This passage was quoted at length at the beginning of Section VII of Chapter 5.

3. *TI*, "How the 'Real World' at last Became a Myth," pp. 40-41.

4. See *WP*, §583(B), p. 314.

5. Clark, 114-15.

6. Haar thinks that in abolishing the real and the apparent world we are left with everydayness, but the horror of existence has little to do with what is usually meant by *everydayness;* Haar, *Nietzsche and Metaphysics*, x-xii.

7. See Section III of Chapter 5.

8. See Section II of Chapter 5.

9. Heidegger, *Nietzsche*, III, 166.

10. *AC*, §23, p. 132.

11. Clark, 24, 221ff. Stack argues that Nietzsche's thought is not metaphysical. Following Lange's standpoint of the ideal, Nietzsche puts forth experimental, hypothetical, or fictive ideas that have a primarily existential significance; see Stack, 16, 21, 39-40, 67-68, 269-72, 293-96.

12. See Section III of Chapter 5.

13. See Sections I-II of Chapter 5.

14. Wilcox (108ff.) argues that there is a passage which suggests that Nietzsche takes the Dionysian to be an illusion. If that were so, then it would follow that Nietzsche takes the Dionysian *horror of existence* to be an illusion. The passage is the following:

> It is an eternal phenomenon: the insatiable will always find a way to detain its creatures in life and compel them to live on, by means of an illusion spread over things. One is chained by the Socratic love of knowledge and the delusion of being able thereby to heal the eternal wound of existence; another is ensnared by art's seductive veil of beauty fluttering before his eyes; still another by the metaphysical comfort that beneath the whirl of phenomena eternal life flows on indestructibly . . . (*BT*, §18, pp. 109-10).

However, the third illusion listed here cannot be identified with the Dionysian. Rather, it is quite clearly the tragic, as is made evident at the end of the paragraph from which the above passage is quoted; see *BT*, §18, p. 110; also compare to §7, p. 59. The tragic gives us an Apollonian veil over Dionysian terror and thus quite properly involves illusion—without in any way suggesting that Dionysian horror is illusion.

15. *Z*, I, "On War and Warriors," p. 47; also IV, "Conversation with the Kings," §2, p. 247. See also *HAH, I*, §77, p. 66.

16. *WP*, §877, p. 469. Nietzsche's views here might be likened to those of Epicurus. For Epicurus, we are not after absolute truth. We certainly do not want truth that disturbs *ataraxia* or peace of mind. Our truths must not contradict the phenomena and must be consistent with *ataraxia*—that is, with our values ("Epicurus to Pythocles," in *Epicurus: The Extant Remains*, tr. C. Bailey [Hildesheim: Georg Olms Verlag, 1975], 57-59). For Nietzsche, we accept as true the horror of existence. It does not contradict the phenom-

ena—there is plenty of meaningless suffering to be found. Moreover, it can make an *Übermensch* possible—it serves our values (compare to Danto, *Nietzsche as Philosopher*, 230).

17. *Z*, "Prologue," §3, p. 13.

18. *AC*, §23, p. 132.

19. *WP*, §§533-34, p. 290.

20. *WP*, §15, pp. 14-15; also §487, p. 269; also §535, pp. 290-91; also §853(I), pp. 451-52. *BGE*, §210, pp. 134-35. *AC*, §50, pp. 166-67.

21. *D*, §62, pp. 37-38. *GS*, §143, p. 191. *WP*, §12(A), p. 12.

22. *WP*, §91, p. 56. Nietzsche also says, "To live alone one must be an animal or a god—says Aristotle. There is yet a third case: one must be both—a *philosopher*" (*TI*, "Maxims and Arrows," §3, p. 23).

23. *AC*, §47, p. 162. Also see, *EH*, "Beyond Good and Evil," §2, p. 311.

24. *WP*, §1005, p. 521.

25. Nietzsche to Fuchs on 18 December 1888, translated in *EH*, p. 344. Also see *WP*, p. 85 and *NW*, XV, p. 241. Also *NW*, XII, §350, p. 170; also §352, pp. 170-71. Also *Z*, IV, "On the Higher Man," §2, p. 287.

26. Nietzsche to Burckhardt on 6 January 1889, in *Selected Letters*, 346. See also *GS*, §125, p. 181.

27. M. Luther, *The Bondage of the Will*, tr. J.I. Packer and O.B. Johnston (Westwood, NJ: Revell, 1957), 209.

28. M. Stirner, *The Ego and His Own*, tr. S.T. Byington (New York: Boni and Liveright, n.d.), 3-4. On Nietzsche and Stirner, see K. Löwith, *From Hegel to Nietzsche*, tr. D.H. Green (Garden City, NY: Anchor, 1967), 185-86.

29. *WP*, §487, p. 269. See also *WP*, §§483-85, pp. 267-69; also §497, p. 273. *BGE*, §210, p. 134. *GM*, III, §24, pp. 148-53.

30. *WP*, §15, p. 15.

31. *WP*, §587, p. 322.

32. *WP*, §750, p. 396. For a different explanation of how we can believe what we know to be false, see Reginster, 92-94.

33. *WP*, §§533-34, p. 290. *HAH, I*, §52, p. 56.

34. *BGE*, §22, p. 31.

35. Is Nietzsche the *Übermensch?* On my reading, an *Übermensch* is someone able to create a new heaven, someone like Vishvamitra, Homer, or Jesus, someone able to construct a new meaning structure, that is, a worldview with the ability to actually succeed for a millennium or so in concealing the horror of existence. If this is correct, there is no way to be sure ahead of time whether or not one has created a new heaven capable of creating meaning for a millennium or so. One can have moments when one believes one has done so, but inevitably there will be other moments when one is not at all sure that one has (also see note 7 of Chapter 4). We have also seen above that Nietzsche wavered in his belief in eternal recurrence—the test of the *Übermensch* (see Salomé, 133 [this passage was quoted in Section II of Chapter 4]; also see note 3 of Chapter 5).

36. *GM*, "Preface," §4, p. 18.

37. One might want to contrast Nietzsche to later existentialists, who also thought that existence was meaningless and that we have to create our own meanings. The big difference here is that for existentialists like Sartre and Camus each of us is capable of finding for ourselves enough meaning to make existence bearable—what we might call small meanings. For Nietzsche, what is needed are grand meanings. We need eternal recurrence and *amor fati*. And we need an *Übermensch* to create them. With the death of god we are in need of a Vishvamitra to create a new heaven. It is as if Nietzsche is still a

religious thinker. It is as if his anti-religiousness is still a form of religiousness—as if he is unable to simply be non-religious (see Section II of Chapter 3).

38. *BGE*, §22, pp. 30-31.

39. See note 14 above.

40. J. Stambaugh, *The Problem of Time in Nietzsche*, tr. J.F. Humphrey (Lewisburg, PA: Bucknell University Press, 1987), 160.

41. E. Heller, *The Importance of Nietzsche: Ten Essays* (Chicago: University of Chicago Press, 1988), 12. It has also been argued that the concept of the *Übermensch* requires a notion of linear time while eternal recurrence requires a concept of circular or cyclical time. For a very interesting rejection of this view, see Loeb, "Time, Power, and Superhumanity," 27-47.

42. L. Lampert, *Nietzsche's Teaching: An Interpretation of Thus Spoke Zarathustra* (New Haven, CN: Yale University Press, 1986), 258.

43. D.W. Conway, "Overcoming the Übermensch: Nietzsche's Revaluation of Values," *Journal of the British Society for Phenomenology*, 20 (1989): 212. Ansell-Pearson (*Nietzsche Contra Rousseau*, 186 ff.) argues against the views of Conway and Lampert. He argues that Nietzsche's principle doctrines do not contradict each other.

44. See, e.g., *GM*, II, §11, p. 76, also §§16-17, pp. 84-87; also III, §7, pp. 107-8; §16, pp. 128-29. *TI*, "Morality as Anti-Nature," §3, pp. 43-44. Also *WP*, §1030, p. 532.

45. *WP*, §§533-34, p. 290. *HAH, I*, §52, p. 56.

46. Also, Section VII and VIII of Chapter 3 explained how will to power is a theory compatible with chaos (which is another way of talking about the horror of existence) and that will to power allows us to understand the build-up of structures necessary to mask such chaos.

47. See Chapter 5, Section VI.

48. See Chapter 5, Section V.

49. *BT*, §21, pp. 127-28.

50. Heidegger, *Nietzsche*, I, Chapters 2-4.

51. Clark, 25ff. On these matters, see the interesting article by Magnus, "The Use and Abuse of *The Will to Power*," 218-35.

52. Soll, "Pessimism and the Tragic View of Life," 119.

53. See Nehamas, *Nietzsche: Life as Literature*, 10.

54. Clark, 266.

Notes to Chapter Eight

1. Schutte, xi; also 162ff.

2. R.C. Holub, "Introduction," *Beyond Good and Evil*, tr. M. Faber (Oxford: Oxford University Press, 1998), xxiii. See also J.A. Bernstein, *Nietzsche's Moral Philosophy* (London: Associated University Presses, 1987), 14-15.

3. Warren, xi, 3.

4. Richardson argues that this is the case with respect to Nietzsche's views on women; see Richardson, 192.

5. *BGE*, §232, pp. 162-64. *HAH, I,* §§235, 457, pp. 161, 246. *AC*, §57, p. 179. At times, he is also racist; see *GM*, I, §5, pp. 30-31. Postmodern thinkers, who are deeply influenced by Nietzsche, nevertheless inevitably differ from him in two important ways. In the first place, they have no notion of the horror of existence. From this it follows that they must have a very different reason for emphasizing perspective and interpretation. Secondly, they tend to ignore the fact that Nietzsche is not an egalitarian—that he opposes the emancipation of women, workers, and others.

6. See Section I of Chapter 3.

7. *WP*, §40, p. 25; see also §90, p. 55; also §684, p. 363.

8. *WP*, §41, p. 25.

9. *WP*, §957, p. 502. For a nearly identical passage, see *BGE*, §44, pp. 54-55.

10. *TI*, "Expeditions of an Untimely Man," §34, p. 86. Quibbling about whether Nietzsche is a conservative or a progressive, for the most part, is pointless. Progressives believe in, hope for, and work to bring about, change. Conservatives think there has already been too much change and would like to change things back to the way they were. Nietzsche rejects the notion of change. Things do not change—or whatever change occurs is not of any significance. Change will not affect the horror of existence. The horror of existence can only be concealed, not changed.

11. Warren dismisses such an interpretation. He thinks that we find the view that suffering is intrinsic to existence only in the *Birth of Tragedy* and that in later writings Nietzsche thinks that social violence is the cause of suffering; Warren, 77.

12. *TI*, "Expeditions of an Untimely Man," §34, p. 86. See also *GM*, III, §15, pp. 126-28. Also *WP*, §55, p. 37. Also *BT*, §18, p. 111. The quoted passage suggests that belief in the possibility of change is closely connected with *ressentiment* and the spirit of revenge. One could not justify one's *ressentiment* or revenge to oneself unless one thought change was possible. At the same time, this passage suggests that at a deeper level one understands that change is not *really* possible and that it is revenge or *ressentiment* itself that gives one what little meaning and comfort one can get.

13. *HAH, I,* §235, p. 161.

14. *WP*, §27, p. 19; see also §751, p. 397. Also *GM*, I, §13, pp. 45-46. See also *CWFN*, XI, 135.

15. *WP*, §965, p. 506.

16. *TI*, "Expeditions of an Untimely Man," §38, p. 92.

17. *WP*, §870, p. 465.

18. *WP*, §874, p. 468.

19. *WP*, §252, p. 146. Also *AC*, §5, p. 117.

20. *WP*, §864, p. 460.

21. *GS*, §325, p. 255.

22. See Section IV of Chapter 5.

23. *AC*, §7, pp. 118-19.

24. *D*, §133, p. 84.

25. Stambaugh argues that the distinction between pity and compassion is one "that Nietzsche could not make linguistically, but also did not make in terms of meaning. . . . There is only one word in German for both of these phenomena: *Mitleid"* (see J. Stambaugh, *The Other Nietzsche* [Albany: State University of New York Press, 1994], 45). However, I do not think Nietzsche was unaware of the concept of compassion. He says of love that "it penetrates to the core, the suffering individual, and suffers along with him . . . " (see *CWFN*, XI, 192; also 373). After all, *Mitleid,* literally, means 'suffering with.' For an argument that Nietzsche does not reject compassion altogether, see Reginster, 185-90.

26. *Iliad*, Book 24.

27. *GM*, II, §10, p. 73. Also see *WP*, §776, p. 407.

28. *HAH, I,* §81, p. 67.

29. *BGE*, §188, p. 101.

30. *BGE*, §229, p. 158.

31. *BGE*, §225, p. 154; see also §208, p. 131.

32. *BGE*, §225, p. 153. See also *TI*, "Maxims and Arrows," §8, p. 23. Also *WP*, §26, p. 19.

33. *Z*, I, "Prologue," §5, pp. 17-18.

34. The passage just quoted from *Z*, I, "Prologue," §5, pp. 17-18 should be compared to the passage quoted at the beginning of Section I of this chapter from *WP*, §957, p. 502—also see the nearly identical passage at *BGE*, §44, pp. 54-55.

35. *AC*, §57, p. 179. See also *GM*, III, §15, pp. 125-26; also II, §10, pp. 72-73. Also *WP*, §776, p. 407. See also *Z*, I, "On the New Idol," p. 48.

36. Here, I prefer Cowan's translation; see *BGE* (Cowan), §228, p. 155.

37. Aristotle, *Politics,* in *Complete Works of Aristotle,* II, 1284ᵃ. See also *TI,* "Expeditions of an Untimely Man," §48, p. 102.

38. "The Philosopher: Reflections on the Struggle Between Art and Knowledge," §46, p. 16. See also *On the Future of Our Educational Institutions,* 12-13, 36, 75.

39. *U&DHL,* §9, p. 111; see also §2, p. 68. Also *CWFN*, XI, 135.

40. *CWFN*, XI, 214.

41. *WP*, §§998, 999, p. 519.

42. *BGE*, §126, p. 87.

43. *WP*, §997, p. 518.

44. *WP*, §1053, p. 544; also §55, pp. 36-37.

45. *WP*, §874, p. 468.

46. *WP*, §252, p. 146.

47. *WP*, §54, p. 38.

48. *BGE*, §258, p. 202. See also *WP*, §26, p. 19; also §246, p. 142; also §660, p. 349; also §859, p. 458; also §866, pp. 463-64; also §877, p. 469; also §895, p. 476; also §898, p. 478. *CWFN*, XI, 294. "The Greek State," 6-7.

49. *GM*, II, §12, p. 78. See also *WP*, §247, p. 143.

50. *EH*, "Preface," §2, p. 217.

51. *WP*, §958, p. 503.

52. *EH*, "Why I Write Such Good Books," §1, p. 259. Also see *EH*, "The Birth of Tragedy," §4, p. 274.

53. *CWFN*, XI, 278.

54. *GS*, §40, p. 107.

55. *GM*, I, §11, p. 43.

56. *WP*, §55, p. 37.

57. *AC*, §3, p. 116. Nietzsche makes it clear here that his concept of the *Übermensch* is not Darwinian—humans are not expected to evolve into a higher type. *Übermenschen* are chance occurrences that can occur in any age. Nevertheless, Nietzsche believes in breeding; see *BGE*, §262, p. 210.

58. *GM*, II, §12, p. 78.

59. *EH*, "Why I Write Such Good Books," §1, p. 259.

60. See section III of Chapter 7.

61. *GM*, I, §15, p. 49. *Summa Theologiae* (New York: McGraw-Hill, 1964 ff.), III, Supplementum, Q. 94, Art 1.

62. *WP*, §27, p. 19.

63. *WP*, §55, p. 36.

64. See, e.g., *Z*, IV, "On The Higher Man," §1, p. 286. *WP*, §246, p. 142. *AC*, §62, p. 186. Schacht defends Nietzsche's views on this matter; Schacht, 327-28.

65. *D*, §62, pp. 37-38. *GS*, §143, p. 191.

Bibliography

Ahern, D.R. *Nietzsche as Cultural Physician*. University Park: Pennsylvania State University Press, 1995.

Allison, H.E. *Kant's Transcendental Idealism: An Interpretation and Defense*. New Haven: Yale University Press, 1983.

Ansell-Pearson, K. *An Introduction to Nietzsche as Political Thinker: The Perfect Nihilist*. Cambridge: Cambridge University Press, 1994.

_____. *Nietzsche Contra Rousseau: A Study of Nietzsche's Moral and Political Thought*. Cambridge: Cambridge University Press, 1991.

Aquinas, T. *Summa Theologiae*. 74 vols. New York: McGraw-Hill, 1964–.

Aristotle, *The Complete Works of Aristotle*. Ed. J. Barnes. Bollingen Series LXXI. Princeton, NJ: Princeton University Press, 1984.

Behler, E., Montinari, M., Müller-Lauter, W., and Wenzel, H., eds. *Nietzsche-Studien*. Berlin: de Gruyter, 1972–.

Berkowitz, P. *Nietzsche: The Ethics of an Immoralist*. Cambridge, MA: Harvard University Press, 1995.

Bernstein, J.A. *Nietzsche's Moral Philosophy*. London: Associated University Presses, 1987.

Bloom, H., ed. *Friedrich Nietzsche*. New York: Chelsea House, 1987.

Breazeale, D. "The Hegel-Nietzsche Problem." In *Nietzsche-Studien*. Ed. E. Behler, M. Montinari, W. Müller-Lauter, and H. Wenzel. Berlin: de Gruyter, 1975, IV, 146-58.

Braddock, G. "Personal Identity, Determinism, and the Eternal Recurrence." *Eidos,* 14 (1997): 33-48.

Brobjer, T.H. *Nietzsche's Ethics of Character: A Study of Nietzsche's Ethics and its Place in the History of Moral Thinking*. Uppsala: Uppsala University, 1995.

Brodsky, G.M. "Nietzsche's Notion of *Amor Fati*." *Continental Philosophy Review*, 31 (1998): 35-57.

Cameron, F. *Nietzsche and the 'Problem' of Morality*. New York: Peter Lang, 2002.

Carr, K.L. *The Banalization of Nihilism: Twentieth-Century Responses to Meaninglessness*. Albany: State University of New York Press, 1992.

Cicero. *Tusculan Disputations*. Tr. J.E. King. Loeb Classical Library. Cambridge, MA: Harvard University Press, 1950.

Clark, M. *Nietzsche on Truth and Philosophy*. Cambridge: Cambridge University Press, 1990.

Combee, J.H. "Nietzsche as Cosmologist." *Interpretation*, 4 (1974): 38-47.

Conway, D.W. "Overcoming the Übermensch: Nietzsche's Revaluation of Values." *Journal of the British Society for Phenomenology*, 20 (1989): 211-24.

Danto, A.C. *Nietzsche as Philosopher*. New York: Macmillan, 1967.

_____. "Nietzsche's Perspectivism." In *Nietzsche: A Collection of Critical Essays*. Ed. R.C. Solomon. Garden City, NY: Anchor, 1973, 29-57.

_____. "Some Remarks on *The Genealogy of Morals*." In *Reading Nietzsche*. Ed. R.C. Solomon and K.M. Higgins. New York: Oxford University Press, 1988, 13-28.

Deleuze, G. *Nietzsche and Philosophy*. Tr. H. Tomlinson. New York: Columbia University Press, 1983.

Derrida, J. *Spurs: Nietzsche's Styles.* Tr. B. Harlow. Chicago: University of Chicago Press, 1979.

_____. *Writing and Difference.* Tr. A. Bass. Chicago: University of Chicago Press, 1978.

Epicurus. *Epicurus: The Extant Remains.* Tr. C. Bailey. Hildesheim: Georg Olms Verlag, 1975.

Euripides. *The Bacchae.* Tr. W. Arrowsmith. In *Euripides V.* Chicago: University of Chicago Press, 1959.

Feuerbach, L. *The Essence of Christianity.* Tr. G. Eliot. New York: Harper & Row, 1957.

Förster, E., ed. *Kant's Transcendental Deductions.* Stanford, CA: Sanford University Press, 1989.

Förster-Nietzsche, Frau. *The Young Nietzsche.* Tr. A.M. Ludovici. London: William Heinemann, 1912.

Foucault, M. "Nietzsche, Genealogy, History." In *Language, Counter-Memory, Practice.* Ed. D.F. Bouchard. Ithaca, NY: Cornell University Press, 1977.

Freud, S. *Civilization and Its Discontents.* Tr. J. Strachey. New York: Norton, 1961.

Gooding-Williams, R. *Zarathustra's Dionysian Modernism.* Stanford, CA: Stanford University Press, 2001.

Goethe, J.W. von. *The Sorrows of Young Werther.* Tr. E. Mayer and L. Bogan. New York: Vintage, 1973.

Green, M.S. *Nietzsche and the Transcendental Tradition.* Urbana: University of Illinois Press, 2002.

Greene, M. "Hegel's 'Unhappy Consciousness' and Nietzsche's 'Slave Morality.'" In *Hegel and the Philosophy of Religion.* Ed. D.E. Christensen. The Hague: Martinus Nijhoff, 1970.

Haar, M. "Heidegger and the Nietzschean 'Physiology of Art.'" In *Exceedingly Nietzsche: Aspects of Contemporary Nietzsche-Interpretation.* Ed. D.F. Krell and D. Wood. London: Routledge, 1988, 13-30.

_____. *Nietzsche and Metaphysics.* Tr. M. Gendre. Albany: State University of New York Press, 1996.

Hales, S.D. and Welshon, R. *Nietzsche's Perspectivism.* Urbana: University of Illinois Press, 2000.

Hamilton, E. *Mythology.* New York: Mentor, 1953.

Hatab, L.J. *Nietzsche and Eternal Recurrence: The Redemption of Time and Becoming.* Washington, DC: University Press of America, 1978.

Hegel, G.W.F. *Aesthetics.* Tr. T.M. Knox. 2 vols. Oxford: Clarendon Press, 1975.

_____. *Grundlinien der Philosophie des Rechts.* Ed. J. Hoffmeister. Hamburg: Felix Meiner, 1955.

_____. *Phänomenologie des Geistes.* Ed. J. Hoffmeister. Hamburg: Felix Meiner, 1952.

_____. *Phenomenology of Spirit.* Tr. A.V. Miller. Oxford: Clarendon Press, 1977.

_____. *Philosophy of History.* Ed. J. Sibree. New York: Dover, 1956.

_____. *Philosophy of Right.* Tr. T.M. Knox. Oxford: Clarendon Press, 1952.

_____. *Vorlesungen über die Philosophie der Weltgeschichte.* Ed. G. Lasson. Hamburg: Felix Meiner, 1968, II-IV.

Heidegger, M. *Nietzsche.* Tr. D.F. Krell. 4 vols. San Francisco: Harper & Row, 1979-87.

_____. *Nietzsche: Volumes III and IV.* Tr. J. Stambaugh, D.F. Krell, and F.A. Capuzzi. San Francisco: HarperCollins, 1991.

Heller, E. *The Importance of Nietzsche: Ten Essays.* Chicago: University of Chicago Press, 1988.

Henrich, D. "Kant's Notion of a Deduction and the Methodological Background of the First *Critique.*" In *Kant's Transcendental Deductions.* Ed. E. Förster. Stanford, CA:

Sanford University Press, 1989, 29-46.

Higgins, K. "Reading Zarathustra." In *Reading Nietzsche*. Ed. R.C. Solomon and K.M. Higgins. New York: Oxford University Press, 1988, 132-51.

Hill, R.K. *Nietzsche's Critiques: The Kantian Foundations of His Thought*. Oxford: Clarendon Press, 2003.

Hodge, R.D. "On Nietzsche's Enigmatic Anti-Kantian Categorical Imperative." *Conference: A Journal of Philosophy and Theory*, 4 (1993): 36-49.

Holub, R.C. "Introduction." In *Beyond Good and Evil*. Tr. M. Faber. Oxford: Oxford University Press, 1998.

Homer. *The Iliad*. Tr. R. Lattimore. Chicago: University of Chicago Press, 1951.

Houlgate, S. *Hegel, Nietzsche and the Criticism of Metaphysics*. Cambridge: Cambridge University Press, 1986.

Hume, D. *A Treatise of Human Nature*. Ed. L.A. Selby-Bigge. Oxford: Clarendon Press, 1967.

_____. *An Enquiry Concerning Human Understanding*. In *Enquiries Concerning Human Understanding and Concerning the Principles of Morals*. Ed. L.A. Selby-Bigge. 3rd edition. Revised P.H. Nidditch. Oxford: Clarendon Press, 1975.

Hunt, L.H. *Nietzsche and the Origin of Virtue*. London: Routledge, 1991.

Jaspers, K. *Nietzsche: An Introduction to the Understanding of His Philosophical Activity*. Tr. C.F. Wallraff and F.J. Schmitz. Tucson: University of Arizona Press, 1966.

Kain, P. J. *Hegel and the Other*. Albany: State University of New York Press, 2005.

_____. "Eternal Recurrence and the Categorical Imperative." *The Southern Journal of Philosophy*, 45 (2007): 105-16.

_____. "Kant and the Possibility of Uncategorized Experience." *Idealistic Studies*, 19 (1989): 154-73.

_____. "Nietzsche, Eternal Recurrence, and the Horror of Existence." *The Journal of Nietzsche Studies*, 33 (2007): 49-63.

_____. "Nietzsche, Skepticism, and Eternal Recurrence." *Canadian Journal of Philosophy*, 13 (1983): 365-87.

_____. "Nietzsche, the Kantian Self, and Eternal Recurrence." *Idealistic Studies*, 34 (2004): 225-37.

_____. "Nietzsche, Truth, and the Horror of Existence." *History of Philosophy Quarterly*, 23 (2006): 41-58.

_____. "Nietzschean Genealogy and Hegelian History in the *Genealogy of Morals*." *Canadian Journal of Philosophy*, 26 (1996): 123-48.

_____. *Schiller, Hegel, and Marx: State, Society, and the Aesthetic Ideal of Ancient Greece*. Montreal: McGill-Queen's University Press, 1982.

Kant, I. *Critique of Practical Reason*. Tr. L.W. Beck. Indianapolis: Bobbs-Merrill, 1956.

_____. *Critique of Pure Reason*. Tr. N. Kemp Smith. New York: St. Martin's Press, 1965.

_____. *Foundations of the Metaphysics of Morals*. Tr. L.W. Beck. Indianapolis: Bobbs-Merrill, 1959.

_____. *Kant's gesammelte Schriften*. Ed. Königlich Preussischen Akademie der Wissenschaften. 26 vols. Berlin: Georg Reimer, 1910-55.

Kaufmann, W. *Nietzsche: Philosopher, Psychologist, Antichrist*. 4th edition. Princeton, NJ: Princeton University Press, 1974.

Kierkegaard, S. *Fear and Trembling*. In *Fear and Trembling and The Sickness unto Death*. Tr. W. Lowrie. Garden City, NY: Doubleday, 1954.

Kofman, S. *Nietzsche and Metaphor*. Tr. D. Large. Stanford, CA: Stanford University Press, 1993.

Köhler, J. *Zarathustra's Secret: The Interior Life of Friedrich Nietzsche.* Tr. R. Taylor. New Haven, CN: Yale University Press, 2002.

Krell, D.F. "Consultations with the Paternal Shadow: Gashé, Derrida and Klossowski on *Ecce Homo.*" In *Exceedingly Nietzsche: Aspects of Contemporary Nietzsche-Interpretation.* Ed. D.F. Krell and D. Wood. London: Routledge, 1988, 80-94.

Krell, D.F. and Wood, D., eds. *Exceedingly Nietzsche: Aspects of Contemporary Nietzsche-Interpretation.* London: Routledge, 1988.

Krueger, J. "Nietzschean Recurrence as a Cosmological Hypothesis." *Journal of the History of Philosophy,* 16 (1978): 435-44.

Lampert, L. *Nietzsche's Teaching: An Interpretation of Thus Spoke Zarathustra.* New Haven, CN: Yale University Press, 1986.

Lange, F.A. *The History of Materialism.* Tr. E.C. Thomas. 3rd edition. New York: Humanities Press, 1950.

Lenson, D. *The Birth of Tragedy: A Commentary.* Boston: Twayne Publishers, 1987.

Loeb, P.S. "Identity and Eternal Recurrence." In *A Companion to Nietzsche.* Ed. K. Ansell Pearson. Oxford: Blackwell, 2006, 171-88.

_____. "Time, Power, and Superhumanity." *Journal of Nietzsche Studies,* 21 (2001): 27-47.

Love, N.S. *Marx, Nietzsche, and Modernity.* New York: Columbia University Press, 1986.

Löwith, K. *From Hegel to Nietzsche.* Tr. D.E. Green. Garden City, NY: Anchor, 1967.

_____. *Nietzsche's Philosophy of the Eternal Recurrence of the Same.* Tr. J.H. Lomax. Berkeley: University of California Press, 1997.

Lukács, G. *The Destruction of Reason.* Tr. P. Palmer. London: Merlin, 1980.

Luther, M. *The Bondage of the Will.* Tr. J.I. Packer and O.R. Johnston. Westwood, NJ: Revell, 1957.

Machiavelli, N. *The Prince.* Tr. T.G. Bergin. New York: Appleton-Century-Crofts, 1947.

MacIntyre, A. *After Virtue: A Study in Moral Theory.* 2nd edition. Notre Dame, IN: University of Notre Dame Press, 1984.

Magnus, B. "Aristotle and Nietzsche: *Megalopsychia* and *Uebermensch.*" In *The Greeks and the Good Life.* Ed. D.J. Depew. Indianapolis: Hackett, 1980, 260-95.

_____. "Asceticism and Eternal Recurrence: A Bridge Too Far." *Southern Journal of Philosophy,* 37, Supplement (1999): 93-111.

_____. "Eternal Recurrence." In *Nietzsche-Studien.* Ed. E. Behler, M. Montinari, W. Müller-Lauter, and H. Wenzel. Berlin: de Gruyter, 1979, VIII, 362-77.

_____. Forward to *Nietzsche's Philosophy of the Eternal Recurrence of the Same,* by K. Löwith. Tr. J.H. Lomax. Berkeley: University of California Press, 1997.

_____. "Jesus, Christianity, and Superhumanity." In *Studies in Nietzsche and the Judaeo-Christian Tradition.* Ed. J.C. O'Flaherty, T.F. Sellner, and R.M. Helm. Chapel Hill: University of North Carolina Press, 1985, 295-318.

_____. *Nietzsche's Existential Imperative.* Bloomington: Indiana University Press, 1978.

_____. "Nietzsche's Philosophy in 1888: The Will to Power and the *Übermensch.*" *Journal of the History of Philosophy,* 24 (1986): 79-98.

_____. "The Deification of the Commonplace: *Twilight of the Idols.*" In *Reading Nietzsche.* Ed. R.C. Solomon and K.M. Higgins. New York: Oxford University Press, 1988, 152-81.

_____. "The Use and Abuse of *The Will to Power.*" In *Reading Nietzsche.* Ed. R.C. Solomon and K.M. Higgins. New York: Oxford University Press, 1988, 218-35.

Magnus, B. and K.M. Higgins, eds. *The Cambridge Companion to Nietzsche.* Cambridge: Cambridge University Press, 1996.

Martin, N. *Nietzsche and Schiller: Untimely Aesthetics*. Oxford: Clarendon Press, 1996.
May, K.M. *Nietzsche and the Spirit of Tragedy*. New York: St. Martin Press, 1990.
McCarthy, G.E. *Dialectics and Decadence: Echoes of Antiquity in Marx and Nietzsche*. Lanham, MD: Rowman & Littlefield, 1994.
Nehamas, A. *Nietzsche: Life as Literature*. Cambridge, MA: Harvard University Press, 1985.
_____. "Will to Knowledge, Will to Ignorance and Will to Power in *Beyond Good and Evil*." In *Nietzsche as Affirmative Thinker*. Ed. Y. Yovel. Dordrecht: Martinus Nijhoff, 1986, 90-108.
Nietzsche, F. *Beyond Good and Evil*. Tr. M. Cowan. Chicago: Henry Regnery, 1955.
_____. *Beyond Good and Evil*. Tr. M. Faber. Oxford: Oxford University Press, 1998.
_____. *Beyond Good and Evil*. Tr. W. Kaufmann. New York: Vintage, 1966.
_____. *David Strauss, the Confessor and the Writer*. In *Untimely Meditations*. Tr. R.J. Hollingdale. Cambridge: Cambridge University Press, 1997.
_____. *Daybreak*. Tr. R.J. Hollingdale. Cambridge: Cambridge University Press, 1997.
_____. *Ecce Homo*. In *On the Genealogy of Morals* and *Ecce Homo*. Tr. W. Kaufmann. New York: Vintage, 1969.
_____. *Human, All Too Human, I*. Tr. G. Handwerk. In *The Complete Works of Friedrich Nietzsche*. Ed. B. Magnus. Stanford, CA: Stanford University Press, 1995, III.
_____. *Human, All Too Human*. Tr. R.J. Hollingdale. Cambridge: Cambridge University Press, 1986.
_____. *Nietzsche Contra Wagner*. In *The Complete Works of Friedrich Nietzsche*. Ed. O. Levy. New York: Russell & Russell, 1964, VIII.
_____. *Nietzsche Werke: Kritische Gesamtausgabe*. Ed. G. Colli and M. Montinari. Berlin: de Gruyter, 1967–.
_____. *Nietzsche's Werke*. Leipzig: Kröner, 1901-23.
_____. *On the Future of Our Educational Institutions*. In *The Complete Works of Friedrich Nietzsche*. Ed. O. Levy. New York: Russell & Russell, 1964, III.
_____. *On the Genealogy of Morals*. In *On the Genealogy of Morals* and *Ecce Homo*. Tr. W. Kaufmann. New York: Vintage, 1969.
_____. *On the Genealogy of Morals*. Tr. D. Smith. Oxford: Oxford University Press, 1996.
_____. *On the Uses and Disadvantages of History for Life*. In *Untimely Meditations*. Tr. R.J. Hollingdale. Cambridge: Cambridge University Press, 1997.
_____. "On Truth and Lies in a Nonmoral Sense." In *Philosophy and Truth: Selections from Nietzsche's Notebooks of the Early 1870's*. Tr. D. Breazeale. Amherst, NY: Humanity Books, 1999.
_____. *Philosophy and Truth: Selections from Nietzsche's Notebooks of the Early 1870's*. Tr. D. Breazeale. Amherst, NY: Humanity Books, 1999.
_____. *Philosophy in the Tragic Age of the Greeks*. Tr. M. Cowan. South Bend, IN: Gateway, 1962.
_____. *Richard Wagner in Bayreuth*. In *Untimely Meditations*. Tr. R.J. Hollingdale. Cambridge: Cambridge University Press, 1997.
_____. *Schopenhauer as Educator*. In *Untimely Meditations*. Tr. R.J. Hollingdale. Cambridge: Cambridge University Press, 1997.
_____. *Selected Letters of Friedrich Nietzsche*. Tr. C. Middleton. Chicago: University of Chicago Press, 1969.
_____. *The Anti-Christ*. In *Twilight of the Idols and The Anti-Christ*. Tr. R.J. Hollingdale. Harmondsworth: Penguin, 1977.

_____. *The Birth of Tragedy*. In *The Birth of Tragedy and The Genealogy of Morals*. Tr. F. Golffing. Garden City, NY: Doubleday, 1956.

_____. *The Birth of Tragedy*. In *The Birth of Tragedy and The Case of Wagner*. Tr. W. Kaufmann. New York: Vintage, 1967.

_____. *The Complete Works of Friedrich Nietzsche*. Ed. B. Magnus. Stanford, CA: Stanford University Press, 1995–.

_____. *The Complete Works of Friedrich Nietzsche*. Ed. O. Levy. New York: Russell & Russell, 1964.

_____. *The Gay Science*. Tr. W. Kaufmann. New York: Vintage, 1974.

_____. *The Genealogy of Morals*. In *The Birth of Tragedy and The Genealogy of Morals*. Tr. F. Golffing. Garden City, NY: Doubleday, 1956.

_____. "The Greek State." In *The Complete Works of Friedrich Nietzsche*. Ed. O. Levy. New York: Russell & Russell, 1964, II.

_____. "The Philosopher: Reflections on the Struggle Between Art and Knowledge." In *Philosophy and Truth: Selections from Nietzsche's Notebooks of the Early 1870's*. Tr. D. Breazeale. Amherst, NY: Humanity Books, 1999.

_____. "The Struggle Between Science and Wisdom." In *Philosophy and Truth: Selections from Nietzsche's Notebooks of the Early 1870's*. Tr. D. Breazeale. Amherst, NY: Humanity Books, 1999.

_____. *The Use and Abuse of History*. Tr. A. Collins. Indianapolis: Bobbs-Merrill, 1957.

_____. *The Wanderer and His Shadow*. In *Human, All too Human*. Tr. R.J. Hollingdale. Cambridge: Cambridge University Press, 1986.

_____. *The Will to Power*. Tr. W. Kaufmann and R.J. Hollingdale. New York: Vintage, 1968.

_____. *Thus Spoke Zarathustra*. Tr. W. Kaufmann. New York: Viking, 1966.

_____. *Twilight of the Idols*. In *Twilight of the Idols and The Anti-Christ*. Tr. R.J. Hollingdale. Harmondsworth: Penguin, 1977.

_____. *Unpublished Writings from the Period of Unfashionable Observations*. Tr. R.T. Gray. In *The Complete Works of Friedrich Nietzsche*. Ed. B. Magnus. Stanford, CA: Stanford University Press, 1995, XI.

_____. *Untimely Meditations*. Tr. R.J. Hollingdale. Cambridge: Cambridge University Press, 1997.

O'Flaherty, J.C., Sellner, T.F., and Helm, R.M., eds. *Studies in Nietzsche and the Judaeo-Christian Tradition*. Chapel Hill: University of North Carolina Press, 1985.

Olafsen, F.A. "Nietzsche, Kant, and Existentialism." In *Nietzsche: A Collection of Critical Essays*. Ed. R.C. Solomon. Garden City, NY: Anchor, 1973, 194-201.

Owen, D. *Nietzsche, Politics and Modernity: A Critique of Liberal Reason*. London: Sage Publications, 1995.

Parush, A. "Nietzsche on the Skeptic's Life." *Review of Metaphysics*, 29 (1975): 523-42.

Patton, P., ed. *Nietzsche, Feminism and Political Theory*. London: Routledge, 1993.

Plato. *The Collected Dialogues of Plato*. Ed. E. Hamilton and H. Cairns. Bollingen Series LXXI. New York: Pantheon, 1961.

Reginster, B. *The Affirmation of Life: Nietzsche on Overcoming Nihilism*. Cambridge, MA: Harvard University Press, 2006.

Richardson, J. *Nietzsche's System*. New York: Oxford University Press, 1996.

Russell, B. "On the Notion of Cause, with Applications to the Free-Will Problem." In *Readings in the Philosophy of Science*. Ed. H. Feigl and M. Brodbeck. New York: Appleton-Century-Crofts, 1953.

Sallis, J. *Crossings: Nietzsche and the Space of Tragedy*. Chicago: University of Chicago Press, 1991.

Salomé, L. *Nietzsche.* Tr. S. Mandel. Redding Ridge, CT: Black Swan Books, 1988.

Santaniello, W. *Nietzsche, God, and the Jews.* Albany: State University of New York Press, 1994.

Sartre, J-P. *Saint Genet: Actor and Martyr.* Tr. B. Frechtman. NY: Braziller, 1963.

Schacht, R. *Nietzsche.* London: Routledge & Kegan Paul, 1983.

Schatzki, T.R. "Ancient and Naturalistic Themes in Nietzsche's Ethics." In *Nietzsche-Studien.* Ed. E. Behler, M. Montinari, W. Müller-Lauter, and H. Wenzel. Berlin: de Gruyter, 1994, XXIII, 146-67.

Schiller, F. *On Naive and Sentimental Poetry.* In *Friedrich Schiller: Essays.* Ed. W. Hinderer and D.O. Dahlstrom. New York: Continuum, 1998.

_____. *On the Aesthetic Education of Man.* Tr. E.M. Wilkinson and L.A. Willoughby. Oxford: Clarendon Press, 1967.

_____. "Concerning the Sublime." In *Friedrich Schiller: Essays.* Ed. W. Hinderer and D.O. Dahlstrom. New York: Continuum, 1998.

Schopenhauer, A. *Essays of Arthur Schopenhauer.* Tr. T.B. Saunders. New York: A.L. Burt, n.d.

_____. *On the Fourfold Root of the Principle of Sufficient Reason.* Tr. E.F.J. Payne. La Salle, IL: Open Court, 1974.

_____. *The World as Will and Representation.* Tr. E.F.J. Payne. New York: Dover, 1966.

Schrift, A.D. *Nietzsche and the Question of Interpretation: Between Hermeneutics and Deconstruction.* New York: Routledge, 1990.

Schutte, O. *Beyond Nihilism: Nietzsche without Masks.* Chicago: University of Chicago Press, 1984.

Shapiro, G. *Nietzschean Narratives.* Bloomington: Indiana University Press, 1989.

_____. "Translating, Repeating, Naming: Foucault, Derrida, and the *Genealogy of Morals.*" In *Nietzsche as Postmodernist.* Ed. C. Koelb. Albany: State University of New York Press, 1990.

Silk, M.S. and Stern, J.P. *Nietzsche on Tragedy.* Cambridge: Cambridge University Press, 1981.

Slote, M. "Nietzsche and Virtue Ethics." *International Studies in Philosophy,* 30 (1998): 23-27.

Soll, I. "Pessimism and the Tragic View of Life: Reconsiderations of Nietzsche's *Birth of Tragedy.*" In *Reading Nietzsche.* Ed. R.C. Solomon and K.M. Higgins. New York: Oxford University Press, 1988, 104-31.

_____. "Reflections on Recurrence: A Re-Examination of Nietzsche's Doctrine, *die Ewige Wiederkehr des Gleichen.*" In *Nietzsche: A Collection of Critical Essays.* Garden City, NY: Anchor, 1973, 322-42.

Solomon, R.C. "A More Severe Morality: Nietzsche's Affirmative Ethics." In *Nietzsche as Affirmative Thinker.* Ed. Y. Yovel. Dordrecht: Martinus Nijhoff, 1986, 69-89.

_____. *Living With Nietzsche: What the Great "Immoralist" Has to Teach Us.* Oxford: Oxford University Press, 2003.

_____. "Nietzsche *Ad Hominem:* Perspectivism, Personality, and *Ressentiment.*" In *The Cambridge Companion to Nietzsche.* Ed. B. Magnus and K.M. Higgins. Cambridge: Cambridge University Press, 1996, 180-222.

_____, ed. *Nietzsche: A Collection of Critical Essays.* Garden City, NY: Anchor, 1973.

Solomon, R.C. and Higgins, K.M. *Reading Nietzsche.* New York: Oxford University Press, 1988.

Sophocles. *Oedipus at Colonus.* Tr. R. Fitzgerald. In *Sophocles I.* Chicago: University of Chicago Press, 1954.

_____. *Oedipus the King.* Tr. D. Greene. In *Sophocles I.* Chicago: University of Chicago Press, 1954.

Stack, G.J. *Lange and Nietzsche.* Berlin: de Gruyter, 1983.

Stambaugh, J. *Nietzsche's Thought of Eternal Return.* Baltimore: Johns Hopkins University Press, 1972.

_____. *The Other Nietzsche.* Albany: State University of New York Press, 1994.

_____. *The Problem of Time in Nietzsche.* Tr. J.F. Humphrey. Lewisburg, PA: Bucknell University Press, 1987.

Sterling, M.C. "Recent Discussions of Eternal Recurrence: Some Critical Comments." In *Nietzsche-Studien.* Ed. E. Behler, M. Montinari, W. Müller-Lauter, and H. Wenzel. Berlin: de Gruyter, 1977, VI, 261-68.

Stern, J.P. *Friedrich Nietzsche.* Harmondsworth: Penguin, 1979.

Stirner, M. *The Ego and His Own.* Tr. S.T. Byington. New York: Boni and Liveright, n.d.

Virgil. *The Aeneid of Virgil.* Tr. A. Mandelbaum. New York: Bantam, 1971.

Warren, M. *Nietzsche and Political Thought.* Cambridge, MA: MIT Press, 1988.

Wilcox, J.T. *Truth and Value in Nietzsche.* Ann Arbor: University of Michigan Press, 1974.

Winchester, J. "Of Scholarly Readings of Nietzsche: Clark and Magnus on Nietzsche's Eternal Return." *New Nietzsche Studies,* 3 (1999): 77-97.

Wood, D. "Nietzsche's Transvaluation of Time." In *Exceedingly Nietzsche: Aspects of Contemporary Nietzsche-Interpretation.* Ed. D.F. Krell and D. Wood. London: Routledge, 1988, 31-62.

Yovel, Y. "Nietzsche and Spinoza: *amor fati* and *amor dei.*" In *Nietzsche as Affirmative Thinker.* Ed. Y. Yovel. Dordrecht: Martinus Nijhoff, 1986, 183-203.

_____, ed. *Nietzsche as Affirmative Thinker.* Dordrecht: Martinus Nijhoff, 1986, 183-203.

Zuboff, A. "Nietzsche and Eternal Recurrence." In *Nietzsche: A Collection of Critical Essays.* Ed. R.C. Solomon. Garden City, NY: Anchor, 1973, 343-57.

Index

Abraham, 66
Achilles, 7, 87, 91, 118
Aeneas, 49, 50, 72
Ahern, D.R., 43
alienation, 5, 10, 98-99, 106-7
amor fati, 48-72, 76, 93, 96, 99, 108, 111, 117-18, 123-24, 146n23
Anaxagoras, 15
anti-Semitism, 153n90
Apollonian, 3-7, 19, 26, 64, 94, 111, 130n23
apparent world, 101-2, 156n6. *See also* real world
Aquinas, T.: *Summa Theologiae,* 124
Aristotle, 1, 5-6, 10, 15-16, 58, 95-99, 117, 120-21, 151n45; *megalopsychos*, 96
art: as a veil, 9, 16-17, 20, 24-25, 64, 97, 120
ascetic ideal, 40, 89-94
ataraxia, 155n16
atheism, 30, 149n86
Augustine, 107

Bach, J.S., 8
Bacon, F., 10
bad conscience. *See* guilt
becoming, 31, 35-36, 54, 74, 84
Beethoven, L., 8
Berkeley, G., 1
Buddhism, 62, 120-21
Burckhardt, J., 105

Camus, A., 156n37
categorical imperative, 69-74, 148n69, 149n71, 149n73
causality, 21, 34, 40, 48, 54, 73, 115
certainty, 107
chance, 1, 62, 72
chaos, 27-42, 54-55, 98, 139n82
Christ. *See* Jesus
Christianity, 5, 10, 12, 19, 25, 27, 30, 45, 47, 63-67, 75-77, 80, 88-94, 97, 101, 106-7, 114-27, 138n30, 143n31, 152n71
Cicero, 154n117
Clark, M., 9, 18, 66-67, 102-3, 112
compassion, 65, 116-19, 126-27, 159n25
Conway, D.W., 108
cosmos: designed, 10, 12, 16, 68, 132n56; horrific, 10, 13, 30, 47, 98, 132n56; mixed, 13; perfectible, 10-12, 30, 68, 132n56

d'Holbach, B., 16
Dante, 129n3
Danto, A.C., 11, 18, 28, 51, 79, 84
Darwinism, 160n57
Deleuze, G., 79, 82, 84
democracy, 80
Derrida, J., 133n20, 134n39
Descartes, R., 1
determinism, 69-74, 102, 109-11
dignity, 6, 58-59, 65, 73, 77, 130n22
Dionysian, 2-9, 26, 64, 98, 111, 130n23, 139n82, 155n14
discipline, 28, 61, 64-65, 76, 81-96, 115-23
domination, 40, 54, 99, 140n94

embarrassment, 66
empowerment, 61-65, 76, 86, 110-11
Epicurus, 155n16
eternal recurrence, 39, 41-79, 93-94, 99-111, 121-25, 142n20, 143n31, 145n3, 146n23, 147n41, 147n45, 148n55; dice game theory, 49-53; great year theory, 49-53; of the same, 49, 52-53, 64, 69, 94, 108
evolution, 19-26, 41, 44, 160n57
existentialism, 156n37

falsification, 20, 31, 38
Faust, 87

About the Author

Philip J. Kain was born in San Francisco in 1943. He received a B.A. in philosophy from St. Mary's College of California and a Ph.D. in philosophy from the University of California at San Diego. He has taught at the University of California at Santa Cruz, Stanford University, and is presently Professor of Philosophy and Chair of the Department at Santa Clara University. He is the author of five previous books: *Schiller, Hegel, and Marx* (1982), *Marx' Method Epistemology, and Humanism* (1986), *Marx and Ethics* (1988), *Marx and Modern Political Theory* (1993), and *Hegel and the Other* (2005).